To PHYLLIS and Wal W9-BUU-286

With my thanks and
best wishes
Ernest   July 18. 2010

Ernest Triumphant!

Also by Ernest Paul

Sara Triumphant!
A Survivor of the Shoah

Praise for *Ernest Triumphant!*

While telling of the many horrors of the Holocaust, the memoir *Ernest Triumphant!* will help readers to understand life before and after the Holocaust.

The story is valuable for students, for it describes very vividly the role of the perpetrators, the collaborators, the victims, and resisters.

Reading the book will also show students the spirit of Ernest as he fights to survive, helping readers to see how resistance was an important part of the Holocaust. After reading *Ernest Triumphant!* I believe readers will appreciate and understand the full cycle of Ernest's life and why his mission now is to educate all about the Holocaust.

—Dr. Paul B. Winkler, Executive Director,
New Jersey Commission on Holocaust Education

The book you hold in your hands is the memoir of a remarkable man.

In the first part, you will learn of his youth in Eastern Europe prior to the Nazi era and of a lost world about which we simply cannot have enough accounts.

You will also learn of his exploits against the Nazis, a hair-raising self-portrait of a fighting Jew. Such memories are important as well. Right after the war, when the contours of the destruction of Europe's Jews became apparent, the prevailing notion was that Europe's Jews had allowed themselves to be led to the gas chambers like lambs to slaughter. That notion led to a parallel disbelief how that could have happened, disbelief, incidentally found also among the native born in the young state of Israel. Only much later did we begin to realize that weaponless people, earlier deprived of livelihood, made stateless, and diabolically isolated from Europe's non-Jews in an ever more tightening cultural, social, and economic noose, did not really have much of a chance at all, especially where bystanders so outnumbered those ready to help, to resist, to lay their own lives on the line.

And yet, and yet…over time these two strands of thought slowly eroded as we learned of the collective heroism of those in the Warsaw ghetto who knew they were going to perish and decided to make a fight of it, against all odds. And beyond that extraordinary tale, the dogged scholarship of Nechama Tec reconstructed the resistance of such partisans as the Bielski brothers—scholarship that would result in a gripping book and in a film (*Defiance*) worthy of the protagonists of this particular story.

Stories also emerged of those, often blue-eyed blond young Jewish boys, who were "runners" for the remarkable work undertaken by the Swedish diplomat, Raoul Wallenberg who would disappear in a Soviet gulag after

World War II, or a certain boy in Holland named Max Léons, who managed to hide hundreds of Jews with a minister's son and did so essentially with a few bicycles and a lot of courage.

Ernest Paul's story fits snugly into this new tapestry, the historic reality that untold numbers of young Jewish men and women, armed only with their own wit and sang-froid, resisted and fought. You will read how sheer luck and a huge amount of personal pluck repeatedly got Ernest through the shoals of war. Like most others who did the right thing, for example, Miep Gies who helped Anne Frank's family, they don't see themselves as heroes but as wanderers through the minefield of providence who simply were lucky. Reading the first part of this memoir will convince you otherwise. Doing the right thing in the face of likely mortality if caught—is that not the essence of what we mean by heroism?

Had the first part of the book stood by itself, you would have had that nagging feeling "what happened thereafter," but here the question is abundantly, even exuberantly answered in the remainder of the book.

There are wonderful stories about the emergence of Israel—especially as Ernest had a front row seat in that national narrative as well.

But Ernest's other traits—his industry his willingness to take risk, and his humanity in dealing in business with a German who will increasingly become large as an actual friend in the story—all shine through, if you care to read between the lines (and you'll have to, as Ernest won't thump his own chest.)

The business details will astound you in the timing of seizing one opportunity after another. On that score, a very successful friend of blessed memory once told me: "Well, we buy for a dollar, sell for 97 cents and live on the interest of the loss." There is, of course, a whole lot more to business than that but the readiness to take a chance, to try the new, and to be nimble certainly are at the core of this second part—a fine primer for anyone who has dreams of import and export.

And then, finally, there is a wonderful rendering of the post-war cornerstones of Ernest's existence: a strong marriage, a commitment to family, and, remarkably free of any post-war bitterness, a decision to seek the sunny side of the street. Now go read—you will, I am sure, be inspired.

—*G. Jan Colijn*
The Richard Stockton College of New Jersey
Pomona 2010

Ernest Triumphant!

Ernest Paul

with Maryann McLoughlin

A Project of The Richard Stockton College of New Jersey
Sara and Sam Schoffer Holocaust Resource Center
and Graphics Production

PUBLISHING

MARGATE, NEW JERSEY

STOCKTON COLLEGE
THE RICHARD STOCKTON COLLEGE OF NEW JERSEY

NEW JERSEY'S
GREEN COLLEGE®
Stockton College is an AA/EO institution.

Published by:
ComteQ Publishing
A division of ComteQ Communications, LLC
101 N. Washington Ave. • Suite 2B
Margate, New Jersey 08402
609-487-9000 • Fax 609-487-9099
Email: publisher@comteqpublishing.com
Website: www.ComteQpublishing.com

ISBN
Library of Congress Control Number

Book/Cover Design by Sarah Messina, Stockton Graphics Production
Back cover photograph by Randee Rosenfeld
Endnotes by Maryann McLoughlin
Copy editing by Pam Cross

Printed in the United States of America

10 9 8 7 6 5 4 3 2 1

To My Dear Family—

My Children:
My daughter, Dahlia,
my son Stewart and daughter-in-law Nancy
my son Gil and daughter-in-law Dali

My grandchildren:
Tara, Ilana, Ari, Eitan, Elite, and Daniel

Our Great-Grandchildren:
Jake, Roman, Cole, Sean, Ryan Sara

In memory of my wife, Sara—
Your mother, your mom-mom, *Savta* Sara

I am dedicating this book to all of you—
I am grateful for your encouragement
in bringing this book to press
as a legacy anda true account.

Acknowledgments

I would like to thank my family for their love, support, and their encouragement to write my memoir. Especially Stewart urged me to undertake this project and assisted me on a daily basis. Moreover, he continually asked me open-ended questions that resulted in details that helped to flesh out my memoir. He also kept asking me to be more reflective about what I experienced and how I felt about these experiences. His loving attention helped contribute to a richer narrative.

I appreciate all the help that was given to me by The Richard Stockton College of New Jersey. From Stockton College's President, Dr. Herman Saatkamp, to the Dean of the College of General Studies, Dr. G. Jan Colijn, to the Director of the Sara and Sam Schoffer Holocaust Resource Center, Gail Rosenthal, all have been very supportive of projects for Holocaust survivors.

The publishing of this memoir was a team project: Dr. Maryann McLoughlin, of Stockton's Holocaust Resource Center, and Sarah Messina, of Stockton's Graphics Production, worked with me to produce this book, a record of my life as well as the fulfillment of my dream to write a companion memoir to *Sara Triumphant!*

Thank you to everyone.

Ernest Paul
2010

Author's Note

When reading Part II, Business Ventures, the reader should view it through the lens of my youth, my participation in the resistance movement, and the establishment of the State of Israel. Those experiences gave me the strength and confidence to start a new life in a new world and to begin creating business opportunities. Moreover, in the resistance and as an immigrant to two countries, Israel and the U.S., I developed a facility in adjusting to new situations, which helped me in establishing international businesses.

My business ventures gave me financial satisfaction, of course, but also the opportunity to reach across different cultures such as the Brazilian and German cultures. From this bridging of cultures, I realized enormous satisfaction.

I also included Part II to show that even after great tragedy, it is possible to have the resilience to create a better future.

Ernest Paul
2010

Blessed is the match consumed in kindling flame.

Blessed is the flame that burns in the secret fastness of the heart.

Blessed is the heart with strength to stop its beating for honor's sake.

Blessed is the match consumed in kindling flame.

—Hannah Senesh, 1944

Table of Contents

Prefaces   i

Part I   Love and Death

Chapter 1   A Bountiful Harvest   1
Chapter 2   My Brother Villie   11
Chapter 3   Cousin Ludvik   14
Chapter 4   Berehove   17
Chapter 5   Budapest   19
Chapter 6   *Habonim*   22
Chapter 7   *Levente*   26
Chapter 8   The Supply Train   29
Chapter 9   An Attempted Rescue   32
Chapter 10   Arrest and Torture   42
Chapter 11   Liberation   48
Chapter 12   A Delegation to Bucharest   52
Chapter 13   Train to Freedom   55
Chapter 14   Sara Kafmanova   57
Chapter 15   Cousin Sara's Story   62
Chapter 16   Marriage in Bucharest   64
Chapter 17   The Long Journey   67
Chapter 18   Carlo Forlanini Institute   70
Chapter 19   Rome to Merano   74
Chapter 20   Aliyah to *Eretz Israel*   77
Chapter 21   Tivon, Our New Home   82
Chapter 22   The IDF   89
Chapter 23   *The Etzel Altelana*   *93*

Chapter 24	The Upper Galilee	96
Chapter 25	*Metzach*	*98*
Chapter 26	*Histadrut*	*104*
Chapter 27	Villie, After the War	109
Chapter 28	First Visit to the U.S.	111
Chapter 29	Rationing in Israel	116
Chapter 30	Sinai War 1956	117
Chapter 31	Stewart and Nancy, "Pioneer"	119
Chapter 32	Revisiting my Hometown	123
Chapter 33	Our Fiftieth Anniversary	126
Chapter 34	A Trip to Remember	128
Chapter 35	Our Marriage of 62 Years	129
Chapter 36	Business and Pleasure	132
Chapter 37	Recognition of Heroism	134
Chapter 38	Ari's *Bar Mitzvah*	*136*
Chapter 39	Eitan, The Peacemaker	140
Chapter 40	Gil and the Hillel Angels	142
Chapter 41	Committed to Education	146
Chapter 42	Sara's Devotion to Family	148
Chapter 43	Five Great Grandchildren	154
Chapter 44	Sara's Last Struggle	157
Chapter 45	Our Final Cruise	160
Chapter 46	In Treatment	164
Chapter 47	Sara's Funeral	170
Chapter 48	Friends	171
Chapter 49	Two *Simchahs*	*175*
Chapter 50	From the Ashes	178

Part II   Business Ventures

Chapter 51	Hula Hoops	181
Chapter 52	Ceramic Glass Housewares	185
Chapter 53	Weigh In!	188
Chapter 54	Business Changes	191
Chapter 55	The Fire	193
Chapter 56	Vacuum Metalizing	195
Chapter 57	Meeting David Chase	201
Chapter 58	Nelson McCoy Factory	206
Chapter 59	Studying the Ceramics Industry	209
Chapter 60	The Smiley Craze	212
Chapter 61	Klaus Schumacher	213
Chapter 62	Klaus, The Pioneer	220
Chapter 63	Business in Brazil	225
Chapter 64	Primex Is Born	228
Chapter 65	My Baby	231
Chapter 66	The Rumpf Project	235
Chapter 67	Avon Products	237
Chapter 68	Hand-Painted Products by Weiss	241
Chapter 69	The Breweries	247
Chapter 70	Brazilian Furniture	251
Chapter 71	The Dean of Furniture	255
Chapter 72	Brazilian Sweets	263
Chapter 73	Oxford Ceramics	265
Chapter 74	Porcelana Schmidt	267
Chapter 75	Tramontina	270
Chapter 76	Our Helicopter Venture	274
Chapter 77	Handicraft Project	278
Chapter 78	Our Successful Business Model	282

Chapter 79	Primex Chile	284
Chapter 80	The Presidential Palace	289
Chapter 81	Chilean Toys	292
Chapter 82	Trade Shows	294
Chapter 83	Scheurich Keramik	297
Chapter 84	Israel	301
Chapter 85	Partnership with Shaul Eisenberg	309
Chapter 86	Crystalline, Israel	316
Chapter 87	Primex Argentina	319
Chapter 88	Primex Colombia	320
Chapter 89	Primex Peru	322
Chapter 90	L'Chaim !	325
Chapter 91	Interview with my Saba-Grandfather	327
Postscript		334
Appendix		337
Maps		340
Works Cited		346
Endnotes		347
Photographs		357

Stewart's Preface

Each time a man stands up for an ideal, or acts to improve the lot of others, or strikes out against injustice, he sends forth a tiny ripple of hope, and crossing each other from a million different centers of energy and daring, those ripples build a current that can sweep down the mightiest walls of oppression and resistance. —*Robert F. Kennedy*

Our dad, Ernest Paul, is charismatic, honest, hardworking, loving, intelligent and unpretentious. This is certainly a tribute that would make any man proud. Thanks to his writing of this book, we have learned so much more about him. Our father's book is a gift to every reader and a precious legacy to his family. It allows us to learn of his depth of character, his experiences, and his triumphs in the face of incredible challenges

My sister Dahlia, my brother Gil, and I grew up in an immigrant middle class home where chasing the "American dream" was usually the purpose of life. We had no grandparents and a relatively small extended family. Mom and Dad filled this void with close friends who in many ways were closer than family. As young children, we knew our parents were different or unusual. Mom and Dad spoke with funny accents. Dad traveled a great deal and worked long hours. Mom was involved in every aspect of our lives. They had expectations of how we should lead our lives but did not lecture. We learned our lessons by seeing how they lived their lives, not by what they told us.

Dad believes in the general goodness of people and in a positive future. He believes bad people can change and it is our responsibility to help them. He is for working hard, doing something you believe in.

He knows that one person can make a difference, armed with knowledge and determination. *Tikun Olam* (repair of the world) was more than just a Jewish tenet. It was and is a way of life for Dad.

After World War II, Mom and Dad immigrated to Israel (made *Aliyah*). They later immigrated to the United States. Throughout our childhood, we were told by my father that we would return to Israel. This was his dream and the source of many family discussions and serious arguments between my parents. My father wanted more than to just build a future for himself and his family. Life wasn't just about how much money you made. It was about the mark you left on the world. It was about the good you could accomplish and the lives you could touch. Mom had always felt that they had sacrificed enough and should be able to live in peace without the constant struggle for survival. She believed that building a strong Jewish family was a worthy enough goal after all that was lost in the Holocaust.

We lived for the future and knew little of our parents' past. As we grew older, Mom would tell us of her wonderful childhood, her horrific experiences during World War II, and her challenging years in Israel. In contrast, my father rarely spoke of the past. We only heard bits and pieces from my mother, family, and friends. When we would ask for more detail from my father, he would either change the subject or give a very limited answer. He was too modest to sing his own praises or tell of his accomplishments.

In 1972 my father founded Primex International Corporation. In 1979 I joined him at Primex. Later, my cousin Steve, sister Dahlia, and brother Gil also joined the company. We all had the privilege to work with him and see how he applied humanistic principles to the business world.

Recently, while my wife Nancy and our two sons, Ari and Eitan, visited him in Atlantic City, we went for a stroll on the boardwalk.

He confessed to Nancy and me that perhaps he had made an error in judgment during his years in the business world. He told us, "It was never about the money. We could have been financially much better off if I had focused on doing what was most profitable." Instead he was always looking to make a difference. Dad didn't just want to make a good living for himself and his family; he also wanted to help others to achieve success. Nancy then spoke up and told him how proud we were of his achievements. She reminded him that while we all had very comfortable lives, the true gifts we received from him were far more valuable than material things. Our sons Ari and Eitan have inherited much of Dad's wisdom, optimism, and character. They too want to better the world and dedicate themselves toward this end.

My father resisted writing this book for many years. It was never in his nature to look back. Almost twenty years ago I approached my parents with the idea of writing their stories. I felt that it would be a tragedy to lose them. Their stories are of exceptional people who were tested in extraordinary times.

Finally, at the young age of 81 my father took on the mission of bringing his experiences and those of my mother to a new generation. At 81, my father again reinvented himself. He has become a writer and a lecturer, dedicating himself to sharing these important life experiences. He travels to schools and social clubs and offers his firsthand perspective about what happened during the Holocaust and what Zionism really means. He draws lessons that are meaningful to the trials we face today, inspiring those who hear his story to do their part in easing the continuing suffering around us. Recently, Gil, Dahlia, and I attended an event at Stockton College where Dad spoke eloquently, with great passion, sharing his experiences with students, professors and various honored guests. It was with great pride and a renewed appreciation that we witnessed the reaction of the audience to Dad's exemplary life.

My mother passed away last year before she was able to complete her book. Dad, with Dr. Maryann McLoughlin, completed the task. Once Dad began writing, he approached this effort as he did everything else in his life, with unwavering determination. Without a formal education and no previous writing experience, he completed the telling of not only my mother's life story, but his own. He knew from a lifetime of success, if you are willing to do the work and apply yourself diligently, you can succeed.

In preparation, Dad read other autobiographies and background materials to refresh his memory and determine the approach he would take. He spent countless hours speaking with friends, relatives and acquaintances about their recollections and shared experiences. The same work ethic, curiosity, openness, and creativity he applied throughout his life to various endeavors were put to productive use in writing his autobiography. This book is yet another testament to Dad's indomitable spirit.

My dear father, Ernest Paul, exemplifies the statement, "One man can make a difference." He made a difference saving lives while in the Hungarian Underground. He made a difference helping establish the new State of Israel. He made a difference by creating work for many, many individuals in different countries through his various business ventures, and he is now making a difference in teaching the importance of tolerance and compassion.

Assisting my Dad to get his special story out was both an honor and a wonderful journey of discovery. I am extremely proud of Dad and his book. How extraordinarily blessed I feel to be his son.

Stewart Paul

Gil's Preface

When I was ten or eleven years of age, a homework assignment required that I give thought to who my heroes were. I was asked to select the one that in my eyes had all of the characteristics a real hero should have.

I remember that I did not for a moment consider any alternatives. I already knew who my hero was. The vision I had of my father as that hero has not faded, neither with my age nor his. This was never a child's idealized view of a common man. Anyone that has ever had the fortune of meeting my father knows he is far from ordinary. He is the real deal. A true hero. For sure, some proof of the merit and measure of my words can be found in my father's youth, serving in the Hungarian Underground during World War II at an age that sees most boys today too busy with video games to consider real world heroism. My father remains my hero, not because of who and what he was those long years ago, but for what he is today.

Things did not come particularly easy to my father, and many of his remarkable accomplishments were hard fought, sometimes achieved for no other reason than his exceptional persistence and desire to succeed. He is not just a survivor but a fighter. He has never given up and I know he never will. Of course, being a hero is not just about fighting the good fight. Being a hero is not just about personal accomplishments. We do not define our heroes by evaluating the sacrifices they have made or their contributions. While all of these traits combined form some measure of how we define our heroes, we also consider how our heroes measure up in the eyes of others.

It is in this trait that my father flies like a superman. I am lucky enough to have not only grown as my father's son, but also as a professional, working for a great man. Working with my father, for all its challenges, has given me the opportunity to see him as everyone else does. I cannot count the number of times or the number of people that have asked me about "Ernie" over the years. I cannot begin to guess how many people have told me, in reverent and emotional tones, how they not only respect my father but also love him. I am not talking about family. I am not even talking about friends. I am talking about people that knew my father only professionally, either as clients or as vendors. So many people, time and time again, have expressed to me the honor that they have felt having had the opportunity to work with him or even to have just briefly met him.

My father will forever be my hero but something more and that so few of us can ever aspire to become—he is a hero to everyone that knows him.

Gil Paul

Part I

Love

and Death

Chapter One
A Bountiful Harvest

White peaches, plums, raspberries, grape vines, wooden vine barrels, snow, a horse and sleigh, challah and *cholent*—all these things remind me of the bountifulness of my childhood.

Our family home was in the small town of Beregújfalu (Nové Selo),[1] Czechoslovakia, in the Okres (District) of Berehovo (Czechoslovakian) in the Beregszász (Hungarian) region.[2] My father, Josef Pal, was born in Nové Selo in 1898. He died in 1942, only forty four years old, because he was critically ill with heart problems and extremely high blood pressure. Special arrangements were made to take him to the Jewish Hospital in Budapest; unfortunately, they couldn't save him.

My father was an extraordinary man. Because he was blinded in an accident while serving in the Czech army during World War I, he had received a medal equivalent to the Purple Heart. After a military discharge with honors, he attended regional schools for the blind, in Užhorod (Ungwar), the state capital, where he learned to read Braille, which opened up opportunities in his life. To the best of my knowledge he had no doctor's degree, even though many times people in town addressed him as Dr. Pal. He was the wisest person in town, so people used to ask for his advice and help. He was willing and able to help many.

Despite his blindness, he was very actively involved in politics. During the Czech regime he used to travel to Praha (Prague) and during the Hungarian regime to Budapest on behalf of the people in our town. Many people also referred to him as their lawyer because he was able to open the doors of regional and federal government offices.

My father composed and dictated letters that impressed all recipients and got results. Despite his blindness, nothing stopped him. He had a male secretary/caretaker who was always with him. His secretary read the updated news to him daily. Communications to authorities were through his secretary.

Father managed the various family businesses with great success. While he always had dependable and capable people reporting to him, he was one of a kind—intelligent and hard working. He demanded that others produce results as he did. With all this, he was a loving and caring father as well as a good provider for our family and many others. He undertook projects such as solving the town water supply problem by constructing a deep well that was named in his honor. While some families had their own wells of water in their back yards, many others had to carry water by buckets from the town well. He succeeded in getting funds from the central authorities to improve road conditions, schools, etc. When he was the *Gabbai* of the synagogue he helped build a new synagogue.[3] My father was well respected and liked.

A note about our father: I have been talking to my sister, Chaya, in Israel and my brother, Emil, in New Jersey: we remembered how our father recognized all seven children—five sons, one daughter, and our cousin Ludvik—by our voices or by height; this is still a mystery among ourselves.

Our home was warm in every aspect. For heating we used hard woods that were chopped and piled up in the yard during the summer for drying in order to be ready for the winter.

My mom, Serana Nani, as she was called, was slim and no taller than five feet, but she moved around like "thunder." She was in charge of our strict upbringing. Mom directed the two in-house helpers we had. She was directly in charge of the grocery store in front of our house. Although she was always busy, she never failed to make sure that the children were properly fed, properly dressed for school, and prepared with our homework. However, when Friday noon came, all the businesses stopped, and her full attention and love was devoted to the family.

We always had a special Friday night candle lighting, and we dressed up to go to services. The special Shabbat dinners started with the blessing of the home baked challah, two long, tasty challah with honey on top.[4] The Kiddush (the blessing of the wine) was always the job of my older brothers, Villie or Emil.[5] These Sabbath dinners were delightful.

On Saturday morning at 9 AM we all dressed up and went to Sabbath services that ended after noon.

By the time we came home, the long, beautiful dining room table was covered with a white tablecloth and set for lunch. My mother and our maids were excellent cooks. During the winter we often had *cholent* made in a red clay casserole of beans with meat placed in a special oven we had in the back yard on Friday before the Sabbath.[6] On Saturday, the *cholent* was mouth watering and ready to eat.

After lunch, during the summers, the whole family took a stroll, visiting friends or just walking along with many other families.

Looking back I must say that we had a wonderful home and a good life—while it lasted.

Villie was my oldest brother; born in 1919, he passed away in Miami, Florida, in 1987. Emil, born in 1924, lives with his wife, Lili, in Marlton, New Jersey. My sister, Chaya, born in 1926, lives in Haifa, Israel, with her husband, Avraham. I was born on January 14, 1928. Two of my brothers did not survive Auschwitz: Laychi, born in 1930, and Feri, in 1932.

Because Villie was the oldest, he often was involved with my dad and mom in the various businesses, such as the farms and wineries that we owned. We had a grocery store in front of our big house, managed by my mom. In the back we had a *Korchma*, a bar, which was also used as a "club"—a hang-out place for the many patrons (99% non-Jews). This *Korchma* was a large hall with three billiard tables; drinks were served starting at 6 AM, five and a half days a week (particularly in winter); we were always closed on Friday at 12 noon and we did not reopen until Sunday morning. Indeed, Sunday was the busiest day. Our *Korchma* was also known as Pal Josef's "town hall."

Emil, Laychi, Feri, and I used to sneak into the back of the *Korchma* when our parents were not watching. Despite strict instructions to the manager not to allow us in, we did go in and were fascinated with the noise, the singing of the drunk patrons, and the billiard tables. As my sister, Chaya, was a beautiful teenager, our parents sternly restricted her from entering the bar.

We had large wine cellars. The driver of our horse and carriage (*fiacre*) took us often to the wineries during the summer vacation and the fruit season months. Sometimes we walked. Harvest season was always beautiful. In addition to the large volume of grapes that we had, my father's company purchased grapes from the smaller growers. The grapes were packaged in special home-made baskets with a flat lid sewn on the top with raffia-grass. The grapes were sold and shipped in rail cars to big city wholesalers across the country.

Father also made his own wines. Our wine cellar contained many large homemade wooden barrels filled with wine and properly dated and stored at the right temperature. A wine master worked for my father; however, my father had to taste every batch to approve or disapprove the wine master's classification. The making of the wine was mostly done by school kids. We had a number of hydraulic presses, a large open wooden-slatted barrel where the grapes were thrown in from the bushel baskets. First the operator turned the handle round to press down the load of grapes. Then followed the fun: after washing our feet, we kids and the hired kids jumped into the barrel with bare feet, dancing around and around, sometimes for hours and sometimes for many days. While the kids were resting, the press was turned around and around again. The grape juice flowed into a large funnel and into wooden barrels. There was much laughter as kids fell down from time to time into the grape juice.

When my wife, Sara, my sister, Chaya, from Israel, and I visited Nové Selo in 1988, we hosted a little gathering with the help of a former employee of our parents. They told us: "We have never had good wine since your father passed on."

In addition to grapes we had beautiful peaches particularly the white peaches (*fahaire barrack*), raspberries, cherries, and plenty of plums. The peaches were to be eaten; the cherries, plums, and raspberries were to make jelly. After the pits were taken out of the plums and cherries, they were washed and cooked to perfection in a large copper kettle (this was called *"Lekvar"*). In the back of our home we had land for farming wheat, corn, potatoes, and vegetables.

Two stables, one for cows and one for horses, were only about a hundred feet from the back of our home. There was a special area for chickens and ducks, even though many times they roamed around the yard. We had lots of fun in the hay stacks where we children often played.

During the winter months our town was covered with many layers of luscious white snow. Lakes and rivers were frozen for months. This did not stop our parents or us. Our parents knew well how to deal with the cold season.

I remember our big open sled, room to seat the entire family, with plentiful blankets. We had warm clothing and handmade knitted mittens and gloves. Our feet were kept warm next to pre-heated red bricks. Away we would go on the sled to Berehovo, our neighboring big city, about forty-five minutes away. We always looked forward to these sleigh rides.

We children loved the winter season. Schools would be closed several times during the winter season because of the weather. We had ice skates that locked onto our shoes with a key, and the frozen lakes were our playgrounds; the hills, perfect for sled rides. Some of us were also privileged to have skis, homemade out of good hard woods. The only one in town that had professional skis and boots was one of our school teachers who came from Prague to teach in the Czech school; he had brought his gear with him, including woolen gloves and hat.

We had in town one bakery owned by our cousins, the Rosners. Uncle Shamu had a neatly trimmed reddish beard; he was a *Shomer Shabbat.*[7] He had a special oven in another building that was used to make kosher matzah, unleavened bread. This was a Jewish community effort. Kids and grownups got up at 3 AM to participate in making the matzah for all the families. If my memory serves me right, the flour was supplied by a few who had their own wheat (as in our case). Baking of the matzah continued off and on for seven days. This was almost a religious ceremony. These were extremely happy days–Pesach (Passover) was coming.[8]

Because our Jewish community was small (only about fifty-five families), we had only one synagogue. Just about every Jewish family was in the synagogue on Friday nights, Saturdays, and all holidays. Listening to the *chazzan* and the rabbi was uplifting.

The first synagogue I remember was a small, old building close to a church. In 1938, my father was the *Gabbai* (organized synagogue services); he donated a piece of land on a small hill about 1000 feet from our home. He solicited help from some of the richer families and in less than a year a new synagogue was ready. It was a two-story building with a red-clay covered roof.

The inside was furbished with comfortable wooden benches and four Torahs in an attractive Ark.[9] In the middle of the synagogue was a wooden podium with three or four steps where the Torah was read, and the rabbi, chazzan, and the *Gabi* sat. The women sat and prayed in the second floor balcony.

It was always a warm experience to go to the synagogue. Everyone dressed up, prayed, and talked. Thinking back I realize there definitely was more talking, certainly among us kids, than praying.

The children often spent time in the yard of the synagogue playing "buttons in the hole." In this game, we shot or slid a button with our finger to the hole in the ground about four or five feet away. On *Succoth* we used to play the same game with walnuts.[10] Five or six kids played, and whoever got his walnut in or was closest to the hole won all the walnuts. Another popular game was hitting a homemade cotton ball with a stick, as far out as we could, almost like baseball; however, we had no special rounded sticks.

The synagogue was on a small hill, so on one side the elevation was about 8 feet high on a 45° angle. This section was cemented and ideal for sliding off. And slide we did; we even had competitions similar to today's skate board competitions. We had lots of fun.

In town we had four schools, in relatively small buildings: Hungarian, Czech, Ukraine, and German schools. Parents decided where to send their children. In our case, my brother Villie attended the Hungarian school, Emil went to the Ukraine and Czech schools, Chaya some years to the Hungarian and other years to the Czech, and I also went a few years to the Czech school but mostly to the Hungarian. That part of the world changed hands from the Hungarian regime to Czech and back to Hungarian in the late 1930's.

At home we spoke mostly Hungarian; however, we also spoke Czech and Ukrainian. In our house Yiddish was not the dominate language, although we spoke some, in particular with our grandparents, Esther and Shimon.

My formal schooling in Beregújfalu was eight years of public school. I had better schooling in Budapest where I moved when I was thirteen years old, living with my aunts and uncles, the Junger family. Much later I had the opportunity to take years of evening classes in Israel. I attended many courses, such as seminars, speech training, political science, socialism, and Zionism.

We did have a cheder, a Jewish school housed in one of the rooms of the synagogue. We did not have many kids in our classes. The one teacher was usually from Berehovo or Munkács; he lived with one of the families and ate every week in another student's home. The teaching level was very elementary, basically focusing on learning to pray in Hebrew. To understand the meaning of the Hebrew, we also learned *Chumash* (Pentateuch: Five Books of Moses) and *Rashi* (commentary on the *Chumash*). The teacher spoke to us in Yiddish often mixed with Hungarian. The cheder also prepared us for our Bar Mitzvahs.[11] The cheder definitely helped me as I moved on to Budapest and joined the Zionist youth movement because this group spoke Hebrew. In fact, to speak Hebrew was a prerequisite to making aliyah to *Eretz Yisrael*.[12] Even before I arrived in *Eretz Yisrael*, my Hebrew was almost as perfect as a Sabra (a Jew born in Israel), for I loved the language and devoted myself to speaking Hebrew as well as possible, knowing and hoping that one day Hebrew would be my spoken language in *Eretz Yisrael*.

I remember vividly these years of my life at home. Our parents were very hard working people. Our mom and dad were strict with us. There were rules of the house that every one of us had to obey:

these rules were about washing ourselves, our eating habits, rules about dressing properly for each occasion, for school and synagogue.

There was time for school and time for playing. Often we boys played among ourselves. Emil was the ring leader because he was the oldest after Villie, who, most of the time, was busy with our father and the business.

We often played hide and seek in our big house or outside. From time to time the boys used to gang up against our sister. These fights sometimes ended with one of us crying, but most times these were happy times. Our home was spacious enough to accommodate five sons and a daughter in addition to our older cousin, Ludvik, who lived with us. Ludvik was like a brother to us. We followed him around and often he played with us, taking us for bicycle rides to the lakes. However, as he was older, twenty years old, so he had his own circle of friends.

Happily, we lived next door to my grandparents. To enter our house, we had to go through two heavy wooden, rustic looking gates. Our house was on the left, and our grandparents', on the right, parallel to ours.

Our grandmother and grandfather were the only ones who spoiled us. They gave us everything we wanted, from candy and chocolates, to walnuts, apples, pears, and other sweet things that were plentiful in their house.

My paternal grandmother, Esther, was one of the oldest people in town. When I left at the age of thirteen, she was eighty-four years old; our grandfather had already passed away in 1935, at age eighty-two. Grandmother loved sitting outside in the summer in a rocking chair, smoking her long wooden pipe. The pipe was unique; she was the only woman I knew that smoked a pipe like this. The pipe was longer than her arms could comfortably reach to light up. The end of the pipe, which from an angle looked like a trumpet, had a metal cap.

She used to stuff the pipe by pressing the dried tobacco in with her finger. Then she asked one of us kids to light the pipe for her. To us this was a funny experience; the tobacco smelled like nothing else we could compare with, but it was fun.

After grandfather died and grandmother was alone, the grandchildren took turns sleeping over in her house. We usually fought over this privilege, for she had all kinds of goodies and sweets in her house. For nighttime, she loved to prepare for herself a big cup of light coffee—the bottom half of the cup was sugar. I used to take her cup while she was asleep, pour the top portion of the coffee into another cup, eat the sugar, and pour back her light coffee. One day she caught up with me. She said, "Don't mess with my coffee. If you want sugar, I will give you all you want." Grandmother loved sugar cubes. The sugar came in packages, and she always had several boxes of sugar hidden in her house. Our parents did not allow us to have much sugar.

Ernest's Father

Father with Villie

Beregújfalu, 1988

Beregújfalu, 1988

Chapter Two
My Brother Villie

My oldest brother, Villie, was very popular. When I was thirteen, he was already twenty-two years old. His nickname was the "pretty rich boy." However, he was a very serious young man. My father, who was blind, kept Villie close to him. As a result Villie was very involved in the family businesses. This shaped his serious personal character. Often his self-confidence and independence created heated arguments between my father and him.

Villie had a mind of his own that sometimes got him into trouble. One day he decided that he did not have all the freedom he felt he should have at home. He moved to the other end of town where he rented a small house. In front of the house he opened a small store to sell yarns, candy, and cigarettes.

This move was to demonstrate his independence, financially and socially. Because he was the son of Joseph Pal, his social life was rich and diversified. He placed no limits on his new found freedom. He was very popular with the girls; therefore, he could not keep the girls out of his store—in particular, one beautiful redhead by the name of Marishka. On a cold, rainy day one of Villie's neighbors, the father of Marishka Gabor, who lived across the street from his store showed up in our house. Neither Mom nor Dad was pleased with his unannounced visit. Gabor stormed into our house, screaming:

"Where is he? Your son Villie! My daughter, seventeen-years old Marishka, is pregnant from your son."

Gabor carried on, screaming and threatening my parents and Villie. "I will kill him," he repeated several times. They served him a couple of drinks to calm him down; however, before he left our house, he repeated, "I'll kill him."

Apparently before Gabor came to our house, he had walked across the street from where he lived into Villie's store. Villie saw him coming through the front, so he snuck out the back door, leaving the store unattended. My father sent one of his people to bring Villie home.

When Villie arrived, both my mother and my father were waiting for him. "Explain yourself!" was my father's cry. Mom asked, "How could you do this to us? How could you do this to the young girl?" Villie's reply was, "I will take care of everything." Very angered, our parents ushered him out of the house. Villie again tried to reassure Mom and Dad; he would take care of everything. The story has been told that Villie paid off the girl's father with a significant amount of money.

Villie contacted the Czech military authorities and volunteered for the army. The storm was still brewing in town. Villie closed his store and disappeared. A month passed before my parents received a letter from Villie apologizing for his actions and for leaving home. In his letter Villie told us that he was in the military in the city of Bilke.

My parents' Jewish hearts were bleeding. They felt that they had treated him too harshly. They felt guilty. Mostly our mother had a soft spot in her heart. She immediately gathered a care package: "We must not abandon the poor kid!"

Our father did not feel sorry for Villie. He said, "Maybe the army will make a *mensch* out of him."

Mother didn't waste time; she told my brother Emil and me about the arrangements she was making for us to deliver a package to poor Villie.

We traveled by train with two medium-sized wooden boxes filled with goodies that Villie loved. When we arrived at Bilke train station, we took a horse and buggy to the military camp. We were a big surprise to Villie; he was very happy to see his two brothers.

Mom's letter that we hand-delivered softened Villie to the point of tears. He told us, "Tell Mom and Dad that I am all right. I have a business here and plenty of money. I have everything I need." From under his cot, Villie pulled out two large wooden military trunks, opened them, and showed us that he was selling to his fellow soldiers a variety of products: cigarettes, razor blades, shoe laces, chocolates, candy, and on and on.

When we returned home, we shared with our parents and the rest of the family that Villie was doing well. My father said, "Villie never ceases to amaze me—his business sense, his independent thinking, his confidence, and his ability to make good even from a difficult situation." Villie was loved by all of us.

A year later as the Hungarians took over that part of the country all the Jews who had served in the Czech army were taken to a labor camp in Germany.

From the German labor camp, Villie and some of his comrades escaped to Russia where he served in the Czech partisan unit until the war ended. From Russia he made his way to Prague, the capital of Czechoslovakia. As a partisan freedom fighter wearing a Czech uniform he had special privileges.

Chapter Three
My Cousin Ludvik

Ludvik was born in Beregújfalu in 1919. His father, Samuel Pal, and mother, Shari, immigrated to the United States in 1934. Their son, Ludvik, was born deaf and mute. The U.S. authorities did not allow him to enter the U.S. because of his handicap.

His parents, my father's brother and sister-in-law, decided to leave Ludvik with us for "a while." When my uncle and aunt arrived in the U.S., they went to Philadelphia. As soon as they settled in the U.S., they started to work on bringing their son to join them in the U.S. For years and years their efforts continued with no results.

Like another brother, Ludvik grew up with us in our home. He was the same age as my brother Villie; these two became the best of friends and the most furious competitors.

While Ludvik could neither speak nor hear well, he was the best student in the entire school—with his way of communicating. My parents used to say: "God made up for his limitations in one way by giving him many other advantages." He had natural talents; he was the first one in town to ride by standing up on the seat and frame of the bike. He performed and challenged my brother Villie and the other boys in town, younger or older; he was a daredevil in more than one way. When the non-Jewish boys picked a fight with my brothers, he jumped in to finish the fight. On his own he learned and became the mechanic in town —a jack of all trades.

Ludvik fixed radios, gramophones, bicycles, furnaces, heating ovens, clocks, and watches. One spring day he showed up in our town with a motorcycle that he had purchased second hand in Berehovo. This caused a big sensation in our small town.

Ludvik here, Ludvik there, Ludvik everywhere. He was a great attraction to the boys that looked up to him in admiration, fear, or jealousy. The girls were always around him as well.

One famous tale about my cousin Ludvik is the following:

A couple of days before Yom Kippur 1940, all the Jewish families were busy preparing for the holiest day of the year.[13] The one synagogue in town was being painted, cleaned, and prepared for the Jewish families and all the children.

We had a *chazzan* and rabbi for the holidays—everyone prayed for forgiveness and for a good year. Our small town did not have a *shochet*, a ritual slaughterer to prepare the kosher poultry, the chicken, geese, and ducks; therefore, the Jewish community had a contracted *shochet* who came every Friday morning to slaughter the poultry for Shabbat. Once in a while it was a lamb, a calf, or a cow.

Needless to say for Yom Kippur, the demand was larger than usual. It was two days before Yom Kippur. The *shochet* had not arrived. Everyone was concerned: "How is that possible? Today of all days?"

Some families were upset and hired horses and buggies to go to a *shochet* in a neighboring town. One day before the holiday the other families were in a panic. Ludvik came to the rescue: by that time he had already upgraded from a bike to a motorcycle. Therefore, when he discovered the problem, he volunteered to rig up baskets and burlap rice sacks on his motorcycle to take the poultry to Berehovo to the *shochet*.

About half way there Ludvik's motorcycle broke down. He was in a panic: "My G-d," he thought, "I need a new tire that I cannot get in time. I will disappoint many families." The only way he could make it back to town on time for the holiday was if he came up with a solution right then and there. Ludvik, the genius, found a solution.

Ludvik took out his folding knife (which was always with him) and started to cut the throats of each of the birds—as he had seen the *shochet* do many times. To make the process credible, Ludvik rejected some chickens as being non-kosher by forcing some green corn stems in the throat of the rejects. Obviously he disappointed some;however, the majority received their "kosher" chickens on time.

The following week on Friday morning, the *shochet* came to town after he had recuperated from his illness. The first question he asked was, "How was it possible that no one showed up last week before *Yom Kippur* with the poultry?"

"No one showed up? Ludvik took thirty hens, chickens, and ducks."

"Where did Ludvik go? I did not see him."

My father and grandfather Shimon, my brother Villie, everyone was looking for Ludvik, who had disappeared when the *shochet* had arrived.

Once they cornered Ludvik, he admitted and told his truth in writing: "My most important concern was not to disappoint the families. I tried to help."

At first, my parents were angry because they felt responsible for Ludvik's actions. But Ludvik apologized with tears in his eyes, so they decided to forget the incident and forgive him.

In late 1943, Ludvik was taken to Auschwitz-Birkenau Concentration Camp with my mother, my sister Chaya, and my two younger brothers, Feri and Lajchi. Ludvik, my mother, Feri, and Laychi were murdered in late 1943 or early 1944.

Chapter Four
Our Neighboring City, Berehovo

The neighboring city of Berehovo (Beregszász) was only forty-five minutes away by bicycle or horse drawn wagon. Someone from the family was in Berehovo every week.

Berehovo had a population of about 50,000 people with about 2,000 Jewish families. The Jewish community was very actively involved and influential in all facets of life. Berehovo was known to be the center for higher education, business, regional government offices, and major sport activities. In the 1930s, it was considered a modern, booming city.

In our small town Beregújfalu, it was common to hear anti-Jewish remarks, spoken in Ukrainian, German, Hungarian, or Czech. From time to time we heard, "Dirty Jew." ("*Budösh Zsidó.*") We Jewish kids never turned the other cheek. Our reaction was immediate and convincing. It was well known that the Jewish kids acted spontaneously, one for all, all for one.

I was a restless kid with dreams beyond Beregújfalu. I had heard from my parents that my father had twelve sisters and brothers in Budapest. I approached them with the idea of my going for a visit. My father reacted strongly: "You are only twelve years old. You have to think of your Bar Mitzvah before you think of anything else."

I knew my father's weak side; I started to hug and kiss him, and he definitely softened up. He turned to me, "If you will learn well your part for the Bar Mitzvah, I'll think about your wish to visit your aunts and uncles, but not before the Bar Mitzvah."

Shortly before my Bar Mitzvah, my Aunt Sharika who lived in Újpest (also known as New Pest, District IV in Budapest, Hungary, located on the left bank of the Danube River) surprised us with a visit. The timing couldn't have been better. I really focused and studied seriously. I thought, "My savior is here; maybe she will take me with her."

My father was a man of his word. After talking to my aunt, he agreed to let me go. She was happy to take me. We never discussed the extent of the visit. We agreed that we would take it as it came; time would tell how long I would be staying.

Chapter Five
My Arrival in Budapest

Budapest was not only the capital of Hungary but also a beautiful and cosmopolitan city. Budapest was known as the Paris of the East. Budapest had become a single city occupying both banks of the Danube River on November 17, 1873; right-bank Buda and Óbuda were united with left-bank Pest. Coming from a small town, I was especially excited to be living in a large city like Budapest.

Upon my arrival to my Aunt Sharika's house in 1941, my Uncle Shamu, and my five cousins, Shari, Lipi, Mano, Tibi, and Fery, made me feel at home from the first moment. Tibi was fourteen, willing to share his room with me and everything he had. Tibi introduced me to his friends.

On the first Friday night, we all dressed up to go to the synagogue with Uncle Shamu. The synagogue, of course, was in walking distance of the house.[14] I was very excited with my new environment. Everything was so much bigger, so much different from back home. The synagogue was huge compared to the synagogue in our town; there must have been two hundred adults and children for services.

The following morning after services I was told of a meeting of young people on the lower level of the synagogue. My cousin Tibi was actively involved with this group. The meeting turned out to be a gathering of *Habonim*. This was my first experience of a lecture by the enthusiastic Arani Asher—on the subject of the Zionist movement.[15] I was very interested; I identified with and liked what I heard.

I had attended a Zionist gathering with my older brother Emil only a couple of times. At these meetings, I heard about *Eretz Yisrael*, our future Jewish homeland. In Újpest I was also invited to the home of József Gárdosh, a friend, one of the leaders of *Habonim*, a Zionist organization. I joined the *Habonim* movement, becoming an active member. I didn't miss any lectures or opportunities to hear and learn about the Zionist philosophy.

I attended school with my cousin Tibi. I was pleased with my new life, eager to study and learn. I think back about how I dreamed of exploring further the Zionist philosophy. Although I adjusted easily to my new home with my aunt, uncle, and cousins, my sense of obligation drove me to seek parttime employment after school hours. I found work in an upholsterer's shop as a delivery boy, driving a tricycle, while at the same time learning the skills of an upholsterer with room and board, enabling me to be independent.

At first my aunt and uncle didn't like the idea; they felt a sense of responsibility for me through my parents. I convinced them to let me try my independence for a couple of months—and they did, despite my being only thirteen and a half years old. Because my place was near my relatives' home, it was easier for them and me. I had many meals in their home as I was there playing with my cousins and their friends almost every day. Friday nights and Saturday I was always with them in their warm home. In the synagogue basement I attended weekly lectures. I made new friends, with kids my own age, and some a year or two older than I.

A year later was a milestone for me—a year since I had come to Újpest. I had learned a lot. There had been difficult days when I was thinking about my family back home in Beregújfalu. Yet I had a strong will and the determination to make my life as worthwhile as possible under the circumstances.

In 1942 we were told during our meetings at *Habonim* about the deportation of the Polish Jews. We also learned about the concentration camps and Hitler's dream of having the world *Judenrein*, a world with no Jews. We also learned about a Hungarian hero, Hannah Senesh, her life, her giving up a warm, loving, and comfortable home to make aliyah to *Eretz Yisrael* in 1939, when she was only eighteen years old. We learned about her philosophy and beliefs: "One person can make a difference." She lived up to what she preached. Soon after parachuting in to war torn Hungary, she was murdered by the Nazis while trying to save Jewish lives. Greatly inspired by her example, we too tried to make a difference.

Chapter Six
Habonim Dror

In 1942, when I was in Újpest, the Nazis were becoming quite visible in Budapest and the surrounding areas. The threatening decibel of the Nazi presence broke upon each dawn and sunset with ever increasing force. And though not yet under the Nazi regime, Hungarian fascism had begun to unleash its propaganda and terrorism against the Jews. We never imagined betrayal by our non-Jewish friends and neighbors.

We, as *Habonim* young men and women, began to train for specific military responsibilities, thirteen, fourteen, and fifteen-year olds met in synagogue basements once or twice a week.

Habonim members went through a training course in the use of pistols, rifles, and grenades. Our trainer was Villi Eisikovics.

Zionism had prepared the way, for Jewish youth to be proud of their Jewish heritage. Additionally, Zionism had prepared us for the eventual goal of making aliyah to *Eretz Yisrael*. Attending Hebrew classes was a requisite. The leaders were graduates of the Hebrew schools in Užhorod and Munkács, with the exception of Zvi Goldfarb who arrived from Poland in 1942. In Budapest he met his future wife, Neshka Szandel, both becoming historic leaders. They survived, made *aliyah*, and became founders and active members of Kibbutz Gardosh-Farod, near the city of Zfat. József Gárdosh and Arányi Asher were the leaders in Újpest; they were remarkable leaders, who infused every meeting with dynamic, radiant energy. Their strength and dedication to the cause and their physical as well as their spiritual presence, inspired us, for we recognized the mark of heroism.

The small Zionist youth groups were scattered throughout the towns and cities of Hungary and organized under a national federation. Regional weekend meetings took place in a village high in the mountains of Budapest. These meetings usually drew about one hundred kids who arrived by bike and train. It took me well over an hour each way because I had to change trains twice in each direction.

József Gárdosh, Arányi Asher, and Villi, as well as other leaders who held national posts in *Habonim*, conducted lectures and training classes. The leaders kept us informed and updated as to the political changes, the probability that the present Hungarian regime would soon fall.[16] They knew of Germany's ambition, under Adolf Hitler, to conquer Europe, including Hungary, so they labored zealously preparing against the inevitable attack on the Jewish community, although we had no knowledge in those early days of the ultimate fate of the Jews.

David Gur, Villi Eisikovics, and Moshe Lazarovics operated some of the several small print shops producing false documents to furnish thousands of Zionist youth, as well as others who opposed the Nazi regime, the protection of "safe" (Gentile) identities.

Gur survived and published Brothers for Resistance and Rescue *(2004). Lazarovics survived the Holocaust and documented his underground activities in* Fight for Life *in Hebrew (1992). Lazarovics died in Israel in 2005. Villi Eisikovics made aliyah to Palestine in 1946; he was one of the founders of Kibbutz Gardosh-Farod , named after József Gárdosh. After a number of years, Villi was sent on a diplomatic mission to Austria, where he died in 2006.*

Dozens of groups throughout Budapest and smaller surrounding cities and suburbs were linked to underground organizations at various levels of activities. In the beginning I knew every member of my group of forty, as well as their activities. However, as times grew increasingly dangerous, we split up into smaller groups for mutual protection; therefore, knowledge of each other became limited.

Through its connections with Israeli-trained commanders in Poland, Hungary, and Czechoslovakia, *Habonim* grew into a tight-knit organization. To protect the individual members of the organization, orders were issued daily at designated meeting points, to two or three people at most. The crowds at the vast Kelety and Nyugati train stations afforded anonymity, so these two locations alternated with a busy public park, as points often utilized for meetings.

Each day I was informed by a runner as to the exact location of the next day's meeting. *Habonim* commanders never disseminated information regarding plans beyond the immediate need to know. One of my direct commanders was Villi Eisikovics, twenty-one years old, self taught, from a religious home in the Carpathian area. As a self appointed leader, Villi initiated plans and was determined to complete all missions.

We had almost weekly gatherings in 1943 and early 1944 on Sundays. The leaders were József Gárdos and Arányi Asher, and later we were joined by Zvi Goldfarb, Neshka Szandel, and Villi Eisikovics. We were given updates of our movement's efforts to organize, train on small weapons, pistols, rifles, and grenades.

We were willing to sacrifice to be ready for the eventual occupation, which we expected because of the unfortunate success of Hitler's regime that continued to gain influence and control. We were told about the concentration camps, about the suffering of the German, Austrian, and Polish Jews. We were lectured about Kristallnacht (The November Pogrom of 1938), about Hitler's "final solution," to have a world with no Jews, the solution of *Judenrein*. We were told about the

Warsaw Ghetto resistance, about partisan underground activities, and about the bunkers in Poland.

As a Zionist movement, we were reminded often about our ultimate goals to live through this war and to help others. However, aliyah to *Eretz Yisrael* was our ultimate objective.

Chapter Seven
Levente

By the beginning of 1944, I had moved from Újpest to Budapest and assumed the name of Wadai Janosh (with false documents). I had found a small apartment on Ershebet utza, shared with a fellow Jewish boy, Josef Rakoshi, whose real name was Josef Rosenberg.

In early 1944 the situation in Hungary became even more dangerous. The Hungarian government under Miklós Horthy had refused to deport Hungarian Jews, except to labor camps. However, in March 1944, the fascist Ferenc Szálasi, leader of the National Socialist Arrow Cross Party, became Hungary's de facto prime minister. From March 1944 on, Germany dictated all procedures in Hungary.

As early as February 1944, there was a "call" by the Hungarian Arrow Cross government to the youth of Hungary: "Your country needs you. Become a *Levente*." The call was to those of pre-military age, all thirteen to seventeen years old, including girls, despite the opposition of the Catholic Church. *Levente* was the name of the Hungarian youth paramilitary unit supporters of the Nazis, similar to the Hitler *Jugend* (Hitler Youth). I was told by József Gárdos that we needed to penetrate this youth movement and that I would be a good candidate. I looked like a typical Hungarian, blonde-haired and blue-eyed. Moreover, I spoke fluent Hungarian.

I found the way to the regional recruiting center. There was a line of about thirty. When my turn came, I entered the office. A young lieutenant asked me my reason for volunteering. My answer was ready:

"*Hive a haza*" (the homeland is calling). I was calm and made a good impression. My papers were processed; I was accepted.

The following Monday I had to report to Andrashi headquarters (Andrashi Avenue is called the *Champs Elysees* of Budapest). From there we were taken by truck to a military camp, about a thirty-minute ride, where we were given uniforms and told about the disciplinary requirements of the training center. The training consisted of walking, marching, and saluting. After a couple of weeks some of us were called out to form a separate unit.

We started to train separately with pistols, grenades, and rifles. For me this was not new; however, I couldn't show off my previous training, so I faked being a "quick learner." We also trained to ride mopeds, Csepel-made.

Throughout the six weeks, we were lectured to about the war effort, challenging our readiness and willingness to assist in whatever capacity was needed. Our group was assigned to office desk jobs, as runners and messengers, and sometimes we patrolled with the Hungarian police. I graduated the course with honors and was given a rank of lieutenant in the youth *Levente* division.

During this whole time, I was in touch with my superiors in *Habonim*. I was given various assignments because I was free to move around. I visited Jewish families before they were forced into the ghettos. The printing presses were working well; therefore, we started to distribute forged documents well before the ghetto in Budapest.

I adopted Hungarian behavior and style. I spoke fluent Hungarian and had inherited my mother's dark blue eyes and her pale blond hair, which I wore long. The patrolling Nazis and the Hungarian police never suspected me of being a Jew. I freely mingled with the Hungarian Nazi youth movement members.

I was very mindful of avoiding the district where I could run into Hungarian ex-friends. I felt no fear, nor did I know at age fifteen and sixteen what fear means. However, it was dangerous to enter Jewish homes affixed with the yellow star or to mingle with people who wore the yellow star.

Often my own mother came to mind. I wondered: Is she still alive? What about my sister and brothers? Who is going to save them? I would force myself to snap out of thinking about those horrible eventualities to go back to being the brave person I had to be.

During the day I had an office desk at the headquarters, and I had twelve graduates reporting to me. I was proud as a Jewish young man to be in charge of twelve non-Jews.

I was under the command of a Hungarian police officer. He was well seasoned, experienced, and strict; he made sure all the time that we knew who the commander—the boss—was.

My schedule began at 8 AM and ended at 5:00 PM, so my duties for the movement had to be completed after my official hours. Supplying the bunker was the most demanding and difficult assignment. I used to alternate; some days I arrived in the bunker at seven or eight at night, other times around 6-6:30 AM.

The year passed slowly until suddenly a gruesome tide of tales from the concentration camps began to sweep over us.

Chapter Eight
The Supply Train

On a raw, silent, moonlit night in September of 1944, I was on a mission. A German-Hungarian supply train was stationed at the depot in Budapest. One car was packed with hand grenades, and the underground had learned the exact position of this particular car. I was given the mission to break into the rail car. Two more comrades were included in this mission, Patu and Zali. We were to gather up as many grenades as possible. First we staked out the place, observing two Hungarian Nazis guarding the front section of the train. Although we had not bribed the guards, as we sometimes did, they did not bother to patrol the rear of the train. We had to distract them and work around them.

One of my *Habonim* companions, Betzalel, distracted the two Hungarian Nazi guards with friendly conversation. Patu and I, using a bayonet and screw driver, the only tools we had, succeeded in breaking the chain and removing the lock from the back door of the rail car. Thousands of grenades were stacked in wooden boxes. Some of the grenades had double heads fastened onto short sticks, like broomsticks. We stuck these into our belts. The single grenades filled our coat pockets. Between the two of us we managed to load up with about thirty grenades, doubles and singles. This was a great haul; grenades were a good weapon for us and easy to handle.

We left the scene silently under cover of night. Each one of us went to a different destination to meet our contacts. I continued to the

Budapest Keleti pályaudvar (Budapest Eastern Railway Station), where I met Villi Eisikovics.

My assignments grew with the advances of the Nazi regime. The leaders of the underground decided to start building bunkers. I was assigned to the bunker in Buda, the western part of the Hungarian capital Budapest. Through the contacts our leaders had made with the Communists, they discovered that one of the Christian communist members owned a small farm in Buda. I became aware of this from Villi Eisikovics. Villie had befriended this person and offered him a deal he couldn't refuse; by now, he had a financial motive in addition to an ideological one.

The house was purchased. Part of the deal was that his mother, about fifty years old, would live in the house. This provided the proper cover for us to start building the bunker in late July 1944.

The small house was self standing. The nearest neighbor's house was about fifty feet away. We started from the inside digging slowly during the night. As we entered the house through the front door into a small kitchen, one bedroom was straight ahead. Facing the entrance to the bedroom was a wardrobe, a two-door clothes closet. The bottom of the closet became our starting point; we dug down about eight feet and dug out the area below the house. Three of us—Gyurie, the owner, and two of us from the underground—worked carefully for more than a month. Gyurie's mother disposed of the fresh dirt without alerting the neighbors—by spreading it on her land and planting a garden of vegetables.

We lined the inside of the bunker with boards that the owner of the building delivered. We built two-tier makeshift bunk beds, just a flat platform. We filled the bunker two or three at a time with a total of twenty-two members of the *Habonim* youth organization sympathizers, young men and women, mostly from the Carpathian region.

They spoke little or no Hungarian.

My additional assignment was to supply the bunker with all daily necessities. To accomplish this, I had a letter, signed by the interior minister and the Nazi commander in charge of the region, authorizing me as a procurement officer. This was a forged document reproduced by our special printers, Lazarovics, Gur, and others. The document looked like the real thing, with the signature as well as the government seal. I was authorized to buy, with special terms, supplies for a military base. This didn't necessarily mean special prices; more important was the preferential availability. Money was provided by the United Jewish Agencies through our movement. Because I was free to travel and had a motorcycle (sometimes with a side car), I was able to acquire bread, condensed milk, lard, sausages, meat (sometimes horse meat or pork), rice, flour, potatoes, and sugar.

One night I dreamed of my childhood in Beregújfalu. In my dream I walked through old familiar streets, but as I would pass everything exploded. I came to my home and it exploded. As I passed the new synagogue my father had built, the synagogue exploded. Nightmares were all too common and sometimes hard to distinguish from reality.

Chapter Nine
An Attempted Rescue

One day I became aware of a large Jewish labor camp under joint Hungarian and German command in Kőbánya, a middle class suburb of Budapest and the site of the largest brewery in Hungary, about a thirty- minute ride by motorcycle from Budapest. I discovered that my brother Emil was in this labor camp.

I communicated with Eisikovics that I needed documents, including a special authorization to go into the camp for the purpose of investigating Emil Pal. The real purpose of course was to get my brother out of the camp. Eisikovics provided me with an "official" letter signed by the Nazi commander. Two days later Villi handed me the letter. Before noon I was on my way to the brewery. At the brewery, I was directed by the guard to the camp barracks in the back yard of the brewery.

I presented my documents to the Nazi commander of the camp, a Hungarian officer. I had no problem communicating with him in my good Hungarian. The commander summoned the sergeant and ordered a roll call of the unit. They were all back in the barracks for their lunch break. Within minutes the unit was lined up. Emil was called to step forward. We hadn't seen each other for over three years. Here I was sixteen years old in a Hungarian Nazi youth uniform with a light semi-automatic rifle hanging from my shoulder.

I signaled Emil to keep a distance from me. They ushered us into a small office where we were left alone. Only then did we hug each other and began to realize our predicament. Briefly I told Emil about my activities. I explained that I had found out that he was in the labor camp a couple of days earlier. Unfortunately I couldn't take him out with me at this time because I had no documents for his transfer. However, I promised I would tell his commander that we would need him for further investigation. I told Emil that I would be back in the next few days after I had the proper documentation to have him released into my custody.

The next day I met with Eisikovics and told him about my meeting with my brother. I asked Eisikovics to prepare the proper documents, so I could go back for him as soon as possible. I also need documents for Emil's four friends from our home town who Emil told me were with him.

The following couple of nights I had to spend in the city where I shared an apartment with my friend, Josef Rosenberg, whose alias was Rakoshi. Josef was arrested in the city during a routine *razzia* (raid), when the Hungarian police circled a given area requesting that everyone show his or her documents. Josef acted scared; therefore, they had taken him into the Andrashi Unit Police Station.

After only one day he broke down and told the police about his friend, a Jew, sharing the apartment—Wadai Janosh (Erno Pal). He was not privileged, so he didn't know about the bunkers of the underground. Josef was from Apshe in the Carpathians, so his Hungarian, as much as he spoke, was with a heavy accent.

When I came home the following evening, police were waiting for me at the apartment. No questions were asked; they took me to the same Andrashi Unit Police Station to a separate cell. Only when they took me in for interrogation did I become aware that Josef was in their hands. They first questioned me about him. They asked what I knew:

"Where is he from?"

"Does he belong to some underground organization?"

"How did he obtain documentation as Josef Rakoshi?"

My reply was, "I know nothing. I did not know of his being a Jew. I would never share an apartment with a dirty Jew. " My investigators were taken aback by my answers.

I continued, "I am Wadai Janosh. I am a volunteer with the *Levente*." I explained that I had gone through training in Budapest, and I had volunteered because the homeland was calling. They did not accept my story, not believing a word I said. They called in another investigator.

They started to raise their voices, grabbing me by my neck and shaking me, "Tell us the truth. We know you are a Jew."

The shaking and screaming were followed by throwing me into the walls, to the floor, kicking me, and beating me with a rubber baton. This went on for hours, almost half a night. In the morning a different crew started all over; only one of the interrogators was from the previous night. In the morning anger showed on the face of the investigator, the same questions:

"Who are you?"

"What is your connection with Josef Rosenberg?"

"He has revealed his true name and admitted being a Jew." They had promised him "free haven" in return for his cooperation. I answered the same repeatedly.

The following day a German Nazi officer was present during the interrogation, along with a Hungarian translator. I understood his questions in German, so my answers were ready when he finished his questions. The beating and kicking intensified. It was nonstop. I was denied food. They shone some strange reflector lights into my face, head, and eyes.

They said, "You have two choices. One is to cooperate and tell us all about yourself. The second choice is that we will beat the truth out of you, the truth of your identity, your relation to Josef Rosenberg, your other contacts, your parents, brothers, and sisters."

I gave them no satisfactory answers. The German showed his anger, raising his voice and repeating the questions. Again he requested me to verify my name and identity as a Nazi volunteer.

The following day I was transferred with some other prisoners that I didn't know to a jail and police station reserved for political prisoners in the mountains of Buda. During the first interrogation session at this high risk facility, they ordered me to drop my pants, forcing me to reveal my circumcision.

They were happy to call me a dirty Jew: "Now we know for sure that you are a Jew. This is the first step; now you are going to tell us the truth about yourself and the organization you belong to."

I raised my voice in anger and told them, "I don't know what you are looking at or what you are talking about." I told them, "When I was fifteen years old, I was infected by a prostitute and suffered from an infection, which was treated in the Red Cross Hospital with hot iron rods and this treatment has left its mark on me. Don't dare tell me I am Jewish!" I insisted, "I am a Nazi youth—*levente tisty fohadnagh*—an officer, a volunteer.

They left me in the torture room; one of the Hungarian investigators came back and told me, "We have decided to contact your unit, where you served as a volunteer about the training course, etc."

This man was an older person; he told me how sorry he was but the Germans were in charge, and they needed to follow their orders. They suspended my interrogation, and I was put in a cell with five political prisoners. These were communists, with whom we had a common enemy—the Nazis. We developed a friendship. After four days I looked out through a small window, realizing we were on the second floor. Outside were trees like a forest, the ground covered with snow, no houses that I could see. We were six in the same room. In the evening I approached my fellow captives with the idea of escaping, by jumping out the window that was just big enough. They agreed to join me.

Early in the morning, about 3 AM, we were awake and ready to jump. We forced the window frame open with two or three metal spoons, using the flat end of the spoons. Looking out the window I decided that I could not make a free jump because the window was too high. Therefore, we took some bath sheets, tying them together. All six were awake and helped. I jumped first, followed by two others. The other three changed their minds. The three of us made it safely down, but we decided to part, each on his own. The night was silent, and the forest was not very thick, so I could see the residential areas a few hundred feet away where some lights were shining in the darkness.

I walked for a few hours, walking to the nearest electric car (tramway) station, *villamoskocsi*. As I walked, the snow was melting and the cold wind blew. I had only a light jacket and pants, no hat, no scarf; it was freezing cold.

I had no money either; therefore, I asked the ticket collector to allow me to ride free, as I must go to see a doctor. There were only a few early risers on the train, so he didn't give me a hard time. I needed to change trains to get to my destination, the bunker. I walked about an hour in the cold. Again I begged the ticket collector to let me ride with no money—this time to the bunker. I got off at the last stop and from there I had to walk through snow covered path ways, between the cultivated farm lands. This took me over an hour. I was walking as fast as I could so as not to freeze to death. I saw not a soul on the entire path.

When I arrived at the bunker, it was about 8 AM. I knew the signal: knock three times. The mom of the bunker, as we referred to her, opened the door. She was shocked to see me, tired, wet, shivering from the cold

"*Jaj istenem*! My G-d, what are you doing here? Where are you coming from? Sit down. Let me prepare a hot cup of tea."

I replied, "I just want to go downstairs; I am tired."

I walked toward the closet, opened the two doors, lifted the wooden board, and walked down. Most of the bunker occupants were still asleep. I collapsed. One, Sara Rasmovich, was awake; she *schlepped* me onto the floor near the bunk beds, covering me with blankets. There I rested and recovered.

When the rest awoke, they were anxious to hear my story; everyone offered me help. I did not share with them all my experiences—the last five days. I didn't want to scare them about what could happen to them if they were caught. After a few hours sleep and hot tea, I felt well enough to think about contacting Eisikovics and asking him to send me new documents and a uniform, so I could go out and resume some of my duties.

Early morning, my co-messenger, Patu, arrived at the bunker on his motorcycle. I told him in short about my exciting couple of weeks. Through him I sent my message to Eisikovics. Three days later Patu returned to the bunker on his motorcycle, bringing me the new documents and uniform. It was early morning, so I dressed. Patu took me right to Eisikovics, waiting at a café near the Budapest *Keleti pályaudvar* (train station).

I was debriefed by Eisikovics and Neshka who was with him. They questioned me about my readiness and willingness, my frame of mind, etc. I was able to convince them that I was ready and not at risk of being arrested again.

The first thing on my mind was my brother Emil. Before my arrest, I had asked for the papers that Eisikovics was supposed to have ready. That same day, a couple of hours later, I met Eisikovics again; this time only he and I met: he handed me Emil's documents in an envelope, some money, and some documents of people I am to take out from the ghetto.

This time I had no motorcycle, so I staked out a place near a bank, in a drive through courtyard. A young man arrived on a small moped. As he jumped off going into the bank, I jumped on and drove through the back exit on my way to rescue my brother. Arriving at the brewery, I was told by the guard that there were no more Jews, no more camp. They had been transferred to the German border to dig ditches. Needless to say I was very upset with myself, deep inside I felt defeated; I blamed myself for not saving my brother. I feared for his survival.

As I resumed supplying the bunker, I decided to stay overnight and to leave early in the morning to do my daily activities. In the early morning, about 4 AM, when it was still dark, even before I got ready to leave and when everyone was still asleep, I heard the sound of many footsteps approaching. The boot steps came closer and closer. They entered the house, grabbing the mom first. By now everyone was awake below. The *Csendörség,* the military police, walked to the closet, lifted the bottom, and walked down one by one, as quietly as they could. They knew their way because Patu was the one who led them to the bunker.

Outside were another six policemen with rifles drawn. We had an escape door, but we couldn't even get to this. Everything happened so fast that we had no chance of self defense. One by one we were forced out the door into two small trucks. They took us to a police station. We were divided into two groups. My identity and name they already knew from the informer Patu. In addition to me, five others were held separately. The others were transferred, we later found out, to the Margit Körút Jail. Among the six remaining in the police station, I was the first one to be taken in for interrogation.

This time they knew about me. They asked me point blank, "Are you willing to cooperate with us?"

My reply was, "My name is Wadai Janosh."

Immediately they started beating me, shouting, "You won't live long to tell us your lies. Your time is ticking away fast. You will tell us everything about your underground, about the bunkers, the leaders, and the whereabouts of other bunkers, how many there are and their locations. Tomorrow morning we want answers to all these questions. It depends on your answers whether you live or die."

They gave me some paper and pencil to write everything down. Then they threw me into a small isolated room, with a mattress and a blanket on the floor. I didn't sleep much. About 9 AM, they opened the cell door and took me to the interrogation room. The first question was, "Do you have all the answers ready? Where is the paper?"

I replied, "The paper is in my room. I have no answers for you. I know nothing."

They became very angry, telling me, "We will waste no time with you, dirty Jew. You traitor, you have one hour. Go back to your room and write down the answers."

I did not reply. They took me back to the room, and about two hours later, they came to get me. It was obvious that they were under pressure to produce results for their commanders. They were not happy with me. I was tossed back into the room, hungry and thirsty. During all this time I had only soup and a piece of bread twice.

Early in the morning, about 4 AM, they dragged me out to a truck, which had four policemen, an officer, and eight other prisoners, who were unknown to me. The police were silent: not a word about where we were being taken. We asked, "Where are you taking us?"

The reply from one of the policemen (the officer was in the front cabin) was, "You will soon find out."

We traveled a total of about thirty minutes, arriving at the Duna River (the Danube) near a small guard house, where we were ordered out. They lined us up in front of the river, but with our backs to it. The police lined up facing us. This took seconds. Then the officer ordered the policemen to aim and shoot.

I was in the middle. As soon as the first shot was fired, I fell to the ground in the pitch dark. Another body fell over me, but I did not move, even when I felt warm blood dripping over me. Soon I heard the officer saying, "Leave them lying until the blood runs out. Let's go across the street for a coffee." Apparently he knew a place open this early in the morning; he had been at this place before.

When I heard them walking away, I quietly crawled away. Soon I was up and running. The Budapest *Keleti pályaudvar* was about an hour's walking distance. I knew a twenty-four-hour coffee shop where we used to meet sometimes with Villi. I arrived there with no money. I went into the rest room to wash myself. I also tried to wash the blood off of my clothes. I got my clothes wet, yet the stains remained. My clothes didn't look good. I sat in a quiet corner and ordered hot chocolate milk and a breakfast roll. I had no money, so I told the waiter, "I am waiting for a friend who will pay you." I waited for an hour or so. I told the waiters, "I will be back soon." I basically snuck out.

There was no phone. In any event, I had no number to call anyone. I walked around, sat and walked some more, hoping that some time Eisikovics or Betzalel, another motorcycle runner, would arrive. At about 11 AM, Betzalel made an appearance with Villi on the back seat; they circled around. Eisikovics approached me cautiously. I asked him to come into the coffee shop. The waiter was still there hoping to see me. My lucky break was Eisikovics showing up. This was not a scheduled appointment. He had heard about my arrest as well as the arrest of the others. I told him how I had survived.

Eisikovics told me, "You must disappear immediately. I am sending you with Betzalel to another bunker." Villi stayed behind because he had another appointment. Betzalel drove me close to the bunker, pointing me in the direction of a junk yard that had a little shed. The entrance was through the shed in the office of the junkyard. A fellow member was on guard with a machine gun; we didn't know each other. I gave him the password, so he directed me to the stairs leading down to the bunker.

Chapter Ten
Arrest & Torture

Eli Slomovics was in charge of this bunker. We knew each other from meetings at the Buda Mountains. I filled Eli in on my perilous five days. I told him what I needed was some food and rest. They had a full house of twenty, but they warmly welcomed me, sharing everything they had.

Unfortunately my rest was short: one morning, three days later, the *Csendörség* surrounded the bunker. Our guard, Martzi, who was on duty, opened fire with his machine gun. He was shot with a barrage of bullets. Then the police threw gas grenades down into the bunker. We had no fighting chance.

One by one we came up to ground-level where we were rushed and pushed into the police bus by police carrying bayonet-mounted rifles. They tied our hands with chains. I thought to myself: Here I go again. This time, in good company with my bunker comrades from Buda. We were taken to the infamous Margit Körút jail

When our bus with the twenty-one prisoners arrived at the jail, we were marched through a long corridor where we were lined up facing the wall. Our hands were tied, raised above our heads. We were forced to stand silently in this position for over six hours, guarded by *Csendörség* police. The minute someone slid down to the floor, the rifle landed on his or her back followed with rubber sticks until the person stood up again. This was their way of introducing us to the harsh treatment awaiting us. At almost midnight they moved us, two or three at a time, to our cells, most of us collapsing on our bunk beds.

We were put in large cells, each with eight to ten people. The prisoners were not necessarily from the same resistance movement; however, in my cell of eight, four were from the bunkers. The girls and women were kept separate. I was in a cell with Eli, Dugie, Ferike, and four communist prisoners who had opposed the Nazi regime.

The cells were large enough to house two-tier wooden beds the size of a single mattress. The toilet was in one corner, a hole in the floor that needed to be rinsed with buckets of water that each cell had to haul from a well in the courtyard. The limited supply of toilet paper was newsprint. The cell smelled unbearable; we had to deal with the odor twenty-four hours a day.

In the same corner, behind a canvas curtain, the toilet was used as our "bath shower." Water was rationed; five cups of water were allocated to each prisoner. One of us had to be responsible for cleaning the cell. We had to wash ourselves. Cleaning and washing with only five cups of water a day; to say the least, this was not the Hilton.

The building, an old stone building, meant cold days and nights; cold and unfriendly by purpose and design, designed to make prisoners feel as uncomfortable as possible. This was part of the torturers' treatment—to soften us up even before we encountered them.

The food was inadequate. The daily menu consisted of small portions of soup, potatoes, corn, and bread. The drinking water was also rationed, hauled in by buckets from the same outside well.

Most days we had about a thirty-minute walk in the courtyard. Fresh air was a life saver. During these walks we were not allowed to speak to each other; however, we saw many of our fellow prisoners because we were marching in groups of about fifty. We were heavily guarded by the police who kept a close watch. During one of these walks we became aware that almost all the leaders of the underground had been arrested and were incarcerated in the same jail. Because they were not in the bunkers, no one knew exactly how they were arrested. Obviously there had been a weak link in the chain of secrecy. To see Zvi Goldfarb, his girlfriend (and future wife) Neshka Szandel, Villi Eisikovics, Arányi Asher, Anschel Einehorn, and others was a shock. We did learn that they were not arrested in one location at the same time. Some were taken first after their arrest to a strictly political jail in the city of Sopron. Later these were transferred to Margit Körút Military Prison in Budapest, the same jail where Hannah Senesh was executed.

In the morning a cup of hot *kimmel* (Yiddish for caraway) soup was served. We had no clock in the cell; watches had been confiscated, so breakfast must have been about 9 AM. Two policemen opened the door and called for Eli to step out. He was the first taken; however, we didn't know where they were taking him. A couple of hours later Eli was dragged back to the cell. From the continual beatings all over his body and his feet, he was unable to walk on his own.

After the potato soup was served at lunch time, the same two policemen opened the door and called for me to step out. They walked me through a long corridor down to the basement level. They took me into one of the rooms that became known to us as the torture room. Two men in civilian clothes, a detective and a policeman, ordered me to sit at a table. They started the questioning.

They had notes before them. Not knowing what information they had on me I acted as calmly as I could. Their first question was my name, "What is your real name?"

At first my answer was, "Wadai Janosh."

They stopped me immediately, telling me they knew everything about me, and if I didn't answer their questions correctly, I would see stars before sunset.

They repeated the question, "What is your real name?"

My answer was the same—"Wadai Janosh." They showed their anger by ordering me to place my hands on the wooden table. The policeman took his rubber baton and smacked me across my hands. When I removed my hands, he ordered me to straighten them out again on the table. He started beating me all over my body. Ordering me to stand up, he kept on beating me until I fell to the floor. Then he ordered me to take off my boots. I was unable to use my hands, so he helped me to remove them. I was ordered to lie face down on a short bench, my feet hanging over. He then began to hit me on the bottom of my feet.

Screaming I rolled down from the bench. One of the investigators asked me if my memory had improved. I was silent—no reply. They repeated the question. Again I kept silent. Their beatings affected me: I was in agony, screaming. After a while they dragged me back to the cell. Ferike was next.

The next day and almost every day after, the torture investigations continued. The methods of torture were intensified. Another method was electric wires fastened to my ears. A manually operated transmitter was turned by the torture specialist. The level of electric current depended on the speed with which the wheel was turned. The first shocks felt as if my brain had exploded. They would keep this up for a few minutes depending on the reaction or cooperation. To get some information from me, they continued the electrical treatment by moving the wires to various parts of my body and to my finger tips. I still told them nothing.

They stopped the electrical treatment. By then I was behaving as though I had lost my mind. They didn't give up; questions were repeated; the interrogators taking turns. I was dragged on the floor, up the stairs, through the corridor, and tossed into my cell. I was unconscious, and my head was bleeding. My cell mates labored to revive me, washing my face, hands, and head for quite a while. When I regained consciousness, I realized that I hadn't told my comrades the details about the torture. I had kept silent.

My turn came again two days later when I was still recuperating. They took me back to the same room. I found out later that they had various interrogation rooms with different teams of interrogators. This jail at the time held many hundreds, even thousands, of prisoners, but not necessarily Jews.

The questions were repeated. I was silent and sick; they ordered me to lie down on a bench. They pulled my pants down and connected the electric wires to my genitals. This treatment lasted several minutes. From this bench I was moved to a "carpenter" table, where they clamped my upper body to one clamp and from the hip down to the other clamp. In the middle of the table was a handle bar. They turned the handle manually, so the two parts of my body were pulled in opposite directions. At one point I felt that they were tearing my body apart. This went on until I passed out from severe pain. More questions. No answers.

Somehow throughout all my arrests and interrogations, I remembered the lectures of József Gárdosh in the Buda Mountains, as well as Zvi Goldfarb preparing us mentally for this eventual possibility. They had clearly stressed that those captured carry the responsibility for safety not only for themselves but also for the movement.

A prisoner must never give in to the police. Revealing any information is the shortest way to a prisoner's death. Once you tell them what they want to hear, they would never free the prisoner as a reward but would dispose of that person. Each member of the movement must be ready and willing to sacrifice! These words kept me strong throughout all the beatings and torture.

The disposal of Josef Rosenberg, my ex-friend, with whom I had shared an apartment in Budapest, and the disappearance of Patu, who had led the police to the discovery of our bunker, were only two of many who paid with their lives for their collaboration with the Nazis. Those of us who went through Margit Körút Military Prison and these extreme interrogations—such as Eli, Neshka, Zvi, Eisikovics, and me— have lived with the scars, pain, and nightmares ever since.

No regrets. I would do it over again!

Chapter Eleven
Liberation

By December 25, 1944, Gur reports, the Russian army had circled Budapest (21).   Day and night the sound of artillery kept us awake. We were hoping that the Russians would blow up the entire jail, kill us along with the Nazi police, so we wouldn't have to suffer any longer. The Soviet army was closing in on our location. We could hear the loud roaring of the tanks. The Jewish prisoners in our jail wing were ordered out into the corridor.   The communist non-Jews remained in their cells. We assumed that the Nazi police had decided to execute the Jews before the Soviets captured the jail.

Suddenly a Hungarian officer and two armed sergeants approached the corridor where we were standing.   An officer of the jail explained that some prisoners would be transferred, and the officer of the squad began to read the names of the prisoners to be transferred. He read forty-five names, among them were Eli Slomovics, Villi Eisikovics, Zvi Goldfarb, Neshka Szandel, and my name, Janchi Pal .

We were confused to hear these names because these were not on our official jail record. We had never admitted to these names. Everyone was tense and shaken.   Soviet artillery sounded closer with each passing minute. We were ordered to line up four in a row. Suddenly some of us realized the police squads were our own people. I recognized one of the officers: Bundi! They had documents to transfer us to another jail in downtown Budapest, an area still under the control of the Nazis and Hungarians.

When we were outside the gates of the jail, the officer ordered us to follow him and not to try to escape. We asked him: "Where are you taking us?"

His reply was, "To Szabadságtér 12." Some of us knew that this was the Swiss Consul. We didn't walk slowly; we gathered our last strength to walk as quickly as possible. At the bridge crossing from Buda to Pest, the Hungarian officer requested documentation from our officer. He presented the "official" letter of transfer, urging us to cross as fast as we could because the bridge was already loaded with explosives, ready to be detonated the moment the Soviets came closer.

After about an hour walking and running, we arrived to the main Swiss Consular building. Inside the gate we were greeted by Yoel Palgi, the Israeli paratrooper, and by Rafi, Pil, and Peretz, all leaders of the underground.

A moment of hugging and kissing went on, all in the atmosphere of accomplishment, of a job well done. We had not sufficient energy to thank the squad properly for their heroic behavior, leading us to safety. We were taken down to the lower level of the building. The basement was well lit and comfortable, the air clean, and food was ready and plentiful. The following day the same squad repeated the mission and freed ninety-one prisoners.

This location was supposed to house about two hundred. The number was more than double. Here we felt safe from last minute Nazi activity. However, they made numerous attempts to enter the official Swiss building, by law declared as foreign territory. The Swiss government shield affixed to the gate didn't deter the Nazi police from repeated attempts to enter and arrest Jews and the leaders of the underground. The fortified metal gates and our brave armed guards managed to keep them out.

Another Swiss house, known as the Glass House, a two-story building with a spacious basement, was owned by Arthur Weisz, one of the respected Jewish community leaders. When the Swiss vice-consul, Carl Lutz, and some of the Jewish community leaders approached Mr. Weisz with a desperate need for additional space for underground activities, hiding Jews, etc., Mr. Weisz agreed to turn over his house (his residence and business) to the Swiss consulate. The Glass House was and is located at 29, Vadász Street, where numerous other consulates were located, thus, ideal for the intended purposes. The Swiss embassy wasted no time, instructing the staff to affix a Swiss government emblem on the gate and the building.

They had moved a working staff onto the second floor and street level of the building. Preparation for adapting the basement to house the overflow of refuges began immediately. Yoel Palgi, the Israeli paratrooper and leader, was one of the first ones to settle into this building. As soon as this protected house became known hundreds rushed inside. Mr. Lutz instructed his staff to issue Swiss citizenship papers to everyone entering. The first few days about three hundred people found refuge in this building. By the time they stopped taking in additional Jews, the house was filled with over a thousand. The various Zionist movements, such as *Hashomer Hatzair* and *Habonim Dror*, each were allocated an area of the basement.

The first secretary to the Swedish legation, Raoul Wallenberg, had arrived in Budapest on July 9, 1944. Wallenberg immediately immersed himself in working with the main Jewish leaders. He felt it his mission to save as many Jews as possible. The Swedish consulate building (with a large basement) was prepared to house Jewish refugees. Swedish citizenship papers were made available to hundreds in addition to the "official" papers printed and distributed by the Zionist groups.

Wallenberg worked tirelessly with the Hungarian government officials, as well as the representatives of the Hitler-Nazi regime. Financial bribes were offered to the Nazis for loosening their grip when dealing with the Jewish issues. Raoul Wallenberg as well as Carl Lutz, the Swiss vice-consul, will be remembered as heroes and fighters for justice. Each saved many thousands of Jewish lives.

The Soviet army liberated Budapest on January 18, 1945. Despite his heroic actions saving over 20,000 Budapest Jews, Raoul Wallenberg was arrested in Budapest by the Soviet authorities in 1945. The Soviets transported him to Moscow where he vanished into the Soviet gulag.

Many efforts were made throughout the years by various Jewish and non-Jewish humanitarian organizations as well as by his family to discover his whereabouts, either in life or death. Even the intervention of the Israeli government did not yield results.

Numerous countries have commemorated Raoul Wallenberg with stamps and monuments as well as with books and films.

The example of Raoul Wallenberg, as well as Carl Lutz, demonstrates that one person can make a difference. Gur explains that Yoel Palgi, Hannah Senesh, and the other paratroopers in the various underground movements believed in the same philosophy of personal service and sacrifice (250).

Chapter Twelve
A Delegation to Bucharest

After the liberation of Budapest, the *Habonim Dror* leadership, among them Yoel Palgi, Zvi Goldfarb, Neshka Szandel, Villi Eisikovics, and Zvi Prizant had a plan ready to send a *garin* (a group preparing for settlement), representatives of the movement, to Bucharest Romania. The purpose was to establish a base for survivors of concentration camps and bunkers, partisans from Poland, and others.

We were assigned to this mission: Zvi Prizant, Moshe Lazarovics, Sara Rasmovich, Sanyi Lazar, Moshe Katz, and I. As the aftereffects of the war were still fresh, the scheduling of the trains was not reliable, particularly traveling from Hungary to Romania. The authorities in each country had their own laws and regulations. At almost every main train station when the train stopped, the local police boarded, checking documents, looking mainly for Nazis.

We were well organized. We traveled as Czech partisans wearing Czech armbands, the colors of the Czech flag: blue, white, and green. We all had false documents as partisans. We had to avoid the newly recruited Hungarian police as well as the Romanian police. The Soviet military police had jurisdiction over the Hungarian police in the Hungarian territory as well as over the Romanian police in Romania. The Soviet military policemen and women were the most vicious. They indiscriminately robbed watches, food, and other belongings.

Prior to our arrival in Bucharest, Romania, the representatives of the major Jewish agencies, The United Jewish Agencies, the Hebrew

Immigrant Aid Society (HIAS), and the International Red Cross with Villi Eisikovics, representative of *Habonim Dror*, met with the new communist regime's appointed mayor. They requested that the mayor make available a building for a refugee center for survivors arriving from the concentration camps. After numerous meetings, a building was made available; the keys of Maria Rossetti 21 were given to Eisikovics. This building was a Nazi regional headquarter. When the war ended, the building had been abandoned.

The entrance to the three-story building was impressive: two massive, gold-painted iron gates. The house was known for its three-story French provincial architecture, eighteen large rooms, a large kitchen, a courtyard in the back, a garage for parking six cars, and a spacious basement.

When we arrived, we were greeted by Villi Eisikovics and taken by a horse-drawn carriage to Maria Rossetti 21.

Zvi Prizant, Moshe Lazarovics, Sara Rasmovich, Sanyi Lazar, Moshe Katz, and I were the first occupants of the building. Zvi was in charge; we sat down to plan our moves. We had room for over one hundred people. We were joined by local representatives of the Jewish agencies to assist us with supplies and food.

Within a few days, the address, Maria Rossetti 21, was circulated by the Jewish agency. Survivors from Germany, Czechoslovakia, Hungary, Poland, Lithuania, and Romania made their way to us. The horrors and scars from the recent past stayed with them. They were hungry, tired, dirty, and confused. Even before the first train arrived we already had over one hundred survivors. Each survivor was a blessing from heaven.

During our daily improvement planning meetings, we said in unison, *"Ken yirbu"* (May there be more). The concentration camps were being liberated. We wanted more survivors for our safe haven, in particular the young ones.

The basic idea was to establish a commune life based on the Israeli kibbutz life. Everyone was equal, shared the daily duties. We established the house as a center of learning with the ultimate objective to make aliyah to *Eretz Yisrael*.

Zvi Prizant and Dov Fierwerger were the Hebrew teachers; scholars and lecturers from the Jewish brigade were frequent visitors. We named the building the Kibbutz Frumka after the name of an eighteen-year old heroic Polish Jewish fighter—a partisan.

The *Mazkirut* (management) of the kibbutz were Zvi Prizant, Sanyi Lazar, Moshe Lazarovics, Josef Steinberg, and I. Kibbutz Frumka became well known. The number of survivors grew within a couple of months to over three hundred. We utilized every corner and every hallway to accommodate the many who arrived at the gates of the building. Among the well known partisan survivors were Abba Kovner, partisan and guerilla fighter from the Vilnius Ghetto, and Yitzhak Zuckerman, fighter during the Warsaw Ghetto Uprising of 1943 and the Warsaw Uprising of 1944.

1945, Bucharest, Kibbutz Frumka
Maria Rossetti #21; L to R, front, Erszi,
Miki, Ernest, and Eli; rear, Eliazer

Chapter 13
Train to Freedom

The representatives of the various organizations, the anti-fascist community headed by Jacob Shmeterer, the *Habonim Dror* representative, and the Red Cross representatives, made a joint appeal to the Romanian, Hungarian, Polish, German, and Czech authorities requesting train transportation to carry survivors of the camps, survivors of the partisan groups, and survivors of Warsaw Ghetto, among them many children, ages fifteen to twenty.

To coordinate all the authorities was a monumental challenge. After intensive efforts, two passenger trains were made available—two trains, thirteen cars on each train, to leave thirty days apart. Each train had a doctor and a nurse on board. In charge of the technical crew was Jacob Shmeterer. Zvi Prizant, Sanyi Lazar, and Moshe Lazarovics were in charge of logistics, representing *Habonim Dror*. The train left from Bucharest to the station nearest to Auschwitz.

The first train was loaded with its precious cargo—460 survivors. When they heard the sound of the locomotive and felt the train moving, they burst into tears and sang at the same time "Hatikva," the national anthem of Israel. The train traveled from Krakow, Poland, to Humenné, Slovakia, to Czechoslovakia, Germany, Hungary and Romania.

It was a long exhausting trip of twelve days because the number of tracks that the train could use was restricted to the scheduled trains. Upon arrival in Bucharest, the receiving committee processed the individuals. Some requested Maria Rossetti 21, the Kibbutz Frumka; others were placed in different preliminary housing or traveled to their home towns to look for surviving members of their families.

The second train left Poland thirty days later. The train ride was very emotional; survivors were still skeptical and concerned as to the destination of the train. Would the different border authorities respect the permits? Each survivor traveled with the hope of a new beginning despite the uncertain final destination. Each had hopes and dreams about surviving family members and their whereabouts.

The morale builders throughout these trips were the Zionist youth movement representatives headed by Zvi Prizant. It took long days and sleepless nights to assure all the passengers that they were free—free to face a new world, a new beginning, and a new life.

Chapter 14
Sara Kafmanova

On board the first train was a Holocaust survivor named Sara Kafmanova, a survivor of Auschwitz-Birkenau and a death march. She was the only one in her family to have survived. Sara had decided to take this train, leaving the concentration camp environment. As she boarded the train, suddenly Sara recognized a familiar face, Zvi Prizant, a young man from a neighboring town, Chust, who often came to Krive, Sara's town, to spread the Zionist ideals and ideologies.

"Zvi! Zvi!" Sara cried out. "Look here. It is me, Sara Kafmanova from Krive."

Zvi paused and looked around. Where was this cry coming from? "Who are you?" he asked.

"I am Sara Kafmanova," was the reply.

Zvi stared at Sara and recognition finally came to him. He clasped his large gentle hands, swayed, and his eyes filled with tears. "My God! What have they done to you?"

Zvi was hungry for any information regarding survivors from Krive, so Sara told him about Edith and Chavie, who could not come on this train but would follow on the next.

"There are survivors from Budapest," Zvi explained, "who were hidden in bunkers and now we have a kibbutz in Bucharest, where we have people recuperating and where you have a cousin. Her mother was your mother's favorite aunt. Her name is a Sara Rasmovich, a survivor from one of the Budapest bunkers and your cousin. But listen, I can't send you there looking like this; first we have to put some meat on your bones. My G-d, what can you weigh? Seventy pounds?"

"Sara, you are the first one from the camps that I knew from before the war. I'll bring you to the kibbutz in Bucharest, but, first, you'll stay with a couple I know in Humenné: Olga and Bála. They will take care of you. I'll be back in approximately thirty days to pick you up when the second train comes through Humenné."

So Zvi helped Sara off the train and brought her to the house of the Slavish couple, Olga and Bála, parents of adult children who no longer lived at home. The house was spacious; Sara was given a separate bedroom. The family received her with open arms. Olga, the woman of the house, was very friendly and caring, looking after Sara. The first thing she did was bring in a large basket of assorted fresh fruit and vegetables from their garden, followed with fresh bread and milk. Sara was surprised to see all this fresh produce. She'd imagined that that world had been destroyed.

The most important subject of conversation between them was food: "What can I cook for you, Sara? Something special?"

Sara had no appetite; she had lost her taste buds. She was not very demanding. However, the fresh fruits and vegetables helped her gradually to increase her appetite for more solid food, such as stuffed cabbage and chicken paprikash with noodles. Sara did gain some weight by the time Zvi returned thirty days later. Yet her hair hadn't grown much, she was still coughing up blood, and her body was hurting all over. Sara was still suffering both physically and emotionally.

Zvi led Sara to the second special train, which she boarded. On the train she met up with some fellow survivors. They formed a group to share and care for each other. They were all sick, some more than others. Some had lost an eye; some an arm or a leg.

Sara felt rich. Olga had given her a pair of shoes and a couple of dresses bundled up in a large scarf. The next day Sara unbundled the scarf and found fruits, a salami, bread, and butter—a pleasant surprise for all of them. On board the train some food rations were provided but nothing like Sara's cache of food. They debated cutting the salami open, or not. They couldn't resist, so they sliced the salami (with a knife that Olga had included). The bread, the butter, and the fruits were shared. They enjoyed the festivities.

Despite being on the train among friendly faces, the survivors were still skeptical, wondering if the train would really arrive in Bucharest or take them back to the concentration camp. Eventually Sara arrived in Bucharest, crying with happy tears.

At the Bucharest train station a part of a corridor blocked off. In this area were representatives of the Zionist organization, HIAS, and the Joint. Zvi and his *Habonim Dror* companions had identified those that would be taken to Kibbutz Frumka at Maria Rossetti, among them Sara.

The others were placed in different homes and hotels, awaiting a destination of their choosing. Some returned to their homes hoping to find family members; others chose different refugee camps in other parts of Europe.

Sara walked in through the iron gate of the kibbutz with Zvi. A welcome committee, including me, waited anxiously. Suddenly we heard a shriek, a cry, "Sara."

"Sara."

Both Saras, the arriving Sara Kafmanova and Sara Rasmovich, the cousin who was already a member of the kibbutz, ran to each other while continuing to scream, "Sara."

"Sara."

For a moment we thought we were witnessing a tragic mental breakdown; both were insane—Sara and Sara.

We quickly realized the situation, helping and embracing the Sara that had just arrived. I supported Sara on one side, guiding her up the wide stairs, her cousin Sara on the other side. We helped her into a small peaceful room with five other girls.

As a member of the *Mazkirut* (management), I initiated a meeting with Zvi, the head of the kibbutz, and others. Sara looked sick and frail. We decided to make Cousin Sara and Eva, Zvi's *chavera* (girlfriend), available to help Sara to recuperate. They were both helpful. Eva remained a lifetime friend of Sara and me.

Sara had many visitors; most of them were well wishers offering assistance. Some came seeking information about their loved ones in concentration camps, asking, "Did you by chance know my sister, Mirel?" "Maybe you met my mother, Shuszi Greenberg, blue eyes like mine?"

Sara lay comfortably on a bed; however, she had developed a fever and was coughing up blood. The girls fed her and bathed her as she told them of her experiences and nightmares. In the communal kitchen Eva and her cousin Sara prepared special food for her, but she had no appetite.

Eva insisted, "Just a couple of more bites. Tell us, Sara. What would you really like to eat? Whatever you want just tell us."

Momentarily piqued by the question, Sara replied, "Scrambled eggs and a sour pickle."

Everyone was surprised by the special order.

At that moment I entered the room. Although I was only seventeen, I was self assured and determined. I was determined not only for my own survival but also for the survival of our people, determined to realize our collective dream of a Jewish homeland. I had for three years fought and outlasted the Nazis. Now my attention was focused on Sara. Eva informed me that Sara would eat eggs and pickles.

I knelt beside Sara's bed, "Eggs and sour pickles? I'll go all over Bucharest until I find them somewhere."

I jumped on my battered motorcycle. Eggs and a pickle was the most urgent mission of the day. Sure enough, later Eva brought Sara a plate of warm scrambled eggs. The eggs were fresh, laid that dawn in some farmer's hen loft. On another plate were sour pickles, thinly sliced, from a deli. In my mind a commitment was born: no other task was more important than to feed Sara. Eva, her cousin, and I committed ourselves to this task.

Our days on the kibbutz were structured and full of hope, for we shared a common goal— to make aliyah, to reach the Promised Land, which awaited its ingathering of souls yearning for renewal. Teachers arrived from Palestine to instruct us about the agricultural demands of the desert. They also prepared the survivors for real kibbutz life, a life in the Holy Land, which promised to be harsh and demanding amid hostile Arab neighbors.

We learned the songs and dances of hope with young people who had avoided concentration camps by enduring underground existences in bunkers.

Each week the Joint Distribution Committee (JDC or Joint) posted long lists of names and addresses of American Jews who were searching for European relatives, and a few people were reunited, but Sara had no American relatives. Cousin Sara Rasmovich spent hours at Sara's bedside, and slowly Sara Rasmovich revealed her story to Sara.

Chapter 15
Cousin Sara's Story

Sara Rasmovich's family had lived about two hours northeast of Krive. Sara had attended boarding school in Budapest, so initially chance had saved her from deportation to the ghetto. Later on a teacher helped her acquire false papers, which protected her for a while—until the day the soldiers came marching with their boots and their guns into her school. She was frightened because one soldier took out a piece of paper and read her name off the paper right there in her history class! Someone had betrayed her! Someone she knew and probably smiled and spoke to! Ach!

Then cousin Sara explained to Sara that she and Janchi (Ernest) had known each other well in Budapest as members of *Habonim Dror*, the Zionist youth organization. The following is what Cousin Sara told Sara Kafmanova:

"Sara, you should know, I owe my life to Janchi. One day he ran into me and told me that my Hungarian accent could cost me my life. It was becoming more and more dangerous outside. I agreed. I jumped on his motorcycle and forty five minutes later we arrived at the bunker. That's how Janchi saved my life.

"The bunkers were underground rooms, just large enough to accommodate sleeping spaces on tiered planks. Evenings, well past sunset, one at a time and while one stood guard, the other young people ventured up through the camouflaged trap door and spent a few anxiety-laden moments inhaling fresh air. All the other hours of the day we remained as motionless as possible.

"We felt the fear and uneasiness natural to human beings forced to endure this existence. Our imaginations were provoked by the dank, dark room, besieged by crawling things whose territory we were sharing. We experienced every discomfort one can imagine. Janchi was our provider, our dependable link to the world outside.

"Janchi (Ernest) saved my life."

Chapter 16
Marriage in Bucharest

When Sara, sixteen years old, arrived at the kibbutz in Bucharest, she could hardly walk. She was a skeleton, yet I saw much more than her physical appearance. During the first days and weeks our mission was to get her as well as possible and as fast as possible. It did not take too long for us to get to know each other because while she was recuperating, I was at her bedside quite often. She drew my attention with her shiny brown eyes and more so her sense of humor and her strength facing a new life.

In early April, when spring arrived, Sara had mildly recuperated. I took her for short walks on the outside. As the sun shone on her face, she reflected a warm, dear response.

One beautiful morning I started to see a young woman. Her beautiful face and smile captured my attention. Her body became stronger. Her hair that she had lost during the typhus illness in the concentration camp started to grow back. My heart dictated a further special friendly relationship.

We lived in the kibbutz under the same roof. Days seemed like weeks, weeks like months because we had no parents to match make for us. Sara was sixteen and I was seventeen when I introduced the subject of her becoming my *chavera*, my girlfriend. This meant eating together, dancing together, and singing together. At first she was cool to my idea. It took a lot more conversation until Sara admitted her "special feelings" for me.

Everyone in the kibbutz and particularly her cousin Sara told her we were a couple from *himmel* (heaven). We loved each other; our love grew stronger every day. We decided we would marry. We met with the head of the kibbutz, Zvi, sharing our decision with him. Zvi was happy for both of us.

We had no rabbi in the kibbutz. Zvi stated that as "captain of the ship," he would marry us. After all he was in charge. "As a matter of fact," Zvi said, "another couple in the kibbutz, Shoshanna and Willy Braunstein, your good friends, also have announced their decision to marry.

Plans were discussed. Zvi stated, "We have a limited budget; we must make this economically affordable. There will be two couples with two bottles of wine at the head of the table. We will bring in an accordion player. We also have a good friend in the kibbutz named Lacy who plays the guitar. Both grooms will receive blue shirts (*chulza*) with two pockets, and the brides will be given white shirts."

The *simchah* (joyous celebration) started slowly at 7 PM and went on until 7 AM. The members of the kibbutz and friends celebrated by singing and dancing all night. These were the first weddings in the kibbutz, ones that had a special meaning to all of us. These weddings reflected new life and renewed hope for the future.

1945, July 13, Bucharest: Ernest and Sara's wedding

When we were already in Palestine (*Eretz Yisrael*), and Sara was pregnant with our first child, Dahlia, she said to me: "We are not even legally married by Jewish law." I promised Sara that one day we would have a rabbi and marry officially.

Almost fifty years later on July 15, 1995, we were officially married in the Tropicana Hotel-Casino in Atlantic city by Rabbi Goldberg from Adat Zion congregation in Philadelphia in the presence of 250 friends, three children, Dahlia, Stewart and Gil, their wives, and six grandchildren, Tara, Ilana, Ari, Eitan, Elite, and Daniel. I had kept my promise!

Chapter 17
The Long Journey

Soon after we were married, I was given orders to go back to Budapest, Hungary, where Sara and I received a new assignment from the leader of our organization, *Habonim Dror*, to manage and supervise an orphanage of twenty-two children, ages two to four. Some of these children had been abandoned by their one surviving parent because he or she had no money to feed them. Sara had great satisfaction in helping others, particularly children. After three months a professional team was hired by the Jewish agencies to relieve us because the number of orphans had increased to sixty.

We continued our journey with new orders to take a group of thirty-four young survivors, between sixteen and eighteen, to Italy to get them on a vessel to *Eretz Yisrael*.

Our first stop in Italy was Trieste and then on to Milano via Unione 5, which was the headquarters of the Jewish agencies. This was a stopover as we awaited further instructions. The Jewish Brigade of the British army took charge of all activities; they worked endlessly to provide the Holocaust survivors with temporary shelter, food, clothing, and medicine. The brigade commander, Meir Swartz, a colonel from Kibbutz Ein Charod, and Mayer Rabinovich, the head of the Jewish agencies, were our liaisons and the negotiators with the Italian government. They worked to legitimize our staying in Italy as well as our moving around throughout the country while waiting for a ship to make sail to *Eretz Yisrael*.

We had a great reunion when a group of our Kibbutz Frumka members led by Zvi Prizant and Eva arrived from Bucharest. They had stayed for a short time in the north of Italy. A month later we were given instructions to travel to the very south of Italy, to a beautiful small fishermen's village, Tricase Porto, located south of Bari, where a refugee camp had been set up.[17] A mansion on the hillside that had previously been the Nazi regional headquarters was waiting for our arrival

This house was also named Kibbutz Frumka (the same as in Bucharest) because the majority of this kibbutz was transferred from Bucharest. The Italian population embraced us, offering all assistance possible. As this was after the war the Italians did not have much to give because of the post-war economy; however, their friendship was greatly appreciated. We raised a Jewish and Italian flag on the poles where the Italian Mussolini and Nazi Germany flags used to fly. In Tricase we saw for the first time orange and tangerine trees full of fresh smelling, tasty fruit. The poor Italian families gladly shared the fruits from their gardens with the survivors. We reciprocated their friendship by giving them food items from the daily rations we had received from The United Nations Relief and Rehabilitation Administration (UNRRA) distribution center that was set up in town to supply our daily necessities.[18] Canned meats, cigarettes, biscuits, sardines, condensed sweetened milk, and chocolate powder were among the most popular items. Along with a UN administrator, our kibbutz management was responsible for the daily functions of the distribution center. Some of the members of our kibbutz, including me, took turns working, loading, unloading, and repacking. Everyone competed for this job because the workers had free access to all they could consume on the job. The ability to share with some of our neighbors and friends in town gave us great satisfaction. A warm friendship grew between the kibbutz members and our Italian neighbors.

Many of the residents of Tricase made their living fishing in the sea. A number of us joined the fishermen at 4 AM. This was my first time fishing or being on a boat. This was a unique experience, although we used to get seasick when the early morning winds tossed around the small, primitive sailboat carrying sizable fishing nets. We felt like conquerors, winning the fight with nature.

The kibbutz became a training school to prepare us better to understand the challenges that would face us in *Eretz Yisrael*. Lecturers from the Jewish Brigade were frequent visitors, as well as *Shaliach* (Hebrew for emissary) from kibbutzim in *Eretz Yisrael*. Members of our kibbutz were eager to learn not only our future language, Hebrew, but also all aspects of life in Israel.

Chapter 18
Carlo Forlanini Institute

During our stay in Tricase, Sara was still ill. The local doctors tried to treat her active tuberculosis with penicillin, which we were able to obtain from the Jewish agencies. We stayed for six months in Tricase Porto. However, Sara was not getting better; on the contrary, she was worse. The Italian doctors told us about a well-known hospital in Rome specializing in healing tuberculosis. They urged me to get her to Carlo Forlanini Institute as soon as possible.

I contacted our headquarters in Rome and the head of the Jewish agency, Mayer Rabinovich. I presented him with the medical evidence of Sara's condition and asked him to save her life by contacting the institute and asking them to accept Sara with no insurance and no money. Rabinovich was referred to the health authorities of the city of Rome, who accepted the medical evidence that Sara would infect others and could die in less than six months unless our request was approved.

I took Sara on the first available train to Rome. Upon our arrival we went to the headquarters of the Jewish agency, where we were provided with the necessary documents for Sara's immediate admission to the hospital.

This clean, spectacular hospital occupied a large park, four square blocks on the outskirts of the city. The beautiful garden with blooming trees and flowers, the walkways between the trees, and the fresh air—these made us feel welcomed. Carlo Forlanini Institute was not only a hospital; it was also a sanatorium, a healing center. We were full of hope that this was the place where Sara could get well. I was permitted to stay overnight in the hospital with Sara.

The staff and doctors were extremely friendly. The examination started the following morning. The examination confirmed the seriousness of the illness Sara was suffering. The doctors predicted a minimum required stay of six to twelve months.

When Sara was receiving treatments, she was told about another new patient, also a concentration camp survivor, Bumi Prizant, Zvi's younger brother. Sara was happy to meet someone who spoke the same language, Yiddish and Hungarian, because her Italian was elementary.

Since they were not bed bound, Sara and Bumi took daily walks in the facilities —part of the healing process. Unfortunately, four months later Bumi Prizant died; he was only seventeen years old, handsome, and smart, hoping to live to reunite with his brother and make aliyah to *Eretz Yisrael*.

Bumi died after catching a minor cold. His death was devastating to his family and particularly to Sara. In some ways she saw in Bumi a reflection of her own story, a friend with the same illness, the same hopes, the same dreams, and the same aspirations to live and enjoy life and health.

As Bumi's life light was extinguished, Sara broke down in my arms, crying, "My chances and my destiny are the same. I will never leave here; after all, my lungs, my tuberculosis, is worst than Bumi's was."

Gathering all my strength I repeatedly assured her: "Your case is different. I love you; I need you. You will get well."

Sara lost her smile, the luster in her eyes, and her will-power. It was not until I solicited the help of her medical doctor, and he ordered psychological treatment that she made progress after weeks of treatments. My favorite times, our walks and our talks, were contributing factors to her healing. I was helping with her progress.

My assignment was at the headquarters of the Jewish agency as a liaison between *Habonim Dror* movement and the Jewish agency. My job entailed among other things being a contact for the other young survivors coming through Rome daily.

After the next three months, Sara started to feel better. She made many friends and learned the Italian language. Sara loved some of the Italian weekly magazines that kept her company during the long, lonely hours during the days and nights.

I visited her daily. I saw her beautiful face, her long brown hair that grew longer every day, her deep brown eyes with a glimmer of hope, and her beautiful posture. The environment helped her to make the best of a difficult reality. She definitely fit in with the beautiful Italian women; however, as time went on my patience grew thin.

I requested a meeting with her medical team. "Psychologically she was handling her situation better; medically, however," the doctors told me, "her tuberculosis is still too active. By now we would have expected more progress."

My persistent question was "What can be done to improve her healing process?"

The doctors asked me to leave the room, so they could discuss the options among themselves.

Their reply was that Sara would need to be transferred to another institution—to Merano, high in the Italian Swiss Alps Mountains in the Northern part of Italy. They said, "Merano is the world's most famous sanatorium; she needs to be transferred there as soon as possible."

The doctors offered to help with the transfer because she was one of their favorite patients; moreover, she had suffered enough.

They said, "We will do everything it takes. For your part you have to do the same."

I thanked the doctors. I sat with Sara for hours as I saw her tears, her anxiety, and her overwhelming disappointment. I took a few deep breaths wiping away her tears and mine. I had to show her how much I cared: "I am stronger right now than you. You can depend on me. You know I love you more than you can imagine. I will get you to Merano. You *will* get well. You must trust me and believe me."

She broke down crying, but I stood near her, as a strong pillar that she could lean on.

I contacted my superiors at the Jewish agency, and I shared with them the situation as to Sara's failing health; they embraced me and promised to do everything necessary to get her to Merano. Their joint efforts with the doctors from Carlo Forlanini resulted in the necessary approval to move Sara. It took fourteen long days until I received money to buy the train tickets and to reserve accommodations to stay with Sara for one week.

Sara and Ernest, Milano, Italy, 1946

Chapter 19
Rome to Merano

The trip from Rome to Merano through Milano-Geneva took almost two days. Then a special chain train took us from downtown Merano to the top of the highest mountain bordering Italy and Switzerland. The sanatorium was located on the top of this mountain. Merano, my last hope for Sara to recuperate, was in a magnificent Italian Swiss architecture-style building, surrounded by lush forest and flower gardens. The best was the warm greeting from the admitting staff.

"Look at this place, Sara." I said. "This is all for you." Sara was wiping the tears running down her beautiful face.

As we toured the facilities I repeatedly assured her, "You will be coming home from here, healthy; you will see. You must believe. You must have confidence that you are in good hands."

Sara settled into a clean, spacious room with big open windows facing the garden where she could see the flowers and feel the bright warm sunshine. These calmed her down; I saw a glimmer of hope in her face.

During a meeting with Sara and me, after evaluating her medical files, the medical staff advised us that her recovery time would be approximately a year.

"Don't be concerned, *mia bambina* (my child)," one of the doctors greeted us in an attempt to lift Sara's spirits and to give her hope. "After all, you are in the best place in the world. We will need you to be strong and positive; we will need your help—confidence and will-power are part of the healing process."

As we settled into Sara's room, we looked at each other, hugged, kissed, and cried.

I told her, "Sara, I love you. I will do everything I can, although I have to go back to work in Rome."

Almost daily, letters were exchanged between us. Every month I visited Sara who looked better and better in this new, friendly environment and with good medical care. The special air, the good doctors, and, most important, her positive attitude were helping her.

Nine months of healing saved her life. During my ninth visit I was overwhelmed and pleasantly surprised when her doctors told me, "Sara is well and ready to go home. The tuberculosis is healed; it is non active. However, she needs to take care neither to smoke nor to drink alcohol excessively" (because she never smoked nor drank alcohol, this was easy advice for Sara to follow). He continued, "Eat well, Sara. Dress well. Avoid catching cold. Enjoy life!" "*Arrivederci, Bellisima*," the doctors warmly bid us farewell, good luck, and a good life.

We left the hospital and decided to spend two days in a beautiful small villa, Hotel Casel in Merano. This was our first opportunity to visit this famous city. These two days and nights became our most treasured happy days. I whispered romantically in Sara's ears, "We are together again. I will never let you out of my sight. We have survived another hurdle in our lives."

After our two days in Merano, I purchased our tickets to Rome where our friends and colleagues waited for us.

A new assignment also waited for me: to go to a kibbutz near Rome, to Ladispoli, a tourist attraction and one of the many beautiful beaches on the Mediterranean, a one hour trolley ride from Rome. [19] This kibbutz was already established with over 150 survivors waiting to continue their journey to *Eretz Yisrael*. During the day, I worked in Rome; in the evening, I traveled to Kibbutz Ladispoli. I was appointed to the *Maskirut*, the management team of the kibbutz together with Chedwa, Tichtal, Santo, and Chaimovics/Ben Ami Chaj.

This kibbutz, as were others, was a learning center for Jewish history and the Hebrew language with an emphasis on preparing ourselves for aliyah to *Eretz Yisrael*. We stayed in this kibbutz for five months.

In the interim I found out that my brother Emil had survived the Nazi labor camps and was in a German transit camp for survivors, waiting to find a new home. I established contact with him through the Jewish agency, inviting him to join Sara and me in Italy, in Kibbutz Ladispoli. After five weeks Emil arrived. What a happy reunion! Emil liked the kibbutz and his new friends, rapidly adjusting. During this process he met a young, good looking woman from Romania—Lili.

Lili and Emil became a couple and eventually married, making aliyah to *Eretz Yisrael*; however, their ship was intercepted by the British forces at the port of Haifa. They were deported to the Greek isle of Cyprus.[20] They were in Cyprus for eleven months before they could get into Palestine. On April 30, 1948, two weeks before Israel's Independence Day, their beautiful daughter, Rita, was born in Cyprus. Emil and Lili have also been blessed with two boys born in Israel: David and Neal, who reside in Denver, Colorado. Emil, Lili, and Rita live in Cherry Hill, New Jersey.

1946, Ladispoli, Italy: Kibbutz group, Ernest first row, second from left

1946, Ladispoli, Italy: Kibbutz members

Chapter 20
Aliyah to *Eretz Yisrael*

Considering Sara's past and my activities in the Jewish agency and *Habonim Dror*, the directors decided to give us special treatment. We were provided newly produced "false" documents, train tickets from Rome to Naples, and two tickets on an Italian passenger ship from Naples to Haifa. The documents were based on the fact that each of us had arrived in Italy before the war, with our Palestinian parents, whom we had lost. We were returning home after we had married.

Because I was too young, they decided to alter my birth date from 1928 to 1926 to avoid the suspicion of the British authorities upon our arrival in Haifa.

This method of aliyah was used selectively by the Jewish agency and was known as aliyah-gimel. Most others made illegal aliyah. Cargo or fishing vessels, contracted from Italian, Spanish, and Greek ship owners, were converted to carry passengers. The lower deck was transformed to three or four-level bunk beds with very limited space between the beds to maximize the capacity. Many thousand wound up in Cyprus because the British authorities restricted entry to Palestine; this was aliyah-beit. Other methods of aliyah were for those who had close relatives living in Palestine. They were able to get official entry as part of unifying families. This was aliyah-alev. Our ship was by no means a luxury cruise ship; however, this was our first time on a ship, so we felt the ship was luxurious. On this relatively small ship, twenty-five to thirty crew members served approximately 200 passengers.

Meals were served three times daily in a clean dining room; the food was plentiful; the service, good.

The journey to Haifa took us fourteen days, ten of these rough days. The ocean was inconsiderate of the Jewish passengers. Because of strong winds, the waves were high. Each wave lifted the vessel and tossed us indiscriminately from side to side. Sara held on to me for dear life. The waves did not agree with her; she was seasick for ten out of the fourteen days. I did not get sick, so I held on to Sara as she vomited. Many of the passengers and some crew members kept company with Sara experiencing the same sickness.

When we arrived at the Port of Haifa, two representatives from the Jewish agency immigration authority, a representative with Haganah Defense Forces, and a representative of *Habonim Dror* came on board ship. They called our names; we were the first two passengers off the ship.

As we were waiting for our luggage, we were briefed by the Haganah representatives about the unrest of the Arab population as well as about our struggle for an independent Jewish state. We were well on our way to nationhood.

The *Habonim Dror* representative was Yitzhak Pundek from Kibbutz Alonim (near Tivon). *Alonim* is the Hebrew word for "oak trees." The kibbutz, in the Jezreel Valley, according to the article "Jezreel Valley," is a valley in the south of the Lower Galilee region, situated in one of the few remaining natural oak forests in Israel. Jezreel Valley is "covered with fields of wheat, cotton, sunflowers and corn, as well as great grazing tracts for multitudes of sheep and cattle."

Yitzhak and I had met in Italy where he was in the British-Jewish Brigade. Yitzhak invited us to join his Kibbutz Alonim.

Sara quietly said, "I am very tired. I cannot go any place now. I need to rest."

The journey on the ship had taken a toll on Sara; her tired, pale face reflected her condition.

The decision was made by our resident receiving committee to put us in a small hotel on the Hadar-Hacarmel on Herzl Street.

In the midst of our settling in, the country began experiencing unrest. A number of Arabs from Lebanon, Syria, Jordan, and Egypt became more than sympathizers of the Palestinians. The call from Arab world leaders challenged the Arab population of Palestine to begin an intifada, or revolt, a struggle to fight the Jewish population with all means. The Palestinian Arabs were promised liberation. That is, if they captured and destroyed the Jewish families living in *Eretz Yisrael,* they would be rewarded with the properties and businesses of these Jews.[21]

The Arabs began downtown, attacking Jews indiscriminately. They had a limited number of weapons and explosives, which were deployed daily. Numerous fires lit up the skies of Haifa. Jewish families' homes and businesses were bombed or burned down.

Fortunately the Jewish defense forces were better trained and organized; Haganah, Palmach, and Irgun were fighting back. In a relatively short time the Arabs realized that they had no chance of defeating the Jews nor of chasing them from their homes. The Jews had no *braira,* no options (an old slogan: *"Ein Braira,"* meaning no alternative) but to fight and protect their turf, their homes, and their families.

Some of the Palestinian Arab leaders panicked. They told the Arab population to flee; some left for Jordan; others to Lebanon and Syria. They were promised that they would be led victorious back to their homes. Arab forces declared war on the Jewish part of Palestine. The rest is history: an independent Jewish state

Jewish defense forces were well organized and stronger day by day. My privilege came on the third day after our arrival in Haifa. I was summoned to the yards of the Technion, an academic institution and one of the Haganah Command centers in Haifa, almost across the street from our hotel. A number of others gathered at the same time when we were given a briefing about the reason we had been called in. They told us that the Arab population downtown was organizing an uprising against the Jewish population. "We need you all to be available to defend the Jewish population. We will meet every Sunday morning to give you your specific assignments."

I was ordered to go the same day to a post established near the Arab market. I was assigned another person, so we headed downtown armed with two hand grenades and one old single-shot British rifle. Our shift was from 12 noon until 10 pm when we were relieved by two others. This assignment was to be repeated each day unless otherwise ordered. As I had weapon training, confidence, and the will to do my part for a safe homeland, I was glad to report to my position.

Sara remained in the hotel resting and waiting for my home coming every day. We were in the hotel ten days. Soon we received instructions from the immigration office that we were assigned to move to Camp Bat Galim, converted from a British military camp to a new observation center in the suburbs of Haifa. By now Sara was happy to move anywhere but to a kibbutz. I had again discussed with Sara my desire to live on Kibbutz Gardosh-Farod, where I had friends from the underground, or on Kibbutz Frumka.

Sara was determined, as she explained to me with tears in her eyes, "I love you but don't force me to a community life in a kibbutz after what I experienced in my life. If you wish to go, I cannot hold you back. I will come to visit you," Sara said in good humor.

I saw that she was upset; therefore, we stopped our conversation on this subject. Sara won.

I told her, "Sara: I promise to do anything to help us to establish a warm, friendly home."

Sara answered, "I am willing to work. You need to find a job for me."

"What can you do with no profession?" I asked.

Sara replied, "I worked as a slave laborer in an ammunition factory. Yes, I know how to make bullets and assemble grenades."

"Great!" I said. "I know there is a factory near Haifa. My sister Chaya is working there underground. The factory is managed by the Haganah defense forces. I will get in touch with them."

Well, the observation camp in Bat Galim was not a hotel; however, it was decent. In a converted wooden military barrack, we had a bed in a room with eight other couples. The food was well balanced: bread, margarine, bananas, oranges, tangerines, pasta, rice, potatoes, and vegetables. We definitely were not hungry. Our modest needs and expectations were satisfied.

Then through my contacts I became aware that new housing was being built for new immigrants. I signed up, and six months later in 1948, we were taken to our new home. I thought that this was great: we needed no money; we had no money, and everything was financed by the immigration authorities. What more could we expect? We were also given a bed, a wooden table, and four chairs. The name of the town was Tivon, fifteen kilometers southeast of Haifa. Across the road was the "old" town of Kiryat-Amal, established in 1937, by German Jewish pioneers.

Chapter 21
Tivon, Our New Home

Tivon grew with hundreds of newcomers. The local population of about five thousand benefited from this growth because the roads in the town were paved and better roads were built leading into the city of Haifa.

The other established town, Kiryat Amal, was a home to settlers from the late 1930s. This was a rural town with nice old cottages and single homes. The homes had small farms of vegetables and fruits, such as pears, cherries, plums, grapes and, in season, some citrus fruits, tangerines, oranges, grapefruits. Sara and I took long walks on *Shabbat*. The scent of the whole town reminded us of our homes in Czechoslovakia. The beautiful trees, gardens, and flowers, which Sara particularly loved, gave us a new perspective on life.

Most of the farmers sold their fresh vegetables and fruit directly to the public. *Shabbat* was the best business day. We had the option of picking fruit from the field or trees. The taste of the fresh fruit and vegetables, particularly the tomatoes, were a big draw from the neighboring towns. The prices were considerably lower than in the stores. Each farmer had an old fashioned hanging scale in his backyard and was ready for business. Within a short time both of these municipalities were united and became known as Kiryat Amal Tivon. This town grew with small hotels and guesthouses becoming a beautiful resort area.

Our daughter, Dahlia, was born July 13, 1949, in Haifa, the nearest hospital to Tivon. From one to three years old, Dahlia was a bad eater. This was her mom's biggest concern and a challenge each day. She prepared all kinds of homemade goodies, for example, baby food for her little precious beautiful child. Sara tried to cajole Dahlia to eat with bells, whistles, and toys. It did not help much.

During the spring and summer days, Sara took Dahlia to a beautiful public garden in Tivon, where ducks were swimming in little ponds, chickens running around, and kids playing in a small playground with swings, rocking horses, and slides. Dahlia loved this garden. Occasionally small planes flew over the park as well as beautiful birds and pigeons. These were good distractions for feeding time because Sara used to run after Dahlia, pleading, "Open your mouth." And, "Look up. Look up."

Sara used to run with the food jars, encouraging Dahlia to eat. In the back of her mind she still remembered the hunger she had suffered in the concentration camps. She succeeded in keeping Dahlia above average weight for her age group. For Sara this was a mission well accomplished.

Our part of town was a new development in Tivon, called *Shikun Olim*, a housing development for new immigrants. The buildings were two stories, in total twenty buildings, each with twenty apartments, ten on each floor.

The land was owned by the National Forest Authority, *Keren KayemetLe Yisrael* (The Jewish National Fund, JNF), located on the opposite side of town from the beautiful individual luxury homes. Before it was developed, this area was a wasteland; the valley had not been settled. Therefore, city services such as paved roads, sewer systems, electric, and water had not been available. Because the buildings were built on an incline, the fronts of the buildings were at street level; however, the backs of the buildings were built on concrete pillars. From the back windows of each apartment you could see a wilderness of forests. Later we learned that the forest was the home of many *shakals* (coyotes). These wild animals cried or screamed all night long, off and on.

In the valley beautiful wild flowers grew by the side of a narrow road that led to Kibbutz Alonim, on a hilltop about three miles away. Our neighbors, who had settled in the valley thirty years before we came to the region, were helpful. A good friend, Yitzhak Pundek, whom I had met while he was serving in Italy as an officer in the Jewish British Brigade, lived in Kibbutz Alonim. We melded in nicely with the others in the municipality.

To supplement our food we learned to raise rabbits under the concrete pillars in back of the house. In Haifa I bought four rabbits, two males and two females, one Friday afternoon. I arrived home with this basket of four rabbits. The rabbits had beautiful, white fluffy soft hair and big green eyes. Sara's first question was, "What are these?

My reply: "Four rabbits, two males and two females."

Sara asked, "Rabbits for what?"

I replied, "I will build them a home and they will multiply as rabbits do. Inexpensive meat! This will help us to make ends meet."

Sara's question: "Is the meat to be eaten? Who will prepare them? And who will eat rabbit meat?"

My reply was, "I will. This will be my pet project."

A couple of blocks from us was a small food market. I picked up empty wooden vegetable crates. I took them home and borrowed a hammer, a few nails, and a small saw from our neighbor Mrs. Shiner. It took me only one hour or so to build two cages.

I had all the instructions on how and what to feed them, how much water to give them, etc. My instructions also included how to handle them and skin them.

I took them into the kitchen cleaned and ready to cook. From there it was Sara's turn. She looked at the plastic bowl where I had the rabbit cut up. She said, "These looks like pieces of chicken."

"Exactly," I replied. "The cooking process is also the same as with chicken."

Sara was softening: "I'll cook the rabbit for you; however, I will not eat it." She prepared the rabbit like a chicken paprikash.

"Good, great," I praised her for her effort.

A couple of hours later, Sara called, "Dinner is ready." Dinner was only for the two of us. For me Sara served rabbit paprikash, whereas she had a separate sauce pan with chicken paprikash. The dumplings and the gravy were the same for both servings. Sara waited anxiously for me to start eating. "The rabbit's delicious," I complimented Sara, for she was an excellent cook. Her cooking and baking were praised by our friends and neighbors, often guests in our home.

The rabbit meat was a bit sweet, a bit softer than chicken, but with all the added ingredients that Sara used, such as medium spice paprika, onions, celery, carrots, black pepper, three tablespoons of chicken soup, and flour—on top of the homemade dumplings—the rabbit really tasted as good as the chicken.

After several attempts I was able to convince Sara to try her new dish. She did, "It's good."

I felt that it was important to win her over, so she would accept rabbit meat as one of our staples.

Sara agreed with one condition: "I would have to prepare the rabbit outside."

I agreed with this, so as not to expose her to the preparation process with the skinning and the blood.

Our rabbits multiplied at a rate beyond our needs. Sara invited my sister, Chaya, and her husband, Avraham, who lived a few doors down from us, for a special *Shabbat* lunch, not telling them that rabbit would be served as the main dish. We ate a delicious "chicken lunch." I had a sense of accomplishment—rabbit meat is good. We sat around the table for a while to let our guests digest their freshly eaten rabbit.

Among other things we discussed family matters, politics, and food prices, especially the cost of chicken. I gradually led the conversation toward rabbits. Both my sister and brother-in law stated they have never eaten rabbits, snakes, or frogs.

When we left the table, I took them outside into the back of our apartment where my fifteen rabbits were playing and eating in their cages. My sister said, "Oh rabbits! Since when do you have rabbits?" Slowly I revealed to them my new hobby—raising rabbits, small and large. They were white and beautiful with soft hair and big green eyes. I took a special liking to them alive, or cooked and served on a plate, as Sara was doing at least three times a week, always varying the recipes. By then I was ready to reveal to our guests that their lunch was rabbit meat—Sara's new special dish. Sara, as well as my brother-in-law Avraham and me, were bursting with laughter, whereas my sister took a deep breath and questioned Sara, "Was it really rabbit meat?"

Sara replied, "Yes, wasn't it good?" No answer.

When we returned from a walk into town, my sister challenged me, "How could you have served us rabbit meat without telling us?"

My brother-in law replied, "The rabbit was delicious."

Then my brother-in law, as well as our neighbors, started to raise rabbits because the rabbits supplemented our food supply and helped us reduce food costs.

The rabbit craze lasted several months. The problem was that the entire housing development became infested with snakes. While the snakes were not poisonous, they caused damage in the gardens and scared children and grownups alike. The young snakes were only about six inches long and skinny; however, they grew to be about twenty-four inches. The municipal health department determined that the waste of the rabbits attracted the snakes; therefore, the municipal authorities ordered the destruction of all rabbits. Growing of rabbits was declared a health hazard and, therefore, illegal in town.

Obviously we all followed the ordinance of the authorities. I felt bad considering the problem I had created, but rabbit meals were good while they lasted.

At the end of 1953, we moved to Haifa to a larger apartment because Sara was pregnant with our second child, Stewart. During Sara's pregnancy, we often discussed the possibility that the second child would be a boy. I said to Sara, "I would like a son; however, if the baby were a girl such as our Dahlia, I would not mind." On March 17, Sara gave birth to a little "gingie," a red head, as my mother was. We named him Shlomo after Sara's father.

My desire for a boy was satisfied, and Sara was just as happy as I. Upon notification from the hospital, I left my office at the *Histadrut* (Israeli labor organization), jumped on my motorcycle, stopped at the florist, and then on to the Rothschild Hospital on Mount Carmel to see Sara and our son.

Sara was eager to confirm that the baby was a boy. We both felt great, particularly considering that some doctors had cautioned Sara about having children. The *simchah* began. As is customary in Israel, I brought fifty cigars, not Havana cigars but cigarillos, to announce my happiness at becoming a father to a boy.

I was privileged to have many friends at my workplace as well as others in Haifa. I discussed the *brit mila*, the circumcision, the time and the date with Shifra Almogi. Shifra was not only the wife of

Josef Almogi, the head of the federation in Haifa, but also she held an important position on her own at the federation. She was in charge of the *Mazkirut*, the pool of over ten secretaries and typists. Shifra was older and adopted me as her favorite son (Shifra and Yosef had two wonderful boys of their own, Yoram and Zvika).

Shifra suggested having the *brit* at the hospital grounds in the famous hand-embroidered tents that were given as a gift to the hospital by the father of King Abdullah of Jordan.

We named our son Shlomo (Stewart in English). Shifra took it upon herself to make the arrangements with the hospital management; furthermore, she said, "I expect to have the honor with Josef to be the *sandeck*, godfather. I was thrilled and so was Sara. Because of the big hoopla in Haifa, they nicknamed my son, Shlomo, little "Ben Gurion." Most of the federation of labor offices were closed for the *brit*.

Sara and I were happy and honored with the family members and many friends sharing in our *simchah*.

Chapter 22
The Israeli Defense Force

On May 16, 1948, two days after Israeli Independence Day, I was called up for active duty. I was eager and proud to serve.

I was assigned to Battalion 22, the northern front. My serial number was 1531, indicating that I was among the very early recruits. Most in our unit were from the city of Haifa and the surrounding towns. Some were members of the *Palmach* and *Haganah*, the pre-statehood's largest defense forces, under the command of Ben Gurion.

Our first assignment was to liberate Haifa from the Arabs that had taken up arms against the Jewish population. The Arabs were organized particularly in downtown Haifa; they had their "clubs" and underground training centers. The Arabs were led by outsiders: Arabs from Syria, Lebanon, Jordan, and Egypt.

For the first couple of days, fighting during the liberation of Haifa was tense. Suddenly the Arabs retreated. We attacked with small forces; our units were split up into groups of twenty or fewer. We had attacked simultaneously their known strongholds, their clubs, their mosques, their businesses, and their homes. The inhabitants who fled their homes were promised by those outside leaders that they would return victorious after the fighting was over. After five days of fighting, the remaining Arabs raised the white flag, bargaining for their safety and the safety of their families.

The first chief of staff of the Israeli Defense Forces (IDF) was the president of the Technion University, Yaacov Dori. The *Palmach* was the strike force of the Haganah, an elite force under the command of Yitzchak Sadeh. Both the *Haganah* and the *Palmach* had special training to fight the British occupation based on political guidelines from the central leadership under the command of David Ben Gurion.

The foundation of the *Haganah* and the *Palmach* were members of kibbutzim (a collective community in Israel, traditionally based on agriculture) and moshavim (cooperative agricultural community) who were believed to have stronger moral conviction. Hidden from the British occupying forces, the kibbutzim and the moshavim had developed physical advantages, weapons, training camps, etc.

Etzel and Lehi were the extreme right, politically motivated force under the leadership and command of Menachem Begin. They had their separate agenda. They were a contributing force to fight the British occupation as well as a force the Arabs had to reckon with.

The traditional Arab armies had an enormous advantage not only in terms of numbers, but also in equipment such as heavy artillery, tanks, cannons, automatic weapons, and unlimited ammunition, whereas the Jewish forces had to improvise and fight with little or nothing compared to their enemies. The Arab forces were trained with the help of the British, whereas most of us had only minimal training in the secret underground.

Many of the new immigrants arriving in Israel from Europe or the prisoners from Cyprus (they were deported by the British forces to Palestine) were mobilized and sent to the front line fighting units with no training whatsoever. Israel's newly established military forces were so outnumbered that the government decided to send as many "bodies" to the front as possible. History will bear witness that we had to fight against the well- established and well-trained armed forces, among them the elite Jordanian Legion as well as the traditional armed forces of Egypt, Syria, Lebanon, and the military units that were sent by Iraq and Libya.

The Arab forces were convinced by their military and political leaders that they would be victorious over the newly established Israeli forces. The Arab military leaders never had doubts of their ability to break the resistance of the Israeli military and political leaders. They planned to eliminate the Jews, drive us into the sea, and declare the entire territory a Palestinian state.

However, our political and military leaders were determined to fight for our survival as individuals and for the survival of our newly declared, independent Jewish state. We had no option—defeat the attackers or die trying.

Our right to survival gave us the strength to fight for victory. Throughout the war, we were fighting simultaneously in the north and to the south, in Jerusalem, against the strong Jordanian forces. Our nation paid dearly with thousands of lost heroes, and many thousands wounded. Their sacrifices will be remembered forever.

Our second assignment was the liberation of the Akko (Acre) Fortress. To capture the city we had to concentrate first on taking the Fortress of Napoleon.

Our base was set up in the neighboring Kibbutz Masaryk. We were about two hundred soldiers, arriving after sunset in trucks. We had been given an orientation about the city and the mountains as well as about our expected enemy. After four days of rigorous fighting, the Israeli flag was raised on top of the Fortress of Napoleon.

Occupying the fortress had been a major challenge. The Arabs had defended the fortress vigorously knowing that if Israel conquered the fortress that the city of Akko would fall to Israel.

The historic city of Akko is surrounded from the east to west and north with the original walls thirty to forty feet high and three feet thick.

These walls were referred to as crusader walls or as a fortress. The old city was and is an interesting tourist attraction. Akko is north of Haifa about seventy miles; the city had a population of about 30,000 Arabs.

The citadel of Akko was used by the British as a prison and as a location for gallows. Many political prisoners, mainly Jewish underground movement activists, such as Zeev Jabotinsky of Betar and Shlomo Ben Yosef, a member of Betar and an Irgun activist, the first Jew to be executed under the British Mandate.

The fight to liberate the city of Akko continued for five days. The fighting was very difficult, particularly in the historic part of the city. The Arabs were well positioned behind the thick protective walls. For the first few days we were fighting building to building, block to block. The Arabs had some automatic weapons. Hand grenades were used by both sides. Many of the Arab fighters had big machetes and used them quite effectively. After the second day of fighting we were especially alerted to their machetes because we had lost several of our soldiers in hand-to-hand fighting.

Chapter 23
The *Etzel Altelama*

The first Prime Minister of Israel, David Ben Gurion, declared an independent state on May 14, 1948. He called on all armed forces to unite under the Jewish flag, with the *Haganah* and *Palmach* as the core of the new army, *Tzva Haganah LeYisrael* (acronym TZAHAL: The Defense Forces of Israel or IDF). This was not a request but a direct order of the Prime Minister David Ben Gurion.

The *Haganah* and *Palmach* joined forces in a moving ceremony headed by General Yigal Allon and swore their loyalty to the united forces. The *Etzel* underground movement (also referred to as *Irgun*) refused to unite, nor would they agree to surrender their weapons. Ben Gurion called on Menachem Begin advising him again, "There will be only one united army in this land." Begin and the *Etzel* movement did not respect nor did they follow the orders of the prime minister.

Etzel was an extreme right-wing organization. Among its commanders and leaders was Menachem Begin, who was elected the sixth Prime Minister of Israel, on May 17, 1977, as the leader of the Likud Party.

On June 15, 1948, the ship *Altalena* arrived at the port of Kfar Vitkin (a small commercially inactive port). On board were weapons and volunteers of the *Etzel* movement from Europe. Ben Gurion ordered the weapons to be transferred to the newly formed military. The *Etzel* leadership offered a compromise: 20% of the weapons would remain in the hands of *Etzel*. Ben Gurion gave them an ultimatum:

"All the weapons must, must, be turned over to TZAHAL, the Israeli defense forces."

Etzel maneuvered the ship to the port of Tel Aviv-Yafo where they were hoping for a large outcry from their sympathizers. On June 22, 1948, Ben Gurion ordered then Lieutenant General Yitzak Rabin to attack the *Altalena*. At *Etzel*'s resistance, Rabin ordered the bombardment of the ship. The ship went up in flames; on board was Menachem Begin, who was arrested with fifteen other detainees.

I was in active military service at the time, so I was chosen and ordered to the military headquarters, the Kiria, near Tel Aviv where my assignment was to guard the "special prisoner" Menachem Begin, who was in isolation.

It was a strange feeling to guard the most important Israeli opposition leader; however, in the army, an order is an order. When I arrived at the Kiria, the military headquarters, I received my instructions from the officer in charge to guard Begin. I was a strong supporter of Ben Gurion's party; therefore, I felt no conflict or guilt whatsoever. My role was only to be a guard, so I had no personal dialogue with Begin during the five days of his arrest. Five years later, during my visit to the *Knesset* (Israeli Parliament) with my friend Moshe Wertman, I was introduced to Mr. Begin as a friend from Haifa. I never mentioned to Begin that we had crossed paths under different circumstances.

On June 20, 1977, Menachem Begin, a Holocaust survivor of the Siberian labor camps, was sworn in as the sixth prime minister of Israel. He was recognized as an effective leader and an accomplished Prime Minister of Israel from 1977 to 1983. In 1978, Prime Minister Begin received the Nobel Peace Prize for negotiating the successful peace agreement with Egyptian President Anwar Sadat—Camp David Accords. Later Begin negotiated the 1979 Israel/Egypt Peace Treaty.

But, in 1948, he was in a military jail and I was his guard.

The resistance ended, but not before thirteen had died, and fifty were injured on the ship. Begin ordered *Etzel* forces to give up fighting and get in line with unity, within the armed forces. As a result, Begin was freed with all others.

I returned to my military unit, Camp Gelemy, on the road between the Haifa and Tivon.

Chapter 24
The Upper Galilee

Our new base was in a small park with dense trees outside of Rosh-Pina. Our next mission was to liberate the Upper Galilee, continuing with the towns of Miron, Gush-Chalav, Tarschicha, and Sasa. This enabled us to break through the Arab strongholds of Manara on the Galilee highway.

Fighting became more and more difficult every day because, unlike us, Arabs had tanks and heavy artillery. While in Rosh-Pina we received a new shipment of weapons—this was a major help, for we had to face the well trained and heavily armed Syrian forces. The shipment was from Czechoslovakia and included the Bren, an automatic light machine gun. As commander of the squad, I was handed the first such machine gun. It was still freshly oiled, factory packed in a wooden crate. The first step was to clean off the oil with cotton rags. Holding and rubbing the Bren, I was talking to myself, how beautiful this new gun is. I gained more confidence with the enhanced fighting power.

The instructor and commander for my unit was a young lieutenant. He handed me a cartridge of thirty bullets and showed me how to load the Bren. The new gun was an enormous morale booster. We were all happy with the first automatic machine gun we had. The instruction leaflet showed two positions in which we could use the machine gun; one is in a standing position and the other laying on the ground. Open the tripod, load, aim, and shoot.

The Bren had a relatively short handle because two thirds of the gun was the barrel (pipe), with air holes throughout the pipe. I grabbed the weapon, loaded the cartridge, and started to shoot in the air. Little was I told or did I know that as I shot, the pipe became burning hot. I learned the hard way; my left palm was burned and felt as if I had held my palm over a burning flame. My lieutenant's answer to my being burned was, "You live and learn." After learning the new machine gun, I used it successfully. It was a great weapon during every attack. The sound was music to my ears—troc, troc, troc.

During a severe counterattack in Sassa by the Syrian army, we had several casualties, including me. I was shot in my left leg, below my knee. Two other wounded and I were taken by ambulance to the Rambam Hospital in Haifa. I was given medical treatment for ten days. From there I was transferred to Beit Havurah Number Three Rehab Hospital on Carmel. I was recuperating for two months; the doctors determined that I was not fit to return to a fighting unit.

The military commander of the hospital, Dr. Nagel, requested my unit commander to transfer me to his hospital staff in charge of security and other duties, because I held a rank of sergeant major. My commander released me to the hospital staff where I stayed for approximately four months. It was a boring job, so I requested a transfer to *Metzach*, IDF military police's investigative section. My transfer was granted.

Chapter 25
Metzach

The Military Investigative Police Unit headquarters was in an old British police building on the hilltop before the entrance to the historic Arab city, Nazareth. *Metzach* occupied only one wing of this large military police station and jail. My commander was a Russian-born colonel; he had immigrated to Israel only about three years before, in 1945. He had reasonable command of the Hebrew language but with a very heavy Russian accent. He also had a law degree from Russia and was studying intensely to pass the bar exams in Israel.

When I joined his staff, he handed me a booklet that he wrote when he assumed command of *Metzach*. He said, "This booklet is your bible; it outlines all the rules and regulations and the responsibilities of the job. You will be examined after thirty days time for the position of an investigative policeman."

Throughout the first thirty days, lectures and seminars were conducted by the various experienced officers, explaining the role of this military police unit. Our headquarters was in charge of all the regional bases throughout the country. The total division of *Metzach* had approximately three hundred people including lawyers and experienced investigators.

We wore military uniforms on some investigations. Other investigations required civilian clothes. As in civilian life we had criminals and thieves in the army. We had "professionals" thieves who were stealing large amounts from the defense forces and other thieves, medium and smaller violators of military law.

One of my first assignments was to trace an active, well organized gang that was stealing from the military large amounts of gasoline from the gas supply bases. This went on in the Haifa area as well as at most of the military bases in the northern part of the country.

Our commander briefed us and explained our mission. He decided to plant two of our detectives on a number of our bases. The commander of *Metzach* made direct contact with the commander of the supply bases, advising them that he would be sending two *Metzach* members to their base without detailing the reason for the assignment. The orders to the base commander were to give us flexibility and assign us to any jobs that we requested.

Shalom Goldenberg and I were assigned to a supply base on the main road between Haifa and upper Galilee, near the town of Nesher. When we arrived and reported to the base command, we discussed with him, confidentially and only with him, our assignment without accusations of wrong doings on his base.

At first he felt insulted that we had chosen his camp; however, he offered every assistance we needed. For the first couple of days we were floating around the camp. This camp had eight gasoline tanker trucks, each assigned one driver in addition to mechanics, security people, kitchen personnel—a total of twenty were on this base.

After mingling with the drivers, snooping around as to the delivery routes and the number of deliveries they each make, I compared notes with Corporal Goldberg and decided to ask the base commander to assign each of us to a different truck. The morning started with observing the pumping and the loading of the trucks from the large underground storage tanks. Each of the tankards had three compartments. We took turns traveling with the drivers; upon our return to the base we compared notes. A couple of weeks passed; we could find neither links nor trails to the criminals. The stealing of gasoline continued.

The first break we got was when I obtained the officially assigned stops for each driver. I compared this list with my notes as to the actual stops the driver makes; these did not match. I realized that a couple of drivers made more drop offs than the documented assigned stops. I instructed my partner, Goldenberg, to make the same comparison with his drivers. We cracked the case by focusing on the drivers who made the extra stops. It became obvious that there were three thieves. We still did not know how they accessed the gasoline they stole because on the loading end of the storage tanks there was a gauge to register the number of liters loaded. There was also a gauge, a primitive gauge but nevertheless a gauge, that showed the unloading liters.

Each driver was assigned to the same tanker (except if the tanker was in for repairs), so we checked the suspicious drivers' tankage to see if these were different from the others. We found the answer to our mystery. The suspicious drivers rigged up a way to pass the gasoline from one compartment into another once the first compartment emptied. The gasoline was moved to the empty compartment that registered officially the delivery quantities assigned to each station. The gasoline station managers were unable to detect the missing quantities, so they signed the receipt issued by the driver.

The drivers had their non military, privately owned gas station customers where they sold the stolen gasoline from the military at thirty percent cheaper than the official prices. We arrested the military drivers, and the civilian owners were turned over to the civilian police. They were all prosecuted within a relatively short time to the fullest extent of the law. The thieves were organized nationally and were all arrested.

Following this campaign the army decided to color the military supply of gasoline with a reddish dye to make it difficult to sell to civilians and made it a criminal offense to buy stolen military colored gasoline. Our mission was successfully completed; therefore, we moved back to our military police headquarters in Nazareth.

Shortly after my return to my base I was assigned another investigative campaign. This time *Metzach* command was advised that large quantities of auto parts were being stolen from the largest military base about ten kilometers south of Haifa. The camp was located right off the highway of Haifa and Tel-Aviv. This was a base with several hundred military and civilian workers.

Security on the base was terrible. Only some of the production and supply were housed in large old military barracks. Many vehicles and larger components were stored under temporary makeshift buildings with metal sheeting. Our assignment was to track down the thieves who were stealing not only valuable components like tires, radios, and others but also completely rebuilt cars. Jeeps were the most popular item.

Before we were ordered to the scene, we were given a detailed briefing as to a possibly large-scale criminal ring. The thieves, ex-military and common criminals, had formed a gang similar to the Mafia; on the other hand, the buyers, Jews and Arabs, worked together. Four of us were assigned to the investigation headed by a captain (I was second in command); the captain made arrangements for all of us to visit the plant and tour the grounds of the base inside and outside. It took three days to observe the storage areas, the requisition process, the processes of ordering, supplying, and preparing for pick-up orders, the control of passengers, the outside storage areas, and the interior base, loosely protected with a relatively low and flexible barbed-wire fence. The front gate, the entrance to the base, was guarded twenty-four hours a day in three shifts of one soldier with a rifle, helmet, a couple of hand grenades, and a flash light.

A few scattered lights were on during the night throughout the base. These were too few and too far in between to be an effective deterrent for non-authorized personnel. A decision was made to stake out the base from the outside during the evening and nights. The base officially functioned from 8 AM to 6 PM. During our observation we saw a few people remain. The first night we had noticed several civilians approaching the base from the back. They were driving what looked like a military jeep with civilian license plates. Well into the evening, about 10 PM, a small truck with only two people drove up and parked near the jeep. It took them no more than thirty minutes to load up and leave, the jeep following the truck.

We had a military car, a French-made Citrone; however, we did not follow them, so that we did not alert them that we were investigating them. The following morning we checked the back of the camp, noticing a very loose wire fence, easily moveable. Around the entire camp there was gravel and hard ground; the nearest building was at least a hundred meters away.

We repeated our stakeout for five nights. We checked with the base commander who had no particular knowledge of the night activities. He was definitely unaware of the criminal ring operating on his base. He was the one to begin with who reported the shrinkage (losses) on his base.

We completed our limited investigation by filing our report to the *Metzach* commander. Because the scale of activities was ongoing and involved mostly civilian workers and outside civilian criminals, the report was turned over to the civilian police authorities for immediate action. The police did an effective job, following and tracing the detailed activities; they arrested the entire gang.

Only two military personnel were involved; they were prosecuted by the military authorities.

We had moved on to other investigative assignments. There was no shortage of crooks. David Ben Gurion, among others, said: "We will not be a state until we have our own generals, our own police, our own criminals, and our own jails. Thank God, we have all the above as other nations do."

I completed my two years of military service and was honorably discharged in May 1950.

Chapter 26
Histadrut

My first real job was at the *Histadrut* (The Federation of Labor) in Haifa, from 1950-1955, representing the youth movement. The *Histadrut* in reality was the government before the State of Israel became an independent state on May 14, 1948. David Ben Gurion headed the leadership of the *Histadrut*, the chairman of the Jewish agency (pre-state), as well as the head of the Mapai Party (the Labor Party) until he became the first Prime Minister of Israel on March 8, 1949. Ben Gurion was a visionary, a strong leader, often compared with other short stature leaders in history such as Napoleon, Churchill, and Einstein. He was charismatic, radiating knowledge, confidence, and determination. Ben Gurion remained the dominating figure in Israel public life well into the 1960's. When he first resigned in 1953, thousands were crying. His comment was: "Instead of crying, you would do better to come with me."

I had the privilege of meeting Ben Gurion previously during the first election campaign in Haifa in December 1948 and January 1949, when he led the Mapai Party to a victory, giving Mapai forty-six seats in the first *Knesset* (Parliament) of one hundred twenty members. As the leader of the largest party he was invited by the first president of Israel, Dr. Chaim Weizmann, to form the first government of Israel. On March 8, the first cabinet was sworn in by the *Knesset*. Ben Gurion led the nation and commanded the defense forces until his first resignation on December 24, 1953, when he stunned the nation and the world with his announcement to settle in *Kibbutz Sde Boker* in the Negev desert of southern Israel.

Ben Gurion chose Kibbutz Sde Boker in the Negev because he realized the necessity of reinforcing the existing settlements in the south of the country.

The south represents 50% of the land of Israel. However, the climate, the land, the lack of water, and the shortage of energy were challenging problems. The government was reluctant to send new *olim* (immigrants making aliyah) to the south where there was little housing and no industry.

Ben Gurion's move to the south was a major breakthrough. The government took advantage of the "Go South" atmosphere created by Ben Gurion's move, immediately allocating a large budget to build roads, highways, bridges, by ways, and housing for newcomers. The government also provided incentives for building factories, thus creating employment opportunities. In addition, the government gave farmers incentives to settle in the south.

The building of a large city, Be´er Sheva, the capital city of the south, became a reality as did the establishment of numerous enterprises as well as Ben Gurion University. Prof. Zeev Hadari paraphrased David Ben-Gurion's philosophy by proclaiming, "If there is no university in the Negev's future, then there is no future for the Negev." Today Ben Gurion University is one of the leading institutions of higher learning with a world-wide reputation. Ben Gurion had re-emphasized the importance of making the desert bloom.

In 1952, I had the privilege of visiting Ben Gurion and his wife, Paula, in their modest three bedroom apartment. While our group of well-wishers and supporters from Haifa chatted with Ben Gurion, Paula served us glasses of hot tea. The book shelves in each room bowed from the weight of such a heavy load of books: history, philosophy, the Bible, and others, in addition to books in Hebrew, Turkish, English, and Russian.

I was fortunate to be nominated to the *Histadrut* in 1950 after completing my military service of two years. In May 1950, my position was secretary of the wood working union in the greater Haifa area. My daily responsibility was to ensure that the labor force, over 3.000 people, employed in this industry were earning fair wages, established by the labor movement, including social benefits, health care, insurance, and participation in the Histadrut pension fund. The challenges of the job were daily because some employers preferred Arab labor or new *olim* (immigrants); their salaries were half of those of organized labor with no insurance benefits.

As a representative of the youth political movement, I was a member of the National Central Committee of the Mapai Party, the leading party in Israel.

The Secretary General in Haifa was Abba Chushi. Abba was also the head of the Mapai Party in Haifa for over twenty years as well as a member of the Central National Committee of the party. In 1951 he was elected mayor of Haifa.

He was succeeded by Josef Almogi, second in the city leadership position. Almogi became a strong leader in his own rights, in Haifa as well as nationally. It was a privilege to work with him; he had a magnetic personality. During World War II, Almogi served in the British Jewish Brigade. His battalion was captured in Greece and taken by the Nazis to prison camps as war criminals. Josef Almogi, the highest ranking officer in camp, was the leader and representative of his brigade facing the German commander in charge of the prison. As a proud Jew with strong convictions, he stood fast against the Nazi camp commander. Almogi requested and achieved many concessions from the Nazi commander: to be treated according to the Geneva

Convention and international laws, protecting the rights of military prisoners, in spite of being Jews. Upon his liberation after three months of imprisonment, he was awarded special recognition for his bravery and leadership. After four years, Almogi was nominated by David Ben Gurion to the post of Acting Secretary of Haifa's Workers' Council (1947-1951), Secretary (1951-1959), General Secretary of Mapai (1959-1961).

Josef Almogi, the director of the *Histadrut* in Haifa, created a young action group of three: Wertman, Glazer, and I were his team, spearheading various important functions during historic labor strikes, such as the Haifa port strike. This was the only major seaport (at the time) in Israel that impacted the entire economy of the country. We were also active in the major ATA strike—the largest textile mill. ATA was the producer of the khaki apparel for men and women that became a household national brand. ATA also produced the first uniform for the Israeli army. We were involved in a strike in the cosmetic industry in Haifa and other sensitive assignments that we were given by our boss, Josef Almogi.

Moshe Wertman, a close friend of mine, became Secretary General of the Haifa Workers' Council (1949-1959). After two years, Wertman was elected to the sixth *Knesset* where he served as majority leader of the *Knesset* between 1966 and 1977. He is now in his late eighties, semi-retired, and the head of an organization for seniors in Haifa. Moshe lives in Haifa with his two sons, Udi and Elisha, and daughter, Nurit. The city of Haifa was nicknamed the "red" city of Israel because of the strong federation of labor, *Histadrut*, as well as the strongest Mapai Party (politically middle left) in the city.

Throughout the year and, in particular, before the national elections, the leaders of the party headed by David Ben Gurion, Moshe Sharett, Eliezer Kaplan, Levi Eshkol, Golda Meir, Zalman Shazar, Dov

Yosef, Shimon Peres, Moshe Dayan, and others loved to come to Haifa where we organized large rallies of party members and sympathizers.

These strikes and rallies ended in smashing successes for the Haifa Labor Union. The strikes were in a large part a showdown between unorganized labor advocates and organized labor. In my own small way, I was always an active part of the local Mapai leadership as well as a member of the National team. I identified and embraced the pioneering spirit of the labor union and helped to enforce the official *Histadrut* policies. My *Habonim Dror* education had prepared me well for the eventualities and challenges in life.

Chapter 27
Villie, After the War

During the war Villie, my oldest brother, served in the Czech army. After the Nazi occupation of Czechoslovakia, he and his unit were taken by the Nazis to dig ditches at the front line between Germany and Russia. After several months he escaped to Russia where he served with other Czechs in the Russian army. Eighteen months later the war was over, so, in his military uniform, Villie traveled to Prague, the capital city of Czechoslovakia, as a Czech partisan. As a privileged citizen he was given a house and a small farm in the suburbs of Prague.

During his stay on the farm, Villie cultivated the land. He discovered that our sister, Chaya, had survived the concentration camps and was married in our hometown Berehovo to a Lithuanian Jewish survivor, Avrahm Arkuski (he changed his name in Israel to Argov). Villie traveled to our hometown, met our newlywed sister, and learned that his girlfriend Manci had also survived. She was back in her hometown Vari near Berehovo.

Without losing any time Villie took a train to Vari. To his surprise he met with Manci's mother, who had also survived the concentration camps. She told Villie that on the following evening, his girl friend was to be married to another survivor.

Villie had with him his new brother-in-law, Avraham. Since Villie was still very much in love with Manci, together the two devised a plan to whisk Manci away. Manci's mother, who had always favored Villie, also assisted them. They hired a horse and buggy and, in the evening, waited for Manci to arrive home. Then away they went to Berehovo where they were married within five days.

After that, they left for their home near Prague. The two couples, Chaya and Avraham and Villie and Manci, lived on the farm for almost a year. They did not particularly like being farmers, so they found their way to a transit camp in Germany where thousands of survivors were waiting for a solution to their future.

Villie remembered having many relatives in the U.S. He was able to make contact with one of our uncles, Uncle Louis Gross, and his wife, Aunt Gussie, our father's sister. Villie wrote to them, expressing his desire to come to the U.S.; however, he told them, he must have proper documents from them— an affidavit asserting that they would not be a burden to the state. The uncle replied with kindness. To gather all the papers took a long and agonizing two years. Villie and Manci received the visas and all proper documentation to immigrate to the U.S.

Villie and Manci arrived in Philadelphia in 1949. Chaya and Avraham had immigrated to Haifa in *Eretz Yisrael* in 1947, where they still live with two sons, eight grandchildren, and seven great-grandchildren.

Chapter 28
My First Visit to the U.S.

In 1954, Villie became ill, so he invited me to visit him in Philadelphia. I told Villie that I couldn't afford a trip to the United States, so Villie said that he would make the reservations and pay for the flight. He asked me to stay with Manci and him for a few months.

I contacted my director at the *Histadrut*, Josef Almogi. I asked for permission to take three months unpaid leave. Permission was granted, and I arrived in New York in March 1955 at JFK Airport. The meeting with Villie was quite emotional because we had not seen each other since I was thirteen years old—in 1942. Villie picked me up in a new Pontiac station wagon. He drove me to his home on Marshall Street in Philadelphia; I met my sister-in-law, Manci, my niece, Miriam, and nephew, Steven.

Before I left Israel, a friend within our circle introduced me to a new business he had just become involved in. The business was a pyramid sales concept (multi level marketing): You buy a booklet of five coupons for five dollars; you need to sell four of the coupons to four different friends who each has to buy an additional booklet (with five coupons) for five dollars to be sold to five other friends. Immediately you have twenty-five customers!

As you go on you could see the multiplication factor—the pyramid grows very rapidly. The founders of the business concept had a redemption center advertising the various premiums a person would get for each of the five one dollar coupons he or she had sold.

The person that sold five booklets originally had earned a premium, resulting from the original sale. The advertising leaflets showed valuable premiums (in those years very valuable) such as electric coffee percolators, toasters, kitchen clocks, mixers, electric can openers, etc. In Israel this business concept took off like a missile.

I had purchased coupons and bought with me all the promotional materials. After being with my brother Villie for a few days, I shared with him and my sister-in-law, Manci, the concept of this pyramid business. Both of them were quite impressed; however, my brother said, "This is too good to believe. I have not seen anyone in the U.S. owning this kind of business."

Villie mentioned a friend of his, Bela Denzinger, who had a printing shop. "I'll ask him to come over to our house. Then you can show him the circulars and coupons. Bela will give you a good price for printing and will also give his opinion about the concept."

A couple of days later Bela came to visit us regarding the business concept. He said, "I cannot comment. This may be a good business. Regarding the printing of the coupons and circulars, I will give you a price tomorrow."

His quote for 2,500 booklets, 5,000 circulars (catalogs), and 5,000 envelopes was $150.00, including set up charges.

The following day I made contact with a wholesale electric appliance house, which provided me with pictures of items I had selected for my mailing. I had purchased only one of each product knowing that the wholesaler had an inventory to back me up.

While I was working in his store during the day, I told Villie that I had decided to enter into this business. But I needed two things from him: one, permission to display my premiums on shelves in his grocery store on Marshall Street. He and Manci were living in the same building on the second floor above the store. Two, I needed to borrow $200.00 for stamps and the appliances. The printer gave me ninety days credit, and I had sixty five dollars.

With no hesitation, Villie agreed to allow me to display the merchandise, my assortment of samples, and to lend me the money. I was in business, using Villie's address. I waited three long weeks to receive my order from the printer. As soon as I received the envelopes and the other printed materials, I took a Philadelphia phone book and started to address envelopes. The first night I had addressed over five hundred envelopes, stuffed them, and had affixed first class stamps. In the morning I took my first batch of envelopes to the red mail box on the corner. The second evening I addressed my second batch of five hundred, mailing them in the morning. I repeated this four times five hundred. There was a weekend in between. I waited for results, phone calls, or visits to the store by some who had received my mailings.

I was anxiously waiting, and so excited that I couldn't sleep. I had multiplied in my head the potential earnings; I counted the money in my head. After a week had passed, I said to Villie, "I cannot understand this—not one phone call; not one visit to the store."

My brother realized that I was anxious and concerned at the same time and said: "Sometimes the mail is slow. Give it a few more days."

It took about fourteen days from the first mailing before I had two visitors, well dressed and courteous. In a strong voice one said: "We are looking for Ernest Paul."

I anxiously replied in my broken English, "Yes, me Ernest Paul."

The other person had a plastic bag in his hand. He said, "Can we sit down?"

My brother joined us and ushered us upstairs to the living room. At this point, both pulled out their badges, stating, "We are from the F.B.I."

I asked them to repeat: "Me don't understand."

They repeated what they had said, "We are from the FBI" and opened the plastic bag. To my shock and surprise all two thousand envelopes were in the bag.

"Did you mail these?"

" Yes." I was proud for a moment.

"It is illegal in the U.S. to use the U.S. mail system for multi-level marketing offers such as this. It is a criminal act, against the law in the U.S."

I almost fell off the chair. I did not know what to expect next. I understood everything they said, but privately I had asked my brother to explain to me in Hungarian what they were saying. At this point Villie was concerned about his involvement causing him to be in trouble with the law.

I walked over to my suitcase where I had the original Hebrew printed materials, coupons, etc., explaining the rules of the "game business." I started to explain with my limited vocabulary and the help of my brother.

"I just arrived about a month ago from Israel, which is a free democratic country as is the U.S." I asked, "Why is it legal in Israel and not in the U.S.?

They replied, "We do not care about Israeli laws; we are here to enforce U.S. laws." Showing the Hebrew version of the sales material did not convince them a bit.

"We'll cut this short. We realize your attempt was innocent; however, we repeat, this is against the law of the U.S. You must stop immediately; no more mailings. You are ordered to destroy or burn these two thousand envelopes. The display has to come down, and all promotional material has to be destroyed. You are out of business as of right now. Is that clear?"

I did not wait for my brother's translation; he was concerned not to be involved in breaking the laws of his new country. My reply was, "Yes, okay. I am sorry. We do not know."

They said, "We will let you off the hook; from here on you must comply with the laws of the land."

"Yes. Sorry again. Thank you."

This was obviously a bitter pill to swallow, not a good way to start in the U.S.

After staying for six weeks I missed my wife, Sara, and my kids, Dahlia and Stewart. I talked to my brother about my going home to Israel. My brother insisted on my staying longer and said that he would send airline tickets for Sara and the kids. Two weeks later they arrived.

In the early years in Israel we faced food rationing from 1948 to 1949. The food we received was not sufficient, so most of the rations were given to our kids, with Sara saying, "I do not want my kids to experience the hunger I did."

Sara was happy in the United States. My brother had a food market in Philadelphia, and food was plentiful. All the food, fruits, vegetables and other goodies were a determining factor for Sara. She decided to take advantage of this "golden land" and remain in the United States.

All my idealism was not strong enough to convince her otherwise. The fact that I was somewhat successful in Philadelphia and provided for my family did not help. The ninety days leave from my job expired; we did not return to Israel.

Chapter 29
Rationing in Israel

On April 26, 1949, the Israeli government declared rationing of the basic food items. The Secretary of Agriculture, Minister Dov Yosef, was nominated to be also the Minister of Rationing. He made a special appeal to the people explaining the program. Each person would receive once a month through the nearest food store the following: 60 grams of corn per day, 58 grams of sugar, 60 grams of flour, 17 grams of rice, 20 grams of margarine, 8 grams of noodles, 200 grams of cottage cheese, 600 grams of onions, 5 grams of cookies, 75 grams of meat per month, and unlimited bread; however, the total cannot exceed 6 Liras, the approximate of 25 U.S. dollars per month.

As Sara had experienced this rationing not long after the concentration camps, she wanted to provide as much as possible to the children, so she chose the "goldene medina" of America. Sara was a devoted mother. After all, she was told by doctors after the concentration camps that she would never have children. She proved everyone wrong; the children were her life's jewels.

I did get a position back in the *Histadrut* (not the same position as before); however, nothing was enough to soften or break Sara's determination to go back to the U.S. My options were limited—my family unity or my country. My love for Sara and the kids won; we returned to the U.S. in April of 1957.

Chapter 30
Sinai War 1956

In 1956, I received a notice from the Israeli consulate in New York calling on all military reserve personnel to go back to Israel. Without considering the possible consequences, I quietly told Sara that I was going back to Israel. Five days later I reported to my military unit. I was proud to join my unit and ready to participate in the war. In a way, however, I was very disappointed because my unit was not ordered to the south of the country, to Sinai where Israel had gone to war against Egypt. Israel decided to go to war following the decision of the Egyptian President, Gamal Abdel Nasser, to nationalize the Suez Canal and Egypt's encouragement of the *fedayeen* to murder Jewish civilians and terrorize kibbutzim and other border settlements.[22] The Jordanian armed forces joined the Egyptians and allowed infiltrators across the borders. General staff commander Moshe Dayan called for an extensive operation. Prime Minister David Ben Gurion approved the campaign.

Our unit was kept in the Haifa area where we were shelled by an Egyptian destroyer, the *Abraham Al-Wal*, for several days,.The Egyptian destroyer created a panic in Haifa. Although the Israeli Navy was in its infancy and the IDF naval arsenal consisted of a couple of small vessels and torpedo boats that had been received from France, the Israeli forces silenced the destroyer and captured the crew of 250.

We were standing by, waiting for orders to join the fighting forces in the south. By then, 90,000 IDF forces were mobilized for this campaign. We were never moved out of the Haifa area, where we were guarding sensitive bases.

Military forces the world over were astonishing by the results of the war. The fighting ended after eight days of heroic fighting by the IDF. The lion's share of the fighting and success is credited to the paratrooper battalion under the command of Lt. General Rafael Eitan and the infantry brigade commanded by Ariel Sharon.

This war was short; we were discharged fourteen days later. Then reality started to sink in: I am in Israel; my wife, daughter, and son are in the U.S. I have no idea how to convey to Sara my decision not to go back to the U.S. I had decided to stay in Israel. The bargaining and negotiations to bring my wife and kids back to Israel began.

Neither my job nor my home had been waiting for me in Israel because I was supposed to be absent only ninety days, yet I had stayed over a year in the U.S. This weakened my bargaining position with Sara. I continued to maintain my position, my desire to raise my children in Israel. I was able to get an apartment temporarily again in Tivon with some friends who owned a small hotel. I had reason to believe that I would get a new job at the *Histadrut* once my family came back. Four months passed, and Sara gave in, returning to me and to Israel.

The adjustment for Sara was painful: she had to give up everything she had and everything she was able to give the children, mainly the unlimited quantity and variety of food. There was no question in my mind that Sara was still frightened and vividly remembered her hunger in the concentration camps and the rationing in Israel.

Chapter 31
"Pioneers" in Israel

My love for Israel and yearning to return to live there was absorbed by my son Stewart, who became a Zionist in his own right. At sixteen, Stewart met Nancy, who shared his love for Israel. They married when Stewart was twenty years old. They completed their education in America. Stewart earned a Juris Doctorate in Law, and Nancy, a Master's degree in Sociology. Life was good; they were on a path to a secure and successful life in America, but they were Zionists and idealists. They wanted to do something more meaningful with their lives.

Attending Rosh HaShanah (Jewish New Year, a High Holiday) services in their synagogue in 1981, they heard the rabbi say, "If you get the opportunity to go to Israel, you should go!" They looked at each other and knew immediately what they needed to do. There would be no one offering them a ticket to travel to Israel or a job to work in Israel. They would have to create their own opportunities. They searched for and joined a *garin* that was part of the *HaShomer Hatzair* movement.[23] They studied together and made plans to go to a kibbutz in Israel that was struggling to live the dream they shared. They chose not to work in their respective fields in Tel Aviv, but to do physical work on a poor kibbutz, surrounded by Arab villages. Kibbutz Yasur was located in northern Israel, east of Acre in the Western Galilee. This kibbutz was established in 1949 by immigrants from England and Hungary who were members of the Zionist Socialist youth movement

HaShomer Hatzair. Nancy and Stewart were welcomed with open arms; however, the members of the kibbutz were surprised that well educated Americans would choose such a life. Typically, those making their way to Israel were fleeing oppression or poverty in their home countries, or were very religious.

I was *shepping naches* (felt proud) to see that my son would fulfill my dream of living on a kibbutz. My wife, Sara, was very disappointed—almost in shock. Nancy's mother and father, who lived a few blocks away from us in Philadelphia, felt the same as Sara.

While I was very proud of their decision, I was quietly proud. What they heard from Sara and Nancy's parents was, "How could you do this?" We wondered why they would give up such an easy and good life for physical labor in basically a farming community. Nancy and Stewart were determined and excited about their decision. Their choice to live on a kibbutz was a testament to their Zionistic ideals; Nancy said she wanted to feel like a *halutza* (pioneer).

True to their words, Stewart and Nancy made aliyah to Israel in 1982. Nancy became an Israeli citizen and was put to work washing clothes in the kibbutz laundry. When Stewart wasn't serving in the army, he worked in the kibbutz furniture factory.

In December 1982, Sara and I and Nancy's mother visited Stewart and Nancy in the kibbutz. Because we arrived during the middle of the week, everyone was working. We walked to the office, asking for Nancy and Stewart, and were told that Nancy was working in the *machbesa*, the kibbutz laundry. We headed for the laundry. When we entered, we heard two big industrial washing machines. But no Nancy. We made our way around the big washers, and then we noticed our precious Nancy climbing up to the washer using a step ladder. The washer was far taller than Nancy. We were all happy to see each other.

"A good thing that you graduated with honors from New York University; this qualifies you to wash the laundry for two hundred people," Sara said.

Stewart worked in the furniture factory of the kibbutz until, at the age of twenty-eight, he volunteered to join the Israeli Defense Forces and received training in specialized computers that gave firing directives to artillery batteries. He earned the honor of "Best Soldier in the Platoon" and was given a field promotion, becoming a corporal in a very short space of time. He served in the Israeli Defense Forces in the first Israeli-Lebanese War in 1982-83.

Nancy and Stewart were very happy to be living a life that was about more than themselves, even though it was not easy or comfortable. They felt their lives were rich with friendships and purpose. As a sociologist, Nancy was able to experience the social environment of a very unique lifestyle that was about as different from life in America as one could imagine.

Our first grandson, Ari, was born in Israel on May 25, 1984. The kibbutz celebrated the birth of their *ben-kibbutz* (son of the kibbutz) with joy. Sara, Nancy's mother, and I traveled to Israel for Ari's *brit-milah*.[24] Nancy's father, Bernie, passed away soon after they had moved to Israel. He had been planning a trip to visit them. Sadly he never made it.

In late 1984, Nancy's mother, Edith became quite ill. Stewart and Nancy returned to the United States, leaving all of their belongings in Israel. Nancy did not want her mother to face her illness alone. It was an unfortunate tragedy: Nancy lost her dear mother when both were so young. Nancy and Stewart lived with us. Sara and I tried to talk them into remaining in the United States for good. I offered Stewart the presidency of my company and a generous salary in the hope of convincing them not to return to Israel.

The decision was a difficult and painful one for Stewart and Nancy. For a long time Nancy said that she felt that she had a foot in each country and wasn't wholly at home in the United States. To this day she sees Israel as her third "child," worrying about it, protective of it, and contributing to its welfare.

Chapter 32
Revisting my Hometown

Sara, my sister, Chaya, and I visited Beregújfalu in 1985. Our visit to town was quite spectacular. We arrived in a beautiful red Mercedes that I had hired, with a driver, in Budapest. The trip from Budapest took us about eight hours.

When we arrived at our home, we realized that the Soviets had given away our home and land—the land and the houses were divided among four families. When we first approached the entrance, one of the women came outside. We were hoping for a warm greeting; however, once we told her who we were, she raised her voice in anger and held onto the gate, saying, "What do you people want? This has been our house for the last thirty-five years!"

We told her that our intention was not to come back and claim ownership and that we were visiting only for sentimental reasons. The woman, Magda, then calmed down, opened the gate and the door to her house, and invited us for a cup of tea. Magda also called in her other three neighbors; only the women were home, the men were working in the fields. After a couple of hours stay and lots of stories we parted on a friendly note; we reassured them that we were not moving back.

When we came out of the house, we saw about fifty people around the car, including some who had known our parents well. That night we drove to Berehovo, a thirty minute drive to a hotel, where we rested comfortably. We told the people in Beregújfalu that we would be back in the morning and that we would spend the entire day there. We had a number of invitations, particularly for my sister who was known because she had been home soon after the war and had met with some ex-neighbors. I suggested to one of our old neighbors that he find a place in a club house (there were no restaurants or hotels in Beregújfalu), and we would come back the next day when we would have drinks for all.

We arrived in the morning. We first visited the municipal office of the mayor. Dr. Biro Busie was a young, friendly woman in her thirties; she already knew about our visit. She told us about herself. After graduating law school and practicing law in Beregújfalu, Novo Selo, and Berehovo, she had been elected as mayor two years earlier. Her parents had known our parents. Dr. Busie went out of her way to offer us any assistance during our stay. She took the initiative of opening her offices to invite some of the townspeople in. In the meantime we spent some time around the town, visiting some people that my sister knew.

At 4 PM around fifty people showed up. I had brought with me five bottles of Absolut Vodka that we had purchased at the duty free shop. Several people had brought bottles of wine with them. The party went on for about two hours. The mayor greeted us and spoke eloquently about my father, Josef Pal, who had contributed so much to improving the lives of the people in the town.

A number of other people came to us and told us stories about our father. I thanked the mayor and the people that had come to greet us and those that had not come and wished them well. The gathering resulted in mixed feelings for us. My sister was wiping her tears away, hugging and kissing some. On the other hand, the people of Beregújfalu had profited from what the Jews had lost. That evening we returned to Berehovo (Beregszász), where we spent the night and the next day. From there we traveled through several towns on our way to Munkács and back to Budapest where we stayed for several days.

1988, Beregújfalu: Ernest

1988, Beregújfalu: Sara, Chaya, and former neighbors
(one was the fiacre, driver, and the other made wine barrels)

Chapter 33
Our 50th Wedding Anniversary

I had promised Sara fifty years ago that one day we would have a "real" wedding with a rabbi to make up for the wedding we did not have. On July 13, 1945, our friend Zvi Prizant in Kibbutz Frumka, Bucharest, recognized by his authority as head of the kibbutz (captain of the ship), "married" us.

Almost to the date I kept my promise; on July 15, 1995, my promise became a reality. We had our Rabbi Goldman, from the Adath Zion Congregation in Philadelphia, come especially to officiate and legitimize our marriage.

The religious ceremony was very moving for Sara and me. Our kids, in particular, were delighted to "legitimize" Mom and Dad's marriage. The presence of my sister, Chaya, and her husband, Avraham, who had come especially from Israel, as well as our dear friends Yochevet (Eva) and Zvi Prizant, helped to bless the day. My brother Villie and Manci's kids, Miriam and Steven; my brother Emil, his wife Lili, and their three kids: Rifka, David and Neal, also celebrated our anniversary. Sara's cousin, Sara Rasmovich from Florida, their son Michel, his wife, Ilene; my friend from the bunker, Andi, his wife, Eta; from Brazil, our dear friends: Ursula and her father, Klaus Schumacher; from Chile, our friend Juan Eduardo Undorrago, Christian Chalgeneao, Isabel Lanas, and Petrito Fernandez; from St. Louis, Don Ranz, his wife, Carrie, and Merie Murphy; our children: Dahlia and her daughters, Tara and Ilana; Stewart, Nancy, and their sons, Ari and Eitan; Gil, Dali, and their daughter Elite; and our cousins the Grosses, as well as the many, many friends from New York and Philadelphia, and our neighbors from the Ocean Club in particular: Barry, Rachel, and their son, Eli, daughters, Tova and Jeannet; our friends Zig and Paula Menash; John Dennes and his wife, Ilene; and all the other many friends (over two hundred fifty), who filled our hearth with love, appreciation, and friendship.

The beautifully decorated banquet hall at the Atlantic City's Tropicana Hotel and Casino, the great Kantor band from Philadelphia, the cocktails, the excellent food, and, above all, our beautifully dressed family members and friends certainly made it worthwhile to wait fifty years. Our anniversary was a most memorable event. We appreciated them and were grateful to all.

We had enclosed the following in the invitations we had sent:

Our Jewish tradition teaches us that in times of celebration, we should always remember those who are not able to be with us. Our 50th wedding anniversary coincided with another historic date, the end of World War II and the 50th anniversary of the liberation of the Nazi camps. As survivors of the Holocaust, during which time most of our families perished, we feel a sense of mission to combine these two dates in a meaningful way. We would appreciate and be very thankful if any gift honoring our 50th anniversary would go as a contribution to a unique educational program which prepares high school teachers to implement Holocaust studies in their classes on the Holocaust and Jewish Resistance.

This project is very important and close to our hearts. Please direct any gifts as a contribution to this special, tax deductible program. Checks should be made out to the American Gathering of Jewish Holocaust Survivors Education.

Chapter 34
A Trip to Remember

For our 50th wedding anniversary our son Stewart initiated and planned a trip for us to travel around the world—First class round trip, with the excellent Australian airline, Quantas.

This three weeks trip started in New York, then on to San Francisco, Honolulu, Melbourne, Australia, to Sidney, and on to Beijing, China, Hong Kong, and Taiwan, finally to Japan and back home. In each city we spent time with professional tour guides.

We immensely enjoyed visiting each country, the museums and the historically rich landmarks. The highlights of the trip for Sara were San Francisco (Sara's first time), Honolulu, Sidney, Australia, and in China, the Forbidden City, the Great Wall, and the mosques, churches, and temples.

The hotel accommodations were all 5 stars. We enjoyed the beautiful beaches, restaurants, and ongoing cultural activities. This three weeks' trip was a once in a lifetime, unforgettable experience.

As I have learned, to get the most out of these trips it is best to hire a local tour guide or go on an official tour in each city. That is the way we did it; there is no better way.

Chapter 35
Our Marriage of 62 Years

Throughout the years we had our ups and downs as have most normal marriages. The beginning was relatively smooth and "rosy" despite the illness of Sara. Despite our differences over the years, we managed to discuss issues as they arose and resolve them amicably.

Sara was in charge of every aspect of the household. She handled the family budget responsibly, paid the bills, and did all of the shopping for food, clothing, and other necessities. Sara was the "Boss" at home. I accepted her role as such—from day one.

Sara was more than that; she was in charge of moving our home numerous times. In Philadelphia we moved three times; then the move to New York, where we moved twice. Sara was in charge of furnishing and decorating our homes, including summer homes in Atlantic City from the Roosevelt Condos to Margate Towers and finally the Ocean Club Condos. Sara's taste and style were reflected in every move.

Sara was also the handy "man" at home; she changed light bulbs, replaced missing screws, fixed the sliding window shades, and on and on She never ceased to amaze and surprise me.

I was never home for any move or to share the daily issues at home. She almost single handedly raised our three wonderful children and suffered with them in their illnesses and pain. I did share the results, the satisfaction and enjoyment we got from the kids on birthdays, graduations, Bar/Bat Mitzvahs, and weddings.

My major concern was always striving to provide a decent living standard for my family and the best education for our kids, even under the most difficult circumstances. Most of my years in business (sixty out of sixty-two years of marriage), traveling overseas or in the U.S., definitely took a toll on both of us and the children.

Thanks to Sara's strength and my determination we managed through "thick and thin," in sunny days as well as stormy days. For the first years of traveling overseas, I always managed to take advantage of some of the duty free shops, buying Sara her favorite perfumes, jewelry—something different from each country, for my kids, in particular dolls from each country for my daughter Dahlia and for granddaughters.

The reunions, the homecomings, were always happy occasions like a honeymoon, a reason to celebrate. After I gained more confidence and made friends in the countries I traveled to most, Israel, Brazil, Chile, Argentina, Peru, Colombia, Germany, Italy, England, and Holland, I invited Sara to travel with me.

We went to Israel at about the same time every year, December 17 to January 2, and then spent about ten days in Tel Aviv, visiting family and friends in Haifa, combined with business (where we had a Primex office).

Sara's travels with me reduced the tension between us. She loved shopping in each country for something specific. Israel was her favorite for Gotex bathing suits, jewelry, and Beged-Or leather apparel. Brazil was known for the wide range of precious and semi- precious stones, such as aqua marine, amethyst and topaz; Argentina, for leather goods, pocket books, leather boots, belts; London, for rain coats; and Italy, for clothing and more shoes and pocket books.

In each country we enjoyed the special foods in the unlimited number of restaurants. Many of the trips were planned around the trade shows which I had to attend; this made it possible for us to spend more valuable time together.

In each country we planned within my time frame visits to museums, theatres, concerts. These were always the carrots that sweetened our traveling, for Sara loved the arts. The last year of Sara's illness I stopped traveling. I dedicated my full time to her, for my love for her grew stronger and stronger every year reaching its peak before her last breath.

Chapter 36
Business & Pleasure

An integral part of my business was traveling overseas to work with our people in the Primex offices in Israel, Brazil, Argentina, Chile, Peru, Colombia, and Mexico. I often traveled with international buyers to attend international trade shows and in the U.S. business required my visiting our clients and some other countries. Whenever possible, I combined business with pleasure, traveling together with Sara on many of these trips.

From time to time the logistics of these trips was difficult, but planning them was always enjoyable. It gave us an opportunity to spend quality time together.

Often we planned our trips to visit famous spas such as in Israel at the Dead Sea and in the Czech Republic at Karlovy Vary (Carlovi-Vari, or Carlsbath) where the natural hot spring water flows from the ground. The baths healed the outside and the water fountains throughout the city were at our pleasure to drink and these healed the inside, according to the doctors. The spas in Budapest, Israel, and Brazil were all a treat.

On these trips to Israel we spent one week to ten days visiting family and friends in Haifa, Tel Aviv, Jerusalem, Chedera, Natania, Tivon, Tiberias, the beautiful Kineret, and Kibbutz Gardosh-Farod. We toured with my cousin Tibi, his wife, and children. Revisiting the Golan Heights was always an emotional experience. We visited the historic city of Acre(Akko) in Western Galilee. We enjoyed the many good restaurants on our way to Kibbutz Yasur, visiting our kids,

Stewart and Nancy, and visiting the Holocaust museum in Kibbutz Mordei Hagetaot where we had numerous friends.

We visited friends in Tivon at Kiryat Amal, and at Netanya, where Sara had her Uncle Shaja and Rachel, her only surviving family. We never failed to visit my cousin Lipi with his wife Shari, who, in the center of Natania, had the best known coffee shop and confectionary, baking on the premises popular Hungarian pastries.

In Chedera, we had (and still have) our loving niece and nephew, Anat and Shalom, with their five children. They lived in a spacious house across from an orange and tangerine plantation. Pardes, their home, was full of love, the garden bloomed with flowers and fresh fruits. Anat's Shaloms and hospitality were always enjoyable.

In Haifa, we visited my sister, Chaya, her husband, Avraham, our nephew, Roni, and his wife, Rachel. They always provided a beautiful Sabbath lunch gathering with their children and grandchildren as well as friends from the old days.

We also attended to business, visiting factories, meeting with suppliers, having fun-loving dinners in my favorite Middle Eastern restaurants or at Shmulik's diner with Joska Givol, Eli Gur and our friends Yochevet and Zvi Prizant. Year after year, trip after trip, the dinners at the home of our dear friends Yochevet, Zvi, and their daughters, Nechema and Zipi, with their children were always a highlight of our memorable visits.

The goodbyes before returning home were difficult as we never knew what the next year would bring. My last visit was November 2008. I hope and dream of returning as many years as possible.

After a long illness, my dear friend Zvi Prizant died on November 20, 2009. May his memory be a blessing.

Chapter 37
Recognition of Heroism

Representatives of the Jewish underground organization, in particular David Gur, and Israeli government representatives conducted ongoing negotiations with the Hungarian government for sixty-two years to achieve recognition for the Jewish underground members as heroic fighters for freedom. The medals of courage and certificates were issued and signed by the Hungarian interior minister, Dr. Monika Lamperth. The medals and certificates were presented to ninety-one individuals, including thirty-two posthumously, in Tel Aviv by Minister of the Chancellery, Peter Kiss,. who visited Israel on April 1, 2004.

2004, Israel: Zvi Prizant accepting the Medal for Courage on Ernest's behalf

During World War II, Hungarian Jewish resistance fighters sacrificed themselves in order to bravely and courageously resist the Nazi fascists and save persecuted Jews.

The reason for the delayed negotiations was attributed to the constant changing of the Hungarian government. Their concern was that financial claims by the medal recipient would follow the recognition. Claims were absolutely never considered by the recipients nor by the Israeli government. Because I was unable to attend, I gave Zvi Prizant power of attorney to represent me and receive my medal.

David Gur's article in "Resistance and Rescue Operations by the Hungarian Zionist Youth" praises Zionist young people for their bravery. Gur, who was among the youth resisters in Hungary, asserts:

The collective endeavor of the Zionist Youth Movement in Hungary during World War II was unparalleled. No other underground movement in German-occupied Europe resembled it in terms of the scope of its activities and the number of Jews it rescued. The activities of the Zionist youth during the German occupation wrote the most glorious pages in the history of Hungarian Jewry in the twentieth century. The resistance-rescue operations of the Zionist youth are an inspiration and a shining example for the present generation.

2004, Israel: Medal for Courage from the Hungarian government

2004, Israel: Certificate awarded by the Hungarian government

Chapter 38
Ari's Bar-Mitzvah

Every year for over twenty years, Sara and I had visited the Moria Resort at the Dead Sea. We became "special guests" and befriended management and staff alike.

Our visits were always around December 17 through January 2. Our dear friends Yochevet and Zvi were always waiting for us at Ben Gurion airport in Tel Aviv. Zvi made arrangements with the same taxi driver every year to take us to Moria, the resort in Sdom. The driver knew to expect four or five oversized suitcases. However, on one of the first trips the driver did not have a canvas to cover some of the suitcases that had to be loaded on the outside top rack of the cab. Two suitcases got wet when an unexpected rain, *gashem shel brache* (a shower of rain or a blessed rain—Rain is usually very welcome in Israel), caught us during the two and a half hour trip south. This only happened once. My Sara was not a very happy camper; with each rain drop her concerns about the clothes getting wet intensified.

Sara used to say to me, "This vacation is for you." For I loved the Dead Sea, the facilities at the spa, the people, the surroundings and the daily planned activities, including ping pong, dancing, and singing.

About three years before our first grandson, Ari, was to become a Bar Mitzvah, we took a trip to Masada, a historic mountain, which was thirty minutes from our hotel.[25] It was 7 AM, and the warm sun was already reflected on the mountain. Being young and daring we decided to walk up the winding path to the top of the mountain, instead of riding up via cable car. It was a strenuous one hour walk. As we knew the history of the place, our anticipation about reaching the summit helped us on the difficult journey.

Once we arrived we joined a guided tour. To be on top of this mountain, so rich in history, signifying bravery and heroism, was exhilarating. Breathing the air, touching the rocks, walking through this special place reminded us of a remarkable chapter in our history.

While on top of Masada, inspired by the surroundings, I turned to Sara and said, "This is where we should have our first grandson, Ari's, Bar Mitzvah. This would be a meaningful venue for Ari, as well as Nancy and Stewart, and the entire family."

When we got back to the hotel I spoke to Mustafa, the manager, about having our grandson's Bar Mitzvah party at the hotel. He reacted with surprise to the idea. At first he said that the hotel didn't host Bar Mitzvah parties. He suggested we meet with the manager in charge of the kitchen and dining room.

The following morning we were invited by the manager into his office. We had known Mustafa for several years. He was a great asset to the hotel, friendly and a top-notch professional, who lived with his Bedouin tribe in a neighboring settlement.

Immediately, Mustafa promised, "For you, Mr. and Mrs. Paul, we will do everything."

Sara and I were touched and appreciative.

"What is the date you require?"

When Sara replied that the great event was approximately three years away, everyone burst out laughing. "Three years? We cannot put anything in writing for something so far away; however, *Insha' Allah* (with God's help), if we will be here, you will have the greatest party ever!"

Nancy, Stewart, and the family were very excited about the idea. It turns out that they were also thinking of making Ari's Bar Mitzvah in

Israel. Ari, after all, was a *ben-kibbutz* (a Sabra born in a kibbutz), and Nancy and Stewart had brought up their children with a love for Israel and Judaism.

Ari studied in a Hebrew Day School through eighth grade and had graduated with the highest honors. He created the school paper, was its editor and chief, and had contributed much of the writing. He also won prizes in science throughout his years of study, beginning with his creation of a working robot in his middle school.

Ari was very mature for his age and gifted at many things. He was a wonderful pianist who delighted us with playing a repertoire of classical and popular pieces whenever we visited their home. He had earned a black belt in Tae Kwon Do and was captain of his high school fencing team. He continued to relish science and lead in competitions throughout high school.

Ari was also an avid reader of all genres, "swallowing ideas whole," as Nancy described it. He could never get enough—always eager for new perspectives. He graduated from the University of Pennsylvania and now works as a very successful trader, writing a popular blog, "Risk over Reward." Ari is studying for his Certified Financial Analyst (CFA) certification.

But I've gotten ahead of myself.

Sara and Nancy happily planned all of the logistics for Ari's Bar Mitzvah in Israel. They loved working on this special occasion together.

Finally, the long awaited day arrived and we traveled to Israel with our kids, Dahlia, Gil and Dali, and our nephew Steven and his daughter, Jill. Nancy, Stewart and the boys were already there. Nancy's sister, Esther, and her family flew to Israel to celebrate with us. Our Israeli family joined us; my sister Chaya, her husband, Avraham, and their sons, Shalom and Roni, and their families. Our dear friends Yochevet and Zvi Prizant, Joske Steinberg and his wife, Sara, Malka and Moshe Wertman, and many others. One hundred family members and friends, including Nancy and Stewart's friends from the kibbutz, came together to celebrate Ari's becoming a Bar Mitzvah.

On June 26, 1997, we all left together for Masada. I arranged for a special bus to take us to a cable car and together we reached the top of this historic mountain.

The rabbi was ready to receive us at the site of the former house of study on Masada. A warm wind caressed our faces. We were all so happy. For me the highlight of the event was listening to Ari read our Torah with conviction and confidence. Looking at Ari and his proud, devoted, and wonderful parents was very emotional for Sara and me. After the suffering, there was joy and new life. A young generation stood on top of this mountain again, singing in Hebrew and reading wise lessons from our cherished Torah.

I presented Ari with a small Torah of his own. Happy tears flowed. Sara and I were so proud. It was truly an unforgettable experience.

The party started at noon. The special effort the Moria staff made was remarkable, beginning with hundreds of colorful balloons, the flowered centerpieces, the artistic ice carvings, the music, and fantastic Israeli dishes. Sharing our first grandson's special milestone with family and friends was a very special and memorable occasion—from the moving religious ceremony on Masada to the lovely party. Sara and I felt so blessed.

Chapter 39
Eitan, The Peacemaker

"Blessed is the peacemaker." Eitan at a very young age committed himself to build bridges of peace between individuals from conflict regions.

An excellent student and national award winning writer, he has garnered numerous awards in Model United Nations competitions in both high school and college. He has assumed leadership positions as President Emeritus of his Model United Nations club in high school and on the Board of Directors of the International Relations Club at Georgetown University's School of Foreign Service, where he is presently a Dean's List Honors student.

His writing has advocated for human rights and peaceful co-existence, challenging China to stop supporting the Bashir government in Darfur to promoting Seeds of Peace, a non-profit program aimed at bringing adolescents together from Israel, Egypt, Jordan, Afghanistan, India, Pakistan, Yemen, and Morocco in the hopes of breaking down negative stereotyping and creating friendships. He has experienced this program first hand as an American Ambassador of Peace, participating in the Maine woods in difficult dialogue sessions and camp life. He continues participating in this worthy program, chairing conferences and continuing the dialogue with those he's met from around the world. He has especially enjoyed the musical collaborations with his peers from conflict areas, where the joy of playing together became the universal language among them, overriding language barriers and helping to change perceptions of the "other" side.

Eitan is an accomplished saxophonist who created the award winning "Jazzy Jamming Jews" with friends. Three years in a row they won the Battle of the Bands, and he continues to play jazz with a Georgetown University ensemble.

As a musician he has performed in many venues to raise money for such worthy causes as Save Darfur, March of Dimes, Victims of Hurricane Katrina and Rita, and Music with a Mission.

The meetings and phone conversations I have with Eitan on a regular basis give me the strength, *naches* (pride), and willpower to live on—to see him graduate from the Georgetown University School of Foreign Service and work in the field of diplomacy. He believes in the ability of one individual to make a difference. I know Eitan will continue to work toward realizing his goal of making the world a more peaceful one and the world will indeed be a better place for his efforts.

Chapter 40
The Hillel Angels

Sara and I first discovered that our son Gil had a motorcycle, when we were at Elite's Bat Mitzvah. Many of his friends and family members attended this on November 14, 2004.

One of Gil's good friends turned to Sara and me asking, "Have you taken a ride on Gil's Harley yet?" Both of us were shocked and surprised.

Sara asked Gils's friend, Shelly. "What motorcycle? What Harley?"

As a fellow motorcycle club member, he proudly repeated, "Gil just got his new Harley, his second bike."

Sara and I were discussing the bike issue and the club that we knew nothing about. We decided not to spoil the party (for us it was a double surprise) but to wait until the party was over to discuss this with Gil. We visited his house, as we did on many other visits during the year; this time I was looking to find the motorcycle. To enter Gil's and Dali's house we often used the garage door entrance. There we found it, well covered under heavy canvas. Removing the canvas, we saw, before our eyes, a beautiful light and dark blue motorcycle, with shiny chrome trimmings—our son's bike.

We questioned him, "How long have you had it? What made you do it?"

Gil answered that he had another motorcycle for a year before he bought the new Harley. "Why didn't you tell us?"

During the previous year we had entered through that garage

many times and had never noticed the bike because it was tucked away—mainly from us.

Among the reasons we worried was the death of our friends' son. We had close friends living near us in Philadelphia, Sara and Betzalel Ben Ami. Their seventeen year old son, Michael, had bought a bike. The first day he rode his motorcycle, he drove out of the driveway, was hit by a truck, and had fallen to his tragic death.

That tragedy lived with his parents and us for years. So the first thought that entered Sara's and my minds was Michel's fatal accident. Once Gil was aware of the fact that we knew about his bike, he told us how much he enjoyed riding. He also told us that he joined a club of Jewish riders—Hillel Angels,and, proudly, that he had become president of the club.[26]

The first mission the Hillel club took on under his leadership was a fund raising ride to Memphis, Tennessee, where they joined with other Jewish riders from the U.S. and Canada. They raised over $55,000 for "The Paper Clip Museum." In a movie, this museum told the story of the six million paper clips that had been collected in memory of the six million that perished during the Holocaust and how that project led to the students' interaction with Holocaust survivors.

The overwhelming reaction to the Hillel Angels' commitment to the museum, particularly because it was a non-Jewish town in Memphis, touched us, made us suddenly proud of our son, the president of a club that had such a noble agenda and mission.

The following year Sara and I lined up in New York on Fifth Avenue watching the 150,000 or so that paraded in support of Israel on *Yom Haatzmaut*, independence day of Israel.[27] For us, the best part of the parade was the Hillel Angels riding in the parade with the Israeli flag billowing from their antennas. Daniel, our grandson, who was eleven years old at the time, proudly participated in the parade, riding on the back seat of the Harley, in full gear, Harley leather jacket, helmet, and the Israeli flag.

As we walked home to our apartment after the parade, I turned to Sara: "How proud I am to see our son Gil committing to a world historic project. All our fears should be lifted with positive thinking, in particular since when I was only fifteen in the Budapest Underground, I too was riding a motorcycle, as well as in Romania, Italy, and Israel where we used to live."

We are proud of his hobby and his commitment and have hope, trust, and confidence in his safety.

The following is a letter Sara and I received from Gil about his commitment and another letter of appreciation for what Gil was doing:

June 7, 2007

Dear Mom and Dad,

This may be the most important project that I will ever be involved with. Making it a reality and a successful program is my promise to you. The attached letter explains it all. This was sent to Mr. Sam Fried who is the founder of the National Holocaust Endowment Fund. You can read more about his organization at www.sixmillionlights.org.

I love you both. Thank you

Gil.

Wednesday, May 28, 2008
From: Sam Fried
To: Gil Paul

Gil,

Even though we only met and spent a few hours together, I feel very connected to you. Your dedication to teaching the lessons of the past to protect the future warms my soul. If I ever questioned the legacy that we survivors would leave behind, seeing you and your fellow JMA riders this past weekend put that question to rest. Your words on Thursday evening were inspiring and the job you did with fund-raising for the HHEF—well, the $55K + speaks for itself. I am still getting donations today from people who were moved by the show of strength and support from the JMA.

Even more important than the money is the fact that you are carrying the torch for those of us who will soon not be able to speak out about the Holocaust and you are educating the next generations to stand guard.

Your mother, of blessed memory, would be so very proud of you. I was serious when I said I wanted to adopt you myself!

I hope the ride home went well and you all arrived safely. It has been an honor to meet you. If you are ever this way, please consider this an open invitation.

All my best,
Sam

Chapter 41
Commitment to Education

I often think about the people who were murdered during the Holocaust. Numbers of those murdered were intellectuals, artists, and scientists. Their deaths deprived the world of their genius and their creations.

Their loss is compounded by the numbers of children who were murdered. As many as 1.5 million children were killed by the Germans and their collaborators, including the disabled, Jewish, Romani, Polish, and children in the occupied Soviet Union.

These children died in ghettos, slave labor camps, death camps, and concentration camps. They were murdered in medical experiments, in reprisals, by the *Einsatzgruppen*, and in the gas chambers. With the murders of these children, the world lost future musicians, artists, scientists, teachers, writers, poets, electricians, diplomats, and on and on.

Moreover, during the Shoah, countless survivors were deprived of educations. Although many of us survived and thrived in various fields, who knows what others would have accomplished in the fields of medicine, science, law, politics, or art, if we had been able to complete our educations?

Because of our staggering losses, we survivors made many sacrifices to give our children and grandchildren the best education possible. We taught our children and grandchildren the importance of education and encouraged them to acquire higher educations. To see the percentage of children and grandchildren who have graduated from the best universities has been gratifying.

That the majority of survivors' children have been well-educated is a testimony to our efforts and care. The contributions of survivors and our families to our chosen country—the U.S.A—is remarkable. We continue the Jewish tradition of *tikkun olam*, or repairing the world. We are grateful for the historic opportunity given to us.

Chapter 42
Sara's Devotion to Family

Because during most of our married life I was traveling, Sara had assumed the double role of mother and father as soon as our children were born.

When Dahlia, our first child, was born, Sara was only twenty one years of age. Somehow she stopped being a child herself and became a loving, devoted mother. The reality of her own childhood, the pain and suffering, the hurt, the hunger of losing her parents at a tender age lived with her during every step of her life.

Sara did not have a normal youth, playing, singing, and dancing with her age group of kids. Sara did not experience the fun of jumping into the water and learning how to swim. She did not have the pleasure of splashing in the clean rivers or lakes. She had to learn to stay afloat in a big ocean of hatred. She clearly knew that beyond the energy of the waves the danger of death was waiting.

Despite the obstacles and against all the odds of her illnesses, typhus and tuberculosis, Sara was determined to embrace the sunshine of tomorrow, the future of building a new family from the ashes, as she used to say.

Dahlia was her sunshine, her first born, the beginning of building a new family. Sara took nothing for granted, she lived for a purpose. She lived to love and give Dahlia, Stewart, and Gil everything she did not have as a child.

Stewart was the second born. He was and is the cornerstone, followed by Gil. Sara was there for all our kids, on all occasions, on birthdays, first days of school, and during illnesses. She was there, taking them places and playing with them in the playgrounds and parks, buying their clothes, cooking and baking each one their favorite things, feeding them, and sometimes force feeding them. She took them for their first haircuts, watched them do their homework, and sang them lullabies at bedtime.

As the kids were growing up, I did help Sara, sharing some of the responsibilities, while I was home between my travels. I felt a great sense of accomplishment every minute I was able to spend with them, playing with them or just walking with them.

Some of my most memorable times were the summers we spent in Philadelphia or spending long weekends on the beaches of Atlantic City.

Sara's love grew stronger with the second generation of our family: the birth of our first granddaughters, Tara, Dahlia's first daughter, and Ilana, Dahlia's second daughter. The four women, Sara, Dahlia, Tara, and Ilana had a special bond among them from their youngest ages until Sara's last days.

To solidify that special relationship when Tara became thirteen and Ilana eleven, Sara took the girls, Dahlia, Tara, Ilana, on a long trip to Europe and Israel. The first stop was London, England visiting museums, the Palace, and other well known tourist destinations.

Everything was an eye opening experience, from the double tiered red buses to the spacious taxis, the many parks, the subway, the restaurants, the department stores, and, for Tara and Ilana, staying in a hotel for the first time.

The second stop was Paris, France, the ride up to the Eiffel Tower, the walk on the famous Avenue des Champs-Élysées, the museums, the zoo, and botanical gardens. From France they traveled to Vienna,

Austria, to the beautiful gardens open to the public, concerts, and guided tours through the city. This part of their trip took fourteen days. Then they traveled from Austria to Israel for an additional three weeks.

Without doubt this was the highlight of the trip, visiting my sister, Chaya, and her family in Haifa. They visited Dahlia's birth place, Tivon, Jerusalem, and most of the country from the North to the South. They still remember that they loved Israel most; Israel felt more like home than any other place. The obvious reason was that they had identified with the "homeland," the people, the climate, and the food. It was helpful that their Savta Sara and their mother, Dahlia, spoke Hebrew.

This trip was discussed among the kids and Sara many times in my presence. It hit a high note when during Sara's stay in the hospital the girls came often to visit and talk about that unforgettable trip, which moved everyone to the point of tears, especially Sara. She just kept on listening and kissing (consciously) the girls goodbye as she was holding on and squeezing my warm hands.

Then along came our first grandson, Ari, Nancy and Stewart's first son, the *Sabra* born in 1984 at Kibbutz Yasur in Israel. Six years later Eitan was born in Princeton, New Jersey. We watched both boys as they grew from year to year and very much enjoyed sharing their lives.

Ari graduated from the University of Pennsylvania in 2006 with a degree in Political Science. He was recruited by a major financial institution where he is successfully employed.

Ari is an insightful thinker and writer and shares his views in a widely read investment blog and newsletter. He also volunteers for the Big Brothers of America Program and enjoys participating in many sports.

Eitan is a student at Georgetown University School of Foreign Service, where he is continuing to study for his Bachelor of Science in International Politics.

Sara's daily phone conversations with Nancy kept her in the loop as to the two boys' daily activities and achievements. Almost every day Nancy had some wonderful news regarding the boys, sharing with Sara stories about their writing, music, or studies.

A story from Europe comes to mind. On Friday night many of our Jewish neighbors used to bring their special casseroles to our outdoor brick oven for baking overnight. This was the *cholent*, the traditional stew for the Sabbath midday meal: beans, potatoes, rice, and meat. Some expected that after the ten hours baking, the casserole would grow. My mother used to say to them, "You only get out whatever you put in."

This story is applicable to Nancy and Stewart as inspirations in their sons' daily lives. For Nancy this was a full time job with great rewards.

The musical education that started at age five was the topping on the cake of an excellent education. At first each one, Ari as well as Eitan, learned to play the piano with the same teacher. Sara and I had enjoyed many visits to their home on weekends when the boys played for Savta Sara her favorite songs. For me they played *"Hava Nagila."* I had a double pleasure, one as they played beautifully, putting their heart into every song for Savta Sara, and the second, enjoyment in watching my wife Sara with a smile on her face humming along as the kids played. That happiness is difficult to describe.

Eventually they both became interested in playing the saxophone. Freshly inspired by their talent, Sara and I looked at each other and told the boys to meet us the following weekend in New York and we would go instrument shopping, and we did.

We loved the sophisticated duets that they played. They gave us numerous concerts at their home as well as in the school bands and orchestras. Sara made a point of going to the plays in school to take pride in their achievements.

She experienced great enjoyment and pleasure from their performances.

Eitan joined the school band; in addition, he formed a Jewish band: Jazzy Jamming Jews, playing for various Jewish community functions, and he continues to play with the Georgetown University Jazz band.

Ari continues to play the piano whenever he come home for a visit, and Eitan still loves playing the sax.

Our son Gil also grew up with love of and the talent for music. When I am at his home, Gil sits at the baby grand and plays tunes for relaxation. It is most enjoyable for me to watch Gil play and listen to the many songs for which he wrote the lyrics and music. In the basement he has a complete electrified orchestra, organs and drums where he composes his music.

Elite was born on October 12, 1992, Columbus Day, when there are sales everywhere. Sara and I joked that Elite would be a shopaholic, and, sure enough, she was every bit the girly girl that we expected. Elite was the first girl to be born to our family for about twenty years, so we suddenly had a new doll to play dress up with and have tea parties with. Sara could not paint our grandsons' nails or share beading tricks after long walks in Manhattan, visiting craft stores. Elite was the perfect companion for anything having to do with fashion. Even at two years old, she already had a very clear image of herself, and during sleepover weekends with us in New York or in Atlantic City, Elite would set the agenda. She is not only our granddaughter but we are *her* grandparents; her possessiveness of us was always obvious. We are absolutely, positively, *her* grandparents and were it up to her, she would not have shared us with anyone—not even her brother Daniel. This was expressed in her name for us: Safti and Sabi, which were Elite's own made up compounds of Safta and Saba, combined with an i-ending that in Hebrew means, "of mine." No doubt about it, Elite is our granddaughter, and we will always be her grandparents. Sara and I watched her grow from a beautiful baby to a beautiful and intelligent young woman, and I know she will find much success in life.

Daniel was born with talent, talent that he is refining every year. He has attended a number of summer camps that offer acting and singing lessons. He participated recently in a school play *Oliver*, when he played the role of the Artful Dodger, singing, dancing, and acting to the pleasure of his teachers, his schoolmates, his parents, and for me it was an extra treat—*shepping naches*.

Chapter 43
Five Great-Grandchildren

Our granddaughters Ilana and Tara, Dahlia's daughters, enriched our lives by giving us five beautiful great-grandchildren.

The first great-grandchild was Jake. Seven days after his birth I held him in my lap for his circumcision. Sara holding on to me for dear life as we looked at each other with happy tears in our eyes, Sara said: "Can you believe this *wuse mir haben derlabt*! What a privilege and honor god gave us to live to be here for this historic event in our lives."

The gathering of the close friends and family was celebrated in the house and the beautiful gardens of the proud grandfather, Fred Bor of Voorhees, New Jersey. Fred's daughters, Ilana and Tara, and Fred's lovely wife, the hostess, Jody, their kids, Andrew, and Connor enjoyed the celebration.

Our immediate family also attended: Dahlia, proud grandmother, Nancy and Stewart and their sons, Ari and Eitan, Dali and Gil and their kids Elite and Daniel, and Joyce and Steven Paul, their cousins, with their kids Jason and Jill. In addition many friends made the event even more memorable to Sara and me.

Our emotions, especially our happiness, were almost overwhelming as we made our rounds to greet and thank everyone for joining with us on this great *simchah* (a joyful celebration or festive occasion).

Jake has grown to be a handsome boy. He is an outstanding student; he has mastered computers and all electronic games skillfully since he was three or four years old. These foreshadowed his interest in school because his favorite subject is science. Lately, Jake is especially drawn the most challenging of the LEGO building blocks, consisting of hundreds of components, many of them mechanical or battery-operated moving parts. This is a further indication of his bright and inquisitive mind. Jake is fortunate to have a hard working, loving, and devoted mom and step-father, Julian, as well as Dahlia, his Savti (grandmother).

Throughout his school years, Dahlia was a volunteering teacher at the Jewish Community Center's early childhood school, so she could spend valuable time with Jake. The bond between Jake and Dahlia is strong and unshakeable. Jake is also outstanding in the sports he loves and actively participates in—soccer, basketball, football, and baseball. He is well disciplined, plays hard, and applies himself to win.

Jake's mother, Ilana, has been working hard for the last thirteen years. After she graduated from Towson University with a degree in Speech Pathology, she spent as much quality time with Jake as possible and the last three years with her precious twins, Roman and Cole. She is doing a magnificent job dealing with the daily challenges of motherhood and speech therapy.

Roman and Cole gave us all, in particular Ilana, Julian, and Dahlia, lots to be worried about. They were born six weeks premature. In the beginning every day was a challenge. Their attending doctor suggested not following the Jewish tradition of circumcision after seven days. For medical reasons they were circumcised in the hospital by a doctor, not by a mohel.[28]

A couple of months later as Roman and Cole gained some strength, Dahlia decided to have a special naming ceremony in her home. She invited a rabbi and close family members and friends. She decided to record this historic moment for Mom-Mom Sara and me. This was an especially moving experience because Ilana and Julian had given the two boys Hebrew names after Sara's two brothers, Nachem and Velvel, who were murdered in Auschwitz-Birkenau Concentration Camp.

At the same time Tara named her daughter Ryan Sara and in Hebrew, Bella. For the entire family it was a very special event and more so for Sara.

Tara's son, Sean, another great-grandchild, is six-years old. He is a handsome, bright kid, and very advanced for his age. He loves playing sports, especially soccer and baseball.

Ryan Sara is a beautiful three year old, big blue eyes and long silky brown hair. She used to be very shy. Fortunately she has outgrown her shyness and become very friendly and attentive. Her hugs and kisses are soft; she touches my heart every time I see her. I hug her and kiss her for Sara and me.

Tara, as a school teacher for about fifteen years, manages to impact their upbringing in a loving, systematic way.

Every time I see our kids, our daughter, our sons, our grandchildren and great grandchildren, the memory of Sara overpowers me with joy and *naches*. Oh! If only Sara could have lived a few more years to watch them grow to become *mentschen* (an especially good person).

2009, Atlantic City: Five precious great-grandchildren,
Bottom, left to right—Cole, Roman, Ryan Sara;
Top, left to right—Ilana, Jake, Tara

Chapter 44
Sara's Last Struggle

On December 15, 2006, I took Sara to our family doctor in New York City. Sara was complaining of losing weight, feeling tired, and having headaches.

Our family doctor, Dr. Mark Newman, had been our doctor for over twenty years. He knew Sara well, her sense of humor, her smile, and the twinkle in her eyes, but not this time.

After an examination and blood tests, Dr. Newman said, "I do not like what I see. "You need to see a specialist."

He referred us to the New York University Hospital's Cancer Department to Dr. Robert Newman (no relation to Dr. Mark Newman). The earliest appointment available was three days later on December 18.

As we took the elevator to the 8th floor, both of our hearts were pounding more and more as the elevator went up, stopping three times. There was no waiting time; the doctor was there, and we were there at 9 AM, with records in hand from the referring doctor. Dr. Newman started his own examination. From one thing to another it took a long half hour.

Then the doctor took us into his office, telling us to be seated and to wait a few minutes until he received some test results from his lab. The fifteen minutes seemed to us like hours. In the meantime I tried to lift Sara's spirits; she was very depressed and concerned, so was I. However, I could not show my real emotions.

The doctor returned to his office and sat down behind his desk in his comfortable chair. Then he dropped a bombshell: "I have bad news, Mrs. Paul. You have pancreatic cancer. Surgery is urgently required."

Sara took a few deep breaths and then told the doctor, "Cancer or no cancer, we are scheduled to leave on a fourteen day cruise on the *Queen Mary 2*, leaving December 22, four days from now. I definitely wanted to go on this cruise and spend my fourteen days with my husband."

The doctor was surprised, flabbergasted, by Sara's reaction. Really, so was I.

"Well, it is your decision against my advice."

The doctor's determination started to sink in with us.

I started questioning the doctor, "How long is this kind of surgery? What are her chances with or without surgery?"

The doctor's answers were not encouraging. "Without any surgery, you will live no longer than six months. The cancer could spread slower or faster. Pancreatic cancer is rarely curable—one in many thousands."

With tears in my eyes, I said to the doctor, "Sara is a concentration camp survivor. She suffered a lot: typhus and tuberculosis. I cannot lose her now. We have three children, six grandchildren, and five great-grand children. She cannot die now."

The doctor stated with confidence, "I will try my very best. I promise both of you."

Sara threw in a few Yiddish words to the relatively young doctor of about forty-eight years old. "He replied in Yiddish: "*I'ch wel dire halfen*" (I will help you).

Sara took a liking to this doctor, "You could be my son. How would you treat your mother?"

158

His reply was, "The same as I will treat you. With love and kindness."

"Okay. We will be back from our cruise on January 9."

Chapter 45
Our Final Cruise

On December 21, 2006, Sara and I flew to Fort Lauderdale. We checked into a hotel near the port. We had planned the trip so we could meet Naomi in Fort Lauderdale. Naomi, the surviving daughter of Sara's cousin, Sara Rasmovich, lives near the port. We had a nice visit with her and her family. On December 22, at 2 PM, with our four suitcases we took a cab to the port to check in at the *Queen Mary 2*. The *Queen Mary 2* is the most magnificent ocean liner ever built (according to the company).

The check in for the cruise took over an hour. The cruise liner served chilled champagne, which I enjoyed for both of us because Sara was not a drinker. On board the *Queen Mary 2* were approximately three thousand passengers and over one thousand crew members. After 3 PM we boarded and were warmly greeted by a host who ushered us to our suite on deck four. It was a beautiful room with a nice sized window facing the ocean, adequate closet space, and a comfortable bed.

The first announcement over the loud speaker instructed all passengers to attend the safety drill with their red emergency gear. After the drill was over, we had time to unpack and rest before dinner. While resting, I focused on Sara's face to see if she was showing signs of pain or concern regarding the surgery awaiting her after the cruise. She had closed her eyes, taking a light nap. I didn't want to fall asleep; I wanted to be aware in case Sara needed me. She slept well; she said that she felt great.

We dressed for the first dinner at 6:30 PM. As we walked into the elegant dining room, we were ushered to our table located conveniently near the entrance and were seated with three other couples. We arrived a few minutes late so the other three couples were already seated. Introductions were made; our first impression was good. There was a couple from Chicago, one from Boston, and another from New York.

We had been on numerous cruises before. We usually size up the others around the table because we would be sitting with them for thirteen nights. The first impression is important.

I sat next to Sara and between courses held her hand under the table. She was a trooper, active in the get-to-know-each-other conversation around the table. After dinner we took a stroll on this beautiful new ship—eight stories with many points of interest, such as the shops on two floors, the theatre, the movie house, photo gallery, the bars, library, the dance hall, and the casino. For the evening program there were several options: movies, a bar with a good live band playing, dancing, or live Broadway size productions.

We chose to go to the first show—a great show *Mama Mia*, which we had seen about a year earlier on Broadway. The music, the singing, the costumes were at a level comparable to Broadway. The show was over at about 10 PM. Exiting, we walked by the dance hall, with a great orchestra and about one hundred people having a good time dancing and singing. We joined this party. I ordered Pellegrino water for Sara and a double Hennessy Cognac for myself.

The cognac was served in a beautiful crystal snifter. What a relaxing feeling to sit and listen to the music, sipping on the cognac, holding and kissing Sara's warm hands. Not for long! Sara with a twinkle in her eyes got up from the chair grabbed my hand and said, "Let's go dancing."

Dancing we did—almost non-stop for an hour and a half. We danced tango, waltz, cha cha, meringue, and samba. We could have danced all night. About midnight we went to bed. Not a word did Sara mention throughout the evening about being ill. We both had a good night's rest.

The morning started at 7:30 AM on the treadmill on the 6th floor at the modern newly equipped gym, with the exerciser's own music and TV—everything you could imagine in a gym. We enjoyed working out for an hour followed by a buffet style breakfast, fresh fruit, fresh juice, vegetables, eggs to order, cheeses, cold cuts, on and on, almost too much.

After breakfast we walked the track on the ship three times around, about four miles. About 10 AM we changed to bathing suits or shorts and relaxed at one of the three pools. Sara loved to read; she immersed herself in reading for hours.

After lunch Sara returned to the deck, sitting under the shade and continuing to read while I was playing ping-pong from 1:30 to 2:30 PM, at which time we returned to our room. Every other day I had a massage at the spa club. At 6:30 PM we went to dinner as we had the first night. We watched a different show every night, repeated our activities, including visiting the casino on board.

The cruise schedule took us from Fort Lauderdale through many islands. We had made a similar voyage with the Crystal Line luxury liner. We did not get off the ship every port stop, such as Curacao, Grenada, Barbados, St. Lucia, St. Thomas, or St. Kitts. We had been to these islands numerous times, so we took advantage of the quiet atmosphere on the ship.

Never during the entire cruise did Sara mention the surgery or cancer. It definitely occupied my mind, particularly when Sara was getting dressed, elegant, astonishingly beautiful, or on the dance floor where she acted and looked as if she had many happy years ahead for her. The jewelry she was wearing reflected her beautiful face and eyes filled with hope and confidence.

Chapter 46
In Treatment

The doctor had scheduled January 11, 2007, at 8 AM, for surgery at New York University Hospital (NYU). We arrived on time, so did the doctor. The nurses started with the preparations for the surgery. Five hours later Sara came out of surgery. For over two hours the doctors worked to wake her and help her recover from the heavy dose of anesthesia.

She finally opened her eyes. Around her were the children, Dahlia, Stewart, Nancy, Gil and Dali, and me. They had arrived while Sara was still in surgery. We were all stressed, hoping and crying, "Has she survived? Did the surgeon clean out the cancer?"

The doctor gave us no indication or sense of success. "We need to wait," he said. Finally the surgeon advised us to go home: "Sara will have to stay in the hospital for a while. In the next couple of days I will be able to share with you more as to her condition."

Sara was admitted to the intensive care unit on the 12th floor in NYU. I stayed with her overnight in the hope of getting some sign or indication from Sara as to her pain or feelings. She was heavily medicated, sleeping throughout most of the night. At 6 AM, Dr. Newman arrived with Dr Goldenberg, a cancer specialist, who, I was told by Dr Newman, was the best in his field.

Stewart arrived from his home in Princeton, New Jersey, around 6:30 AM followed by Gil. We tried to get more information from the doctors. The only information we got was, "We will do everything possible for her. She will need to stay in the hospital for a couple of weeks."

After three days Sara was moved from the intensive care unit to the 16th floor, the cancer patient's floor. Sara received good care from the doctors and nurses. Her cardiologist, Dr. K. Kraus; her lung specialist, Dr. Tobias; and her liver specialist, Dr. Camelhair, were notified of Sara's hospitalization. They made daily visits and kept an eye on Sara because she had been their patient for over twenty years. What made a bad situation more difficult was that she had a heart murmur and a dangerously high cholesterol level (over 300); moreover, Sara had been diagnosed a few months earlier as a high risk diabetic.

I was at her bedside from 5:45 AM (waiting for the scheduled visit of the doctors at 6 AM) and stayed until 8 PM. I was relieved by a private night nurse I had hired.

Sara's wound from the surgery was healing; however, she had no appetite and sleepless nights. Her worries and concerns kept her in pain: "What about the children and grandchildren? Do they know I am here?"

At first she did not realize that the children were there every day; her concern for them overshadowed her pain. Four days later with the help of the nurse we started to walk the long hallways of the hospital.

Sara was hooked up to monitors and had to receive intravenous fluids and medications. I decided that the next thing she needed was to eat. I bought in fresh food from the cafeteria: chicken soup, blintzes, grilled chicken. She nibbled away a little more each day. Although a dietician from the hospital staff came to her bedside, asking her what would she like special, the hospital food was not to her liking: The dietician told Sara, "We will be glad to make anything you like."

On the fifth or sixth day before I left the hospital that evening, Sara ordered me: "In the morning please bring me my folding mirror, my blue bathrobe, my slippers, my makeup kit, two hair brushes, and my tooth brush and tooth paste.

I was so glad to get her order because this was a signal of hope and will power; this was the Sara I knew. Even while facing serious illness, she never lost her desire for an impeccable appearance. That gave her confidence.

Before we left the hospital the surgeon, Dr Newman, told us that he had done his utmost to clean out the cancer: "However," he said, "in these cases, there is no 100%. Let's hope for the best. You will now be in the hands of Dr Goldenberg, an oncologist, for treatments."

Dr Goldenberg gave us his card with the name and address of his clinic New York Medical Associates at 157 East 32 Street, six blocks from our home.

Sara stayed in the hospital for a total of fourteen days. We lived only five blocks from the hospital on 37 Street and First Avenue; therefore, it was easy to take Sara home.

After a few days, we showed up in Dr Goldenberg's clinic where the nurses had Sara's files with instructions as to the treatment prescribed. Sara was sat in a comfortable chair among ten other cancer patients.

The nurse rolled up Sara's sleeve and looked for a good vein, which was difficult to find because some had collapsed, so they decided to place a port in her chest for easy daily access to her veins.

The chemotherapy treatment was painless. The treatment took two hours until the large bottle, drop by drop, was emptied.

After the first treatment, Stewart, Sara, and I took the elevator to the 4th floor to meet with Dr Goldenberg.

We asked many questions: "How long and how often will Sara have to take these treatments?"

"We will see how she reacts," answered the doctor. "For now she will have treatments every day. Often we need to adjust the medication depending on the patient's reaction. As to the timetable? At this stage we cannot predict this. We will take one day at a time."

We took Sara home. She felt dizzy, so we put her in bed. In the evening she had a 102° temperature. The doctor had cautioned us that this was to be expected.

Nevertheless, I called the doctor in the evening. He told me to give her two Tylenols and return in the morning. Next morning during her visit to Dr. Goldenberg's clinic, Sara's fever subsided, so treatment was repeated. In the evening she was hot again, showing over 101° temperature. We repeated the Tylenol dose. She had a restless night and no appetite.

The doctor told us the following morning, "This is to be expected."

He prescribed a sleeping pill and relaxing medication. The fever continued.

After the first week the doctor told us that he would change the mix of her medications and would continue to adjust as needed.

He also told us, "You also must realize that in a few weeks you will gradually lose your hair." Sara was not a happy camper.

For six weeks after daily treatments, Sara did not get better. The doctor told us that additional lab tests were required: an MRI, CAT scans, etc. Dr. Goldenberg readmitted her to the hospital for a few days. While in the hospital, chemo treatments continued for six days in NYU. Sara realized no noticeable improvement.

Then treatments resumed in the doctor's clinic. By now Sara had made good friends with all the staff, receptionist, and nurses. She became a "favorite" patient, referred to as the model of elegance. Every day Sara amused the staff and the other patients with her elegance and her chic appearance. Her dress had to match the high leather boots or shoes and her pocketbook. A different glittering pin in her lapel every day was a surprise.

As if in a fashion show, Sara walked gracefully and proudly.

She became well known and loved in the clinic. Sara tried to hide her problems with her appearance. She not only carried her slim body gracefully but she also became a healing spirit with her unusual sense of humor. When she was getting treatments, she sat between two other patients, and she always carried on uplifting and encouraging conversations with these other patients. Every one rushed to be near her.

The nurses told me, "She is a healing element. The place lights up when Sara walks in. She tries to make the best of a difficult and depressing situation."

As for Sara herself, she continued suffering from a lack of appetite and continued loss of weight and hair, which occurred faster than expected.

One day Dahlia, our daughter, took her mom to a custom wig place. She convinced Sara to have one made from human hair. Sara wore the expensive wig once. The following day she donated the wig to some patient that wanted a wig but could not afford one.

Sara did not like the wig and neither did I. I helped her brush the few hairs she had left. Hair loss did not bother us. The bigger picture was my concern—Would she survive the cancer?

Sara continued getting the chemo treatment for ten months, but on November 18, 2007, she became very ill. The treatments had not answered our prayers.

She was readmitted to NYU Hospital. The doctor's shared with us that the treatments had failed to improve her condition. Various new tests were made, trying to establish a different treatment.

Sara was very sick. I watched her for days, weeks, and months fading away. I stayed in the hospital at her bedside, watching her pain and suffering. Then I broke down.

I was hospitalized in the room next to Sara's for three weeks. At first the diagnosis was exhaustion. Next the doctors told me that my breakdown had been followed by a series of small seizures in my brain, the impact of waves of electrical shocks.

When the children came to visit Sara, they had found us in adjacent rooms. Sara and I visited each other in wheel chairs.

Sara's illness had taken a heavy toll on me. My watching her suffering for almost a year weakened my strong immune system and my personality. I had lost over twenty-five pounds by watching her helpless suffering.

Sitting side by side in wheel chairs, crying, Sara poured her heart out to me, speaking with a weak fading voice, "Oh, G-d, how much I would like to live to see my granddaughter Elite on her sixteenth birthday and above all to attend my youngest grandchild Daniel's Bar Mitzvah."(Daniel is Dali's and Gil's son.)

I pulled myself together wiping her tears and trying to find encouraging words, as I always did, but not this time. I choked, and suddenly I became speechless, knowing we had reached the end.

Then Sara completely stopped eating. The doctors stopped the chemo treatments, and, day by day, she continued to fade away.

On January 17, 2008, at 3:30 AM, Sara was pronounced dead.

I had lost a partner of sixty-two years. My kids, grandkids, and great-grand kids had lost a loving Mom-Mom Savta, the best in the world.

Our loss will stay with us forever and ever.

Chapter 47
Sara's Funeral

At the Goldstein Funeral Home in Philadelphia on January 21, 2007, there was a moving outpouring of friends and family, almost three hundred people honoring Sara and her life.

The eulogies delivered by our children and grandchildren were delivered with tears, but with love from the depths of their hearts. They reflected on their mom, Mom-mom Sara: How much they loved her, how much they respected her, how much she meant to them, and how much they would miss her forever.

The service at the cemetery was followed with sitting shivah at the house of our daughter Dahlia in Cherry Hill, New Jersey.[29] Many friends came to her house during this week.

The hundreds of sympathy cards, the special touching letters, and testimonials from friends in the U.S .and from numerous countries that Sara had touched during her life: Israel, Brazil, Chile, Peru, Colombia, and Mexico were received.

We lived the first thirty years after our arrival to the U.S. in Philadelphia where we belonged to the Adath Zion Congregation on Friendship Street in Philadelphia. We had purchased our graves in Northeast Philadelphia where Sara is resting for eternity.

May she rest in peace.

Chapter 48
Friends

Sara Paul, Lili Herskovich, and Rachel Ickovich—these three good friends had one and the same destiny. In December 2006, Sara was the first one to be diagnosed with cancer. Rachel was diagnosed in early 2007; Lili, in February 2008.

Friendship among the three of them, all Holocaust survivors, had a beginning in Haifa, Israel, in the early 1950s. They all lived near each other; their friendship continued and grew stronger and stronger for over fifty years. Only death parted them.

The strongest common denominator among them was their children: Rachel's three children, Ely, Tova, and Jeanette; Lili, two wonderful sons, Michael and Howard; Sara with three extraordinary, loving, caring children: Dahlia, Stewart, and Gil. May G-d bless all the children.

The age differences among the kids were only a year or two. Many weekends were planned together among the families. During the winter was sleigh riding in Pennypack Park; summers in sunny Atlantic City. The beach was a playground for the kids— digging in the warm sand and running to the ocean.

At one point we had over ten children to watch out for— all for one; the three moms were there with their watchful eyes. During many years we all rented rooms in the same house, Marika's, on Dover and Atlantic Avenues, one block from the ocean. The kids mingled, playing happily.

My sister-in-law, Manci, was the link to Marika for they were the best of friends. Manci was the first to arrive in Atlantic City with her two kids, Miriam and Steve. As my brother Villie had a business to run in Philadelphia, he came mostly for long weekends, which was the experience of all the husbands. As Manci was the senior among us, she took charge of the kitchen, allocating kitchen time for the others. Often she even told the others what to cook and how to cook it. She was known to love to taste everyone's food. She was a great cook and had a good heart to share with everyone. Manci had a special soft spot for Sara. Their close relationship was remarkable.

Guests from year to year used to come down every summer—most were survivors. There were the Pauls: my brother Emil, Lili, and their three, Rifka, David, Nir; Rachel; Barry Ickovich with their three; Sara and Zali-Ben Ami and their son, Moishe; Frida and Moske Davidovitch with daughter Chanele; Sara and Josef Katz with daughter, Rifkele, and son, David; and Fruma and Jo Fridman with daughter Billa and son Ira.

At the beach we all sat together. We often shared fruit and lunches, and of course we had ice cream for the kids and some adults as well.

The women cooked up a storm in the one kitchen shared by all. Before sunset, we came back to a house scented by the various dishes cooking and baking—many Hungarian specialties.

When the children were back in the house, there was never a dull moment. One, two, or three cried; they had some sunburn. All the mothers were there with their remedies.

After showers and early dinners, everyone got ready to go for the daily parade on the boardwalk. The evening walks on the famous boardwalk were always challenging. The kids were running for the ice cream store, followed shortly by the visit to Roth's candy store.

The women dressed elegantly. The husbands always knew the difference between those that were staring at our beautiful children or our beautiful wives. Shimi, Lili's husband (who passed away in 2006), Barry, Rachel's husband, and I always walked behind them or before them carrying the smallest of the children.

As we looked at all the children, we were remembering that despite Hitler and the Nazis, what a future generation we have!

Around 8:00 PM everyone was back at the house. The kids were put to bed one by one. For the adults card playing was the past time, and cards they played! During the winter we continued to meet every weekend—each family took turns to host the card games.

A friendly family atmosphere always prevailed; the snacks and particularly the Hungarian special pastries were the "icing on the cake." The wives cooked basically the same wonderful dishes and baked the same delicious cakes. At some point, Sara, Rachel, Lily, Frida, and Manci matched the color of their hair. I think this was a statement of real deep friendship and identity.

There were few days during the years that the five did not phone each other. There was always something to say, always something to share. At the end, the illness of each affected the others.

Philadelphia, 1957: Sister-in Law, Manci, Sara, and my sister Chaya

Manci passed away first. In 2008, we lost Sara; four months later, Lili, followed by Rachel five months later—all in one year. Their common suffering impacted each other. May their good memories be celebrated forever.

Only Frida of the five has survived. She and her husband, Moshke, live in Philadelphia; their daughter, Dr. Helen Ehannele and her husband, David, in Pittsburgh.

Sara, Rachel and Lili are resting near each other in the King David Cemetery in Bensalem, Pennsylvania. Manci is resting close by.

Chapter 49
Two *Simchahs*

During the last years of Sara's illness, she had often mentioned two important events that she would like to live to see—to *shep naches* from her youngest granddaughter Elite's Bat Mitzvah and grandson Daniel's Bar Mitzvah.

Elite's Bat Mitzvah, on November 18, 2004, was almost like a wedding atmosphere. As beautiful as she is, she was glowing as if a beautiful sunrise was on her face. Her dress and earrings magnified her dark, big, beautiful brown eyes. Her parents Dali and Gil, her brother, Daniel, and her many friends helped her to celebrate an important milestone in her life. It was wonderful that Sara and I were able to share this day.

When it was Daniel's turn to stand at the bimah, I told him, "It's a shame that Savti couldn't live to see you.[30] To attend your Bar Mitzvah was one of her last wishes, and she spoke of this even in her last days."

Daniel attended Solomon Schechter Hebrew School. For his Bar Mitzvah, he had started to prepare a year earlier.

Throughout the year I often questioned him: "Are you ready?"

He was ready months before the date. Daniel was more than ready. He was superb on Saturday night, December 19, 2008. He led the services with a good Hebrew accent. His mother, the sabra Dali, his father, Gil, his sister, Elite, and I were very proud of him, as he read from the Torah the weekly chapter, "Berashit," the dreams of Josef. He led the services at Neve Shalom Synagogue in Metuchen, New

Jersey, while his Rabbi Zelizar and the *chazzan*, Cantor Lewin, stood on the bimah beside him.[31]

His Savta Edna, his Aunt Eti, his cousin Rotem, who came from Israel, were all very proud of Daniel's reading in Hebrew. This was a reflection of his maturity.

On Sunday at 2 PM at Neve Shalom, the religious part of the Bar Mitzvah started. The rabbi and chazzan officiated. The rabbi spoke very highly of Daniel as he was passing on to him a siddur, a prayer book, a gift from the congregation. The rabbi reminded him that he was becoming a man that day and was expected in the synagogue for years to come.

The ceremony was moving and emotional because Daniel's reading was full of confidence and grace. That touched us to the point of happy tears.

The open buffet was ready after the services, a buffet, *Kyad Hamelech*, as served by the hands of the king, with love and filled with emotion. The rich variety of food and drinks in addition to the music was overwhelming. Two hours later the doors of the banquet room opened: the setting, the balloons, the flowers, the candles, the centerpieces, the numerous artistic ice block carvings all contributed to a lifetime memorable event.

The input of my daughter-in-law Dali and my son Gil was obvious starting with the unique invitations, the music, the food, and centerpieces all reflected love and a sense of accomplishment—the first important milestone in their son Daniel's life: his Bar Mitzvah.

The young friends of Daniel as well as the old fogies talked about the well organized and well executed affair. Until late into the evening, everyone had a great time. The only sad note was Savta Sara's absence; her dream and wish to be at this affair was cut short by her death a few months before the Bar Mitzvah.

After Schechter School, Daniel continued his Jewish education at Neve Shalom Synagogue. He is fluent in Hebrew, as is his sister, Elite.

Daniel's talent for music and art is remarkable. After the Bar-Mitzvah he was tested in school for his abilities to sing and act.

We are very proud of him.

Chapter 50
From the Ashes

As Sara used to say, "G-d punished us with impunity. The deaths of our parents, brothers and sisters, uncles and aunts—six million of our people perished, others suffered unbearable pain and illness! Despite the Nazi regime's plan to have a world with no Jews, *Limrot Ha-kol* (despite everything), G-d has given us much.

Those of us that were liberated and survived were given a new chance at new lives. We took that opportunity to build new families and rebuild the Jewish nation.

From the ashes—after our suffering, worries, and illnesses—we married had children, grandchildren, and great-grandchildren. We are among the fortunate, having three wonderful children, Dahlia, Stewart and Gil. Each of them has two children: Dahlia's Tara and Ilana, Stewart's Ari and Eitan, Gil's Elite and Daniel.

Their Savta Sara passed away on January 17, 2008. She did live to see them all at their tender ages. I have the pleasure of watching my great-grandchildren grow and talking complete sentences. Their "crazy" young mom-mom, my beloved daughter, Dahlia, devotes to them her love and time—more than the average grandmother does, I think. I believe she is trying to make up for their loss of Savta Sara.

I owe my gratitude to my daughter Dahlia for enabling me to share with her our precious family treasures, our great-grandkids, as well as my appreciation to all my grandchildren, and their spouse's grandchildren for keeping a warm spot in their daily lives for me.

I give my special recognition to Steve Herman, Dahlia's fiancé.

Thanks to the continuous efforts of my daughter, Dahlia, I am able to see my great grandkids on a regular basis. During the winter she picks me up in Atlantic City to shop and visit the kids as they all live near each other in Cherry Hill, New Jersey. During the summer months they frequently spend their weekends in Steve and Dahlia's big summer home in Margate, New Jersey.

This gives me the opportunity to spend some valuable time with them, playing with them at the beach, taking them for a walk on the boardwalk, visiting their favorite candy store, followed with ice-cream after dinner.

As I am enjoying the precious time I have with them, there is no day I don't think of Sara and the short time she had to enjoy our growing extended family.

Part II

Business

Ventures

Chapter 51
Hula Hoops

One Sunday evening in 1958, I watched *The Ed Sullivan Show* where the major attraction was a hula hoop act. It was a very impressive display.

That Monday following was my day off. I went downtown and as I passed John Wanamaker's Department Store on Market Street in Philadelphia, I noticed several hundred people in a line.

I joined this line asking, "What is the line for?"

The reply from the person next to me was, "There is a sale on the hula hoops that were shown last night on the *Ed Sullivan Show.*"

I positioned myself in the line to buy a hula hoop for my son, Stewart, 3 years old and my daughter, Dahlia, 8 years old.

The price was right; instead of $3.98 the promotion price was $1.98. After two hours, I reached the front of the line and happily bought my little darlings a hula hoop as a gift.

I gave them their gift and they had lots of fun trying to hula hoop. Oh! How much fun it was to watch Dahlia show Stewart how to hula! After the kids were put to bed both Sara and I tried unsuccessfully to hula. It seemed so easy and so much fun on *The Ed Sullivan Show.* After numerous attempts I had an idea—a big "idea."

I took a screwdriver and a pair of pliers, opened the two staples that held the plastic tube with a wooden dowel connecting both ends. These hula hoops reminded me of large wooden rings that we kids had back home. However, instead of rolling them around our hips, we chased the wooden rings with small sticks in our hands, hitting and advancing them along the side of the road. These rings were used by wine barrel makers to hold the staves of the barrel together; sometimes we used metal rings that were used by wine barrel makers for the same purpose.

Suddenly it occurred to me that the hula hoop was nothing but a piece a garden hose held together with a piece of wood and two staples one on each end.

The following morning I shared with my brother my "discovery" about the hula hoop that when taken apart is nothing more than a piece of garden hose. I told Villie that I was planning to call my uncle and buy garden hose. Hancock Gross, owned by my Uncle Lou Gross and one of the largest manufacturers of garden hoses, was located in Philadelphia. When I called my uncle, I discovered that the company had been making hula hoops for ten days. (The original inventor of the hula hoop was a California firm.) My uncle told me, "It is the hottest item we ever made. We cannot make them fast enough."

I borrowed my brother's station wagon and drove down to my uncle's factory. When I asked my uncle about garden hoses, he told me to discuss buying those with my cousin Jack, who was in charge of sales. Jack asked me, "Why do you want to buy garden hose?"

I replied: "To make hula hoops."

He then told me, "I can sell you complete hula hoops for $12.00 a dozen."

I asked him for the price of the hose not a finished product; he reluctantly gave me a price of $ 5.40 a dozen.

I immediately agreed, "I am pulling up my station wagon. Please have someone load it up with random lengths of hose." We filled the station wagon to the maximum possible, fifty dozen, unfinished, at $5.40 a dozen.

When I came back to my brother's store with my load, I asked his permission to use the store's meat cutting electric chain saw that we used to cut meats and bones.

He replied, "Okay. But only during the night when the store is closed."

I went to the nearest hardware store and purchased wooden dowels sufficient to cut 600 2" length pieces. I also purchased a hand stapler and staples for a total of $16.00 (an electric stapler was too expensive). I also bought a rubber stamp with my brother's store address and phone number on it.

When the supermarket closed, I was ready for business. At 8 PM I started to cut the wooden dowels and stapled both ends of each hose. At midnight Sara joined me. We worked until the 7AM opening of the store.

I loaded up the station wagon drove to Columbia Avenue where there were stores and outdoor peddlers, selling half of my products in two hours for $12.00 a dozen. The balance of my products I sold in Germantown thirty minutes away.

I issued my business receipts to my customers with my brother's address and phone number. Before I had even returned to my brother's, the phone was ringing off the hook. My customers were selling the hula hoops for $1.99 versus department stores that sold them for $3.99. I returned quickly to my cousin loaded up the station wagon again with fifty dozen and drove off, ready to assemble and manufacture all over again. Overnight we repeated this. The same for the next ten nights! Then I rented a small pickup truck with the capacity for 250 dozen at a time.

Sara's hands were so swollen that she could not hold a stapler. Because my profit margin was excellent, I hired five Puerto Rican young men to help me in my "factory." Only in America!

This money machine continued for six weeks until the hula hoop craze cooled off. The demand and the prices dropped. I closed my business having earned good, hard cash in a very short time.

Chapter 52
Ceramic Housewares

With the hard-earned cash, I was able to search for my next business venture. A friend of my brother Villie, Armin, who was in the housewares business, mentioned to me a good business available for sale in the wholesale district of Philadelphia. A meeting was set up for that weekend with the seller of the business, seventy-eight year old Mr. Miller. After a two hour meeting, we had an agreement in principle to buy the business. Within fourteen days I took over the Philadelphia China Company.

The business was located in an old four-story building with a manually operated elevator. This business bought second and third quality ceramic dinnerware and glassware from factories located in Scio, Ohio; Jeannette ("the glass city"), Pennsylvania; Palestine, West Virginia; and Mount Clemens, Michigan, a suburb of Detroit. One of the early challenges was to drive ten to twelve hours to the factories.

The ceramic dinnerware that we bought from the factories was packed in apple bushel baskets. The purchase price was so much a bushel of plates, cups, cereal bowls, etc. Most of the pieces had chips or minor cracks. Once we brought home a load, we had to process each piece to make them safe and saleable. We had to ground away the chips or the minor hairline cracks. This was not easy, no piece of cake. Then after sorting through all the pieces, we assembled sixteen or twenty piece sets: four dinner plates, four mugs, four salad plates, and four cereal bowls. In the case of twenty piece sets, instead of the four

185

mugs, we included four cups and four saucers. We had also purchased drop proof boxes for these sets and sold them at a good profit to numerous retail chain stores in Philadelphia, such as Wanamaker's Bargain Basement, Gimbels, W.T. Grant, F.W. Woolworth, and independent retailers.

The glassware we purchased was already in boxes. At the factories these boxes had been loaded on wooden pallets, but often the boxes fell off the forklifts or moving belts. These boxes were immediately separated and stamped "Rattlers." For rattlers we paid so much a box.

When we arrived home, we opened each box and took out the broken pieces and replaced them to fill the boxes, selling them to the same retailers as we had the dinnerware.

We learned this business well. At a certain point, we even purchased small electrical kilns and decorated the white dinnerware to enhance sales and profits.

As business was good, I took two partners into the business: Barry Ickovics and Miki Deutsch, who were newcomers from Israel. Thus, I had help with the physically hard work of loading and unloading and driving to the factories. The pressure on me eased up a bit.

Being a small business, we closely watched the operating expenses. The biggest challenge I had was when I made a decision to economize the trips to the factories. Instead of traveling every week with a twelve foot pickup truck, I rented a forty foot rig tractor trailer..

I arranged the pickup time for 4 AM, arriving at Germantown Avenue with Barry, one of my partners. For the first time in my life, I looked closely at the size of a tractor trailer, one that I had committed to drive to Ohio, my first stop. I was shocked and amazed as I climbed up to the cabin of the tractor; the height, the length, and the width surprised me more.

However, I did not back away when I received the keys from the truck rental person. I started the engine placed it in gear and the rig moved out of the parking lot. The parking lot was on the west side of Germantown Avenue where electric trolleys were running on steel tracks. At 4 AM, as I suddenly rolled out onto the street, a trolley was crossing the avenue at the same time. I tried the brakes which did not work. The trolley stopped, but I bumped into it from the side. Happily, there was no major damage to the trolley nor to the truck.

The trolley driver was nice and calm; he did not hit me but only called me "stupid." The rental truck attendant was upset with me for rushing out of the parking lot. Little had I know that the truck needed to build up air pressure for the brakes to function. Barry was sitting quietly; he didn't understand a word of English. Anyway it was too early in the morning for Barry; he was still half asleep.

The rental agent took five minutes to explain the air gauge and the pressure. The excitement was over. Barry and I were on our way.

After a couple of stops, ten hours later we arrived at the Ohio factory. At the factory we were directed to the loading docks to back in our truck. I tried numerous times to maneuver the tractor trailer, to no avail. I had to ask one of the workers to back the trailer in for me. Arriving at the second and third factories, I did not waste my time but asked the factory workers to back up the tractor trailer for me. On our third stop, at Jeannette Glass Company in Jeannette, Pennsylvania, we were finally fully loaded and ready to return to Philadelphia.

Chapter 53
Weigh In!

When we were on the PA turnpike, I was discussing with Barry the size of the load and the potential profits. Although it was pouring rain, dark and foggy, we both felt really good about the trip.

As I was driving, I suddenly noticed some blurry lights at the bottom of the hill. I slowed down, thinking it must be a hold up. As we rolled closer to the light, I tried to stop the truck; however, the load we carried and my lack of experience prevented me from stopping. I passed the blinking light by at least a 100 feet. A big guy in a yellow rain coat and a big Pennsylvania state trooper hat, that not only covered his head but also most of his face, flagged us down. The police officer was decidedly displeased because I had almost run him over. Neither were we in the truck pleased.

The big hat, the flashlight, the strong voice of the police officer screaming, "You so and so. You almost killed me," scared us. The officer continued, "Don't you know you just passed a weighing station? You are supposed to stop and drive the truck onto the scale. So back the damn trailer up and get on the scale."

I was shivering. We were both very scared. I started to mumble trying to tell the policeman, "Me can only go forward."

The policeman did not understand my broken English. "Back up he shouted."

I started explaining that I did not know how to back up. The policeman ordered us out of the tractor trailer cabin. His anger was obvious; he jumped in, backed up the truck, and drove it onto the scale.

Barry and I were walking back and noticed in the guard house another policeman, who yelled, "You guys are crazy."

We did not know what to expect next. Would they kill us? Or would they first arrest us and then kill us?

The policeman who had driven the truck onto the scale stated, "You guys are damn lucky."

He requested our documents: driver's license, rental agreement, and receipts for the merchandise. Everything was legitimate. The load on the truck was 500 pounds below the limit of 40,000 pounds. Both policemen had calmed down, realizing they did not have two gangsters in front of them.

Because my English was better than Barry's (Barry had no English), I tried with my very limited vocabulary to explain that we were newcomers to the U.S. and only trying to make a living for our families.

Both policemen softened up explaining the scale. They told us that in the U.S. throughout the highways, there are scales for trucks to make sure that their loads do not exceed the weight limit regulated by law.

I explained to the police that our intention was to do nothing against the law in our new home, the U.S.A. Barry and I thanked them for their patience and explanations.

They handed us back all of our documents and told us we were free to go. They told us, "Drive carefully and good luck." At the end they were very nice to us. We thanked them again as we drove off.

Upon our return to our warehouse in Philadelphia, Miki, our third partner, was anxiously waiting for us. We arrived at 7AM.

Now the job of unloading and processing of the merchandise began. We discussed the next trip for which the designated driver was Barry because he was experienced; he had been a truck driver in Israel where he had driven and owned a gasoline tanker. True, that was not a forty foot tractor trailer; however, he had more experience than I had. I had only driven a car.

Chapter 54
The Business Changes

Business was good and we repeatedly expanded by importing Czechoslovakian fine handcut crystal and giftware. In addition to the wholesale business, we opened retail factory outlets in three farmers' markets in the Philadelphia area and later a store on Germantown Avenue, which was managed by my wife, Sara, and Miki's wife, Luci.

The retail outlets required us to work in the evenings and on weekends when the wholesale business was closed. We were three hard working young men. Working long days, seven days a week, did not deter us. The business was growing reasonably well after only two years, our wives were good partners, and we appreciated each other's efforts.

One day Miki one of my partners came in and told me that he and his wife had decided to move to California where Miki had a friend who was very successful in the electric construction business and had offered Miki a great opportunity because Miki was a trained electrician from Israel. After visiting their friend during the winter season, they had fallen in love with Los Angeles and the climate.

We paid out Miki for his share of the business, which left two partners—Barry and me. Shortly after, Barry decided that he wanted to sign up to learn to be a beautician. He had a friend in the business who claimed becoming a beautician and owning a shop was certainly much easier work and had the potential of a good salary. I agreed to buy him out. Barry's beautician course took him three months. Then he purchased an ongoing beauty shop; a year later, another shop. Barry became successful and happy. He loved the new business. Instead of driving a truck, loading and unloading, lifting bushels and boxes, his new environment was women. He loved every minute of this. I was happy for him and we have remained very close friends until this day.

My business was going well; it was hard work but going well. I had a brother in Israel, Emil, who wanted to come to the U.S. because he had two brothers here. So I invited Emil to join me in the business. He did and was a great and reliable partner.

Chapter 55
The Fire

The business continued to grow into houseware products and gifts until one cold, rainy November night. At 9 PM, at home, I received a call from the fire department, "Your warehouse is in flames." I could not believe what I was hearing. This was one and a half months before Christmas; the warehouse was loaded with merchandise and we did not have adequate fire insurance. I called Emil and thirty minutes later we arrived at our warehouse in South Philadelphia.

We saw the flames from far away. When we arrived the captain of the fire department told us the fire had started in the next building, on the top floor, and had consumed our old warehouse building like a match.

If it had not been for the Red Cross that arrived shortly after Emil and I had arrived, we would have died from the combination of shock, the smoke inhalation, and the bitter cold, wet night.

I broke down crying. I had lost everything, four years of hard work. To me this was not only a question of lost money but also I felt a personal defeat.

The Red Cross gave us warm blankets and hot tea during the night. Most of all I vividly remember the Red Cross team embracing us, trying to calm us down from our shock and big tragedy. We hardly salvaged any merchandise. With no insurance, it did not amount to anything; we could not recover. Every dollar we had, we had lost in the business—in the warehouse.

All our savings were invested in the wholesale business, and we had lost everything. We were out of business.

The fire affected other businesses. The outlets in the markets that depended on merchandise from our own warehouse could not survive.

I needed to do something. Both Emil and I had families with kids.

One night I sat down with my brother Villie: "Villie, you are aware of our situation. I need you to give me a loan."

Villie was good hearted; he offered me $10,000 dollars as a loan. I was very grateful as this was a lot of money in the late 50's.

I also spoke to some of my first cousins, asking them for a loan. The rich ones made no effort to help. The one that had the least, Leonard, offered me $3,000 dollars.

With $13,000 dollars cash I contacted my bank the First National Bank of Philadelphia, Girard Avenue Branch. They made available to me an additional $7,000 dollars credit line. With this capital, we weighed the options—to restart the same business or turn to something within our financial limitations. To restart the previous business I needed much more capital.

I decided to follow the lead of a friend of mine. Buying and selling on public auctions, general merchandise, housewares, ceramics, glass, etc. This business started off slowly; fortunately, I had some good contacts from the previous business. I worked hard to make a living for my family as well as for my brother, Emil.

Chapter 56
Vacuum Metalizing

One day I came across an advertisement for the sale of a business in Kansas City. I called the seller to find out details about the business. I paid no attention to the two brothers' names: Hugo and Hines Oswald; we agreed that they would send me more details. The business was a vacuum plating shop. A new German technology had been developed during World War 2 to make strong reflecting mirrors, "reflectors" used against airplanes.

The two Oswald brothers came to the U.S. in 1961. Otto was an engineer who applied basic technology to vacuum plate metal components primarily used by lamp manufacturers. The technology to apply the process of gold plating or silver plating to glass gift items, ceramic, and plastics was also improved by them

We did limited research. However, this technology was unknown. There were other methods of plating, such as electroplating, but these were much more expensive.

That morning I called the Oswald brothers to give them my flight number. Kansas City here I come!

The same day on November 22, 1963, I was in my car and the radio was on: "We interrupt our regularly scheduled broadcast. The President of the United States, John F. Kennedy, was shot during a reception parade in Dallas, Texas, at 1:25 PM."

I pulled off to the side of the road and kept listening to the repeated broadcast. Suddenly I heard that the police had arrested Lee

Harvey Oswald as the accused shooter. I asked myself, "My G-d, could this be the same Oswald family I am meeting with tomorrow morning in Kansas City?"

The radio repeated information about the tragic shooting. The President was pronounced dead at 2 PM.

I got to my office on Sixth Street in Philadelphia to make a call to the Oswalds.

I asked them, "Are you guys in any way related to the Oswald, the killer of the President (he was my favorite President)."

"No. No." Otto replied, "Definitely not."

I pressed on the phone- breathing hard and heavy. Should I believe them? Should I go to meet the Oswalds?

After discussing with my brother Emil and others, I kept to my schedule. Upon my arrival, I saw Otto waiting for me with my name on a sign. As we approached his car in the parking lot, I again questioned Otto about the family relations with the killer, Lee Harvey Oswald.

By now Otto was offended. With his heavy German accent, he said, "You do not believe me, Mr. Paul?"

He then told me about his family in Germany until he had convinced me that they could not be related.

We put the subject to rest. We arrived at the vacuum plating shop, where I was given a tour while Otto was showing and explaining the production process to me. This was something I had never seen before. In one phase, in the dipping room, the vapor of the lacquer used in the process of production made my eyes tear.

The other parts were clean. The "gold" and "silver" glittered. However, it looked like hard physical work to lift the dipping fixtures with lacquered components mounted on them. The vacuum chamber worked ceaselessly. They showed me all the details, including costs, structure, margins, and profits. I made notes to be digested later.

I spent the entire day with the Oswald brothers; they were good hosts, friendly and very businesslike. We discussed in detail the price, the shipping cost to Philadelphia, raw material suppliers, customers, etc. Both brothers took me to the airport in time to catch my 7 PM flight back to Philadelphia.

During the flight back, I tried to better understand the details we discussed. As I looked over my notes, I questioned myself: Did I really want to venture into this business? It would be hard work. I did not know the technical process of production, but the bottom line-profit margins looked good.

The following day I discussed with my brother Emil potential new business possibilities. We made some contacts in Philadelphia with some potential customers. We were getting positive feedback.

With the new technology and new process, vacuum metalizing looked tempting. As we evaluated all aspects of the new business, Emil said, "Do not worry about hard work. That does not scare me." Emil knew he would have to manage the shop.

After a week I called the Oswald brothers and told them: "Yes, we are genuinely interested. I will come back to Kansas City to discuss all the details."

However, Otto would have to come to Philadelphia to teach us the production process. This would take a month. Second, the asking price was $50,000. I offered $40,000, including Otto's time for thirty days, including installation and set up time.

After back and forth negotiations, they accepted my offer. I had very limited funds; therefore, I negotiated $20,000 down and $20,000 to be paid out in monthly installments of $2,000 a month. They accepted my offer because Otto was ready to go back to Germany.

Emil looked for a place to house the new business. We were lucky; he found a suitable small, one-story building readily available, approximately 15,000 square feet, with high ceilings. Two weeks later we hired a truck and loaded up the "factory." Twelve hours later we returned to Lehigh Avenue in Philadelphia. Otto was with us.

The unloading went smoothly. Yet it still took the entire day to find the proper location for each piece of equipment. The most important piece of equipment was the 48" vacuum chamber, which had been originally manufactured in Philadelphia by Stocks Machinery Company. This was a great company. When we called them, advising them that we had purchased one of their chambers, they offered their expertise and services. The same vacuum chamber was used for other industries.

It took Otto and Emil a few days to get everything hooked up, including electricity and water. During the set up time I made my rounds to a number of lamp manufacturers.

I was able to contract work for some lamp companies. They gave me components to be plated. Business grew steadily. Within a few months we had built up a solid customer base. While the contract work covered the expenses, I was looking for the bigger picture, buying inexpensive glass gift items and plating them to sell with better margins.

The first item I purchased was a bud vase from Anchor Hocking Glass Company in Lancaster, Ohio. The price per dozen, F.O.B. (freight on board) was $ 1.44 (12 cents each) and freight at 2 cents. We plated the first 100 dozen with no problem. I sold them to a wholesale florist company in Philadelphia for $12.00 a dozen.

Our profit was good. Our cost for the finished goods was about $6.00 a dozen. We sold the same vase to the Philadelphia regional buying office at the F.W. Woolworth Company. The first order was for 500 dozen; these gold and silver vases sold like 'hotcakes." We received a reorder after ten days for 720 dozen.

I had asked the regional buyer to call the national buyer in New York to tell him about our new "'hot selling" item, so he would give me an appointment.

Two days later I was in the New York Woolworth headquarters, the thirty-two story Woolworth building, a well known landmark across from New York City Hall.

I had a 10 AM appointment. By 10:30 AM I was on the phone with Emil telling him about an order for 2000 dozen (they had over 800 stores at the time). It took a lot of guts to approach such a potentially big customer.

This was good news and bad news. The good news was we had received an order from a financially strong company; the bad news was we did not have the financing needed to buy the vases and process them. We had 60 days to deliver. With the order in hand, I contacted the glass factory to negotiate a credit line. They agreed to ship the 2000 dozen on an open credit line.

Now we needed more working capital to buy raw materials and boxes and to cover payroll.

We already had three employees in addition to Emil and me. I contacted my bank and showed them the signed purchase order from the F.W. Woolworth Company. We asked them to loan us $10,000.

The loan officer of the bank, who had known my brother Villie for years, got up from his chair went into his boss's office. After a few minutes the loan was approved.

They gave us a $10,000 dollar credit line against the order for $24,000.00. This was our first major break. We delivered this order within the sixty days. Within ten days of delivery, we received payment. We paid both the suppliers and the bank on time. We had established a good credit rating.

To meet the delivery dates with all customers, Emil and I worked every day 6 AM until 6 PM, six days a week. We had proved to ourselves that our investment was worthwhile.

We continued to expand our product line and our customer base. We exhibited our products in national trade shows and hired commissioned sales reps.

We were on our way to nationwide distribution!

Chapter 57
Meeting David Chase

During one of my stays in New York I had dinner in an Israeli club, Avramels, in the village. The club had good Israeli music—The Five Ruskies—and good food. I met an Israeli named Yakov; in between drinks, food, and music, he told me about his cousin in Hartford, Connecticut: David Chase.

Yakov and I took a liking to each other, so I invited him to my home in Philadelphia. During a Friday night dinner conversation Yakov mentioned his cousin again. Yakov told me, "David Chase is one of the most successful builders of apartment houses and shopping malls throughout the country. You need to meet him. He is our age; you will like him."

A few days later I was invited to Hartford. The offices of David Chase were downtown in a relatively new twelve-story building known as the "Chase Building," which he had built and owned. The Chase offices, with very impressive modern furnishings, occupied the top floor.

We spent approximately one hour with David Chase. He invited me to stay overnight at his home, which was a "palace." I met his wife, Rhoda, and his two small children, Cheryl and Arnold. After dinner, which was served by a housekeeper, we retired to his study. David asked me more details about myself and my business.

David surprised me, telling me about his newly built shopping center in McKeesport, Pennsylvania (near Pittsburgh). His anchor store was a Kmart owned and operated by the S.S. Kresky Company, headquartered in Detroit. David told me that after the ribbon cutting ceremony, he had played golf with Mr. Cunningham, the chairman of the S.S. Kresky Company. Mr. Cunningham offered for sale a ceramic dinnerware factory located in Mt. Clemens, Michigan (a suburb of Detroit). The factory was known as the Mt. Clemens Pottery Company.

The Kresky family was concerned with unemployment in the city and decided to build this plant in 1910 to create employment for several hundred people. The S.S. Kresky Company headquarters in Detroit was very involved in the community. The U.A.W., the auto workers' union, "organized" the factory. The Kresky Foundation would have nothing to do with organized labor unions; therefore, they were looking to sell the Mt. Clemens factory as soon as possible.

I mentioned to David that I knew the factory very well. I had visited them often to buy their second quality ceramics.

I said: "What a coincidence! As a matter of fact, I had spoken a couple of days ago with another friend who owns Sabin China Company in McKeesport, Pennsylvania, and had made an offer through the real estate division of S.S. Kresky to buy the factory."

David responded, "Oh, what a small world! Who is this Sam Sabin?"

I replied, "I have known him for a couple of years; he is an extremely nice person and a good Jew."

David asked me to contact Sam and invite him to Hartford for a meeting as soon as possible. I called Sam told him about my meeting with David Chase, and told Sam, "David would like to meet you regarding the Mt. Clemens factory."

Sam asked for David's phone number. He said, "I want to talk to him before I make a trip."

Sam and David had their phone conversation. Two days later the meeting took place in Dave's office in Hartford. Both David and Sam invited me to be present at the meeting.

David started the meeting by saying, "I am interested in buying the factory, which was offered to me with the right of refusal by Mr. Cunningham, the chairman of the company."

Sam stated that he had made an offer with a deposit of $100,000.

David replied, "They will not necessarily accept your offer; I am dealing directly with the chairman." David questioned Sam about his business and his interest in buying the factory.

Sam explained, "My existing business is decorating. I buy approximately $30,000 dollars per month of white plates, cups, saucers from Mount Clemens, and then I decorate them with various decal designs. I sell my finished ware to department stores across the U.S." Sam stated that he employed sixty people and his annual turnover was three million dollars.

David was impressed with Sam, saying, "I want to do business with you. Send me your financial statements for the last three years, receivables, payables, inventory, and orders on hand, and we will have another meeting. Ernest will coordinate the next meeting which should be in the next ten days." Sam agreed to submit all details as requested.

I knew that for Sam to buy that huge factory that employed over 300 people would be a big stretch. Sam had told me confidentially that he had lined up a potential partner, a plastics manufacturer, Mr. Kline. I had met Mr. Klein through Sam in Chicago during one of the trade shows. Behind the scenes I spoke to Sam encouraging him to let David buy the factory. "You are buying a headache with the labor union."

Sam was receptive in principle to back out from his offer. "Let David buy. You will be running the factory as well as continuing the business in McKeesport."

Sam submitted all requested information. David had a chance to evaluate and to consult with his legal counsel and financial advisors.

The follow up meeting took place ten days later. One of Dave's attorneys was present at the meeting.

David was ready to make an offer, "I will buy your company in McKeesport, and, Sam, you will be the president of the new company that will include the McKeesport operation as well as the Mt. Clemens factory."

"How much Sam?" David asked.

Sam asked David to make the first offer, based on the statements and details he had submitted.

David said, "I spoke again with the Chairman of S.S Kresge, Mr. Cunningham. He told me, in confidence, your offer is too weak and will not be accepted."

This strengthened Dave's position and his bargaining power; he pressured Sam to come up with a reasonable offer. After a few minutes, Sam said, "The price needs to be worthwhile for my family and me: $1,250,000 and assume my payables of about $100,000 dollars."

David explained that his interest in the factory was mostly the land and the real estate. After some back and forth, David offered $1,000,000, including inventory.

The attorney drew up an intent of sale agreement, telling us "*Mazel Tov*!" The agreement was initialed by all parties, with me as a witness.

David stated he would engage his head corporate attorney, Mr. Donovan, to negotiate the deal with the Kresge Company.

I became part of the deal. David offered to buy our company in Philadelphia, Vacuum Plating Company, offering my brother Emil and me jobs—me as Vice President in charge of marketing, and Emil, in charge of warehousing.

We were offered a good deal and we accepted the offer. The amount was relatively small; however, good executive positions made the deal interesting.

We continued our business for three months until the deal was signed and sealed. While visiting the ceramic factories, I became aware of another interesting ceramic factory in Roseville, Ohio, fifty miles east of Columbus, Ohio.

Chapter 58
The Nelson McCoy Factory

My next venture with David Chase involved a ceramic factory in Roseville, Ohio (near Zanesville). The McCoy Factory, which produced complementary kitchen items such as cookie jars, mixing bowls, and flower pots, was seventy-five years old. This factory occupied over 250,000 square feet (including storage area) they had two hundred and fifty workers. They had good products and good clients such as Sears, Montgomery Ward, and many other major retailers. However, the factory was in financial trouble because imports from Japan came in at lower prices than the U. S. prices.

In one of my conversations I had mentioned to David Chase that the McCoy Factory would be a good buy especially because the product complemented items being produced at the Mt. Clemens factory; therefore, they had basically the same customer base. The merger of the two factories would strengthen both companies. There would be significant savings with joint marketing sales reps and exhibition costs at the major trade shows. David asked me to get all the financial details to him. I contacted the president of the company, Nelson McCoy, Jr., who was about fifty-five years old and third generation in the McCoy factory. I also contacted a number of major raw material suppliers, who confirmed that McCoy had serious financial problems.

At a meeting with Nelson, I asked him point blank, "Would you consider selling your company?"

Nelson's face reddened, trying to hide his emotional reaction; he was sad about selling the company that had been in his family for so many years.

He took off his glasses and said, "Yeah, at the right price."

Nelson made no mention of his financial difficulties. He was barely paying suppliers and was in a dire position with the Bank of Zanesville, where he served as a member of the board.

I told Nelson about my friend David Chase who had recently bought the Mt. Clemens factory from the Kresky Foundation. Nelson became more and more interested. He had inherited the business twenty-five years ago; his family was well off. The family had a beautiful home in Zanesville, Ohio, extensive land, and a sizeable stable of riding horses.

Nelson was a well known and respected leader in the community. He was the largest employer in town and the neighboring town Roseville, located ten miles to the south of Zanesville.

At first he was hesitant to disclose details of his business. I convinced him that all details would be kept in strict confidence. He promised to provide me with all pertinent statements and details, and he did. I passed on this information to David and urged him to consider an offer.

David's attorneys looked through the statements and discovered a loan of $150,000 dollars due. Nelson had personally guaranteed the loan, which the factory was in no position to pay off.

The attorneys began negotiations with the bank. The bank was very interested in helping to facilitate a deal. The deal was signed within forty-five days; the bank was happy to get $100,000 dollars and roll over the balance of $50,000 for three years. This was another sweet deal for David. The deal was for him to pay all creditors and pay the McCoy family $100,000 dollars a year for ten years.

This gave David ownership of the factory, the land, and the sizeable inventory.

Nelson's personal deal: he was to remain president until all the payments were made. I took over marketing and sales for the McCoy factory and became vice president of the joint companies.

My brother Emil moved the Philadelphia plating shop to the Roseville factory and his family: wife and three children, to Zanesville, Ohio, where they found a small but warm Jewish community. Emil was in charge of warehousing, shipping, and receiving.

Business grew; we built up sales to six million dollars a year from two and a half million under the previous ownership. We had a good work force of over two hundred people with no labor union issues.

After four and a half years, we received an offer from a large glass factory in neighboring Lancaster, Ohio, to buy the Nelson McCoy factory. David Chase, our chairman, instructed his attorneys to negotiate with the Lancaster management, and a deal was made for the McCoy factory. They had offered David a price he could not refuse.

Chapter 59
Studying the Ceramics Industry

When I joined the management team, I became aware that the ceramic industry was very "secretive." There was an active ceramic industry association that held meetings four times a year, when they discussed general subjects such as the business climate in the ceramic industry. Most of all these association meetings were social. Over two hundred people from all over the U.S. participated in these meetings, including the suppliers of raw materials and packaging suppliers.

I was new to the industry, so I was introduced during the first meeting I attended as vice president of the two factories and as the confidential representative of David Chase—the new owner of Nelson McCoy and Mount Clemens Factories.

Before the meeting ended I had met most of the competitors in the industry. To their surprise, I invited my competitors to visit our factories, prioritizing the most successful companies in the business, among them Pfaltzgraff Pottery from York, Pennsylvania, our number one competitor, Lennox China, Hager Pottery, and others. They accepted my invitation, and we set up appointments.

Because I was new, I felt the need to know what the successful factories were doing, the type of equipment they were using, raw materials, etc. My expectation was that they would reciprocate inviting me to their factories. I was pleased when they did.

I had a big challenge on my hands with these two ceramic factories, so I spent three days a week in each of them. Some parts of the factories worked 24 hours, seven days a week. My day started at 6 AM on the production lines to learn the manufacturing process; the office hours were 9 AM to 5 PM; however, I seldom left before 7 PM and worked many weekends. Time is money, so it was imperative that I learn quickly. I realized that because both of the factories were old, they needed some new machinery to be more competitive and profitable for my new boss—David Chase.

The major U.S. retailers imported many of their products in the 1960s. Imports grew very strongly, so I needed to understand how they were making competitive products overseas at 30% lower than U.S. producers. This 30% lower was after landing in the U.S., after paying duty and freight costs.

I also learned that a large number of small and medium sized U.S. companies had closed their doors between 1960 and 1965. At that time there was no trade agreement yet with China. China first penetrated the U.S. market in the late 1970s. So China of today was Japan in those days.

I decided to make a fact-finding trip to Japan. The Japanese Consulate in New York was very helpful in facilitating and planning my trip. I flew to Tokyo, from there I traveled by rapid train to Osaka City, the main center of the ceramic industry.

I learned a lot during this trip. They had much more sophisticated machinery, standardized production, specialized production lines, and the hourly wages were $1.00 U.S. dollar. Hourly wages in the U.S. were $1.60 in Ohio and $ 2.50 in Mt. Clemens, Michigan. On my return I gave a detailed report to our management including David Chase. At that time I also reported on my visits to our U.S. competitors. I felt my learning tour was not over. I decided that I must visit two other important ceramic industry centers: The U.K. and Western Germany. In England the main ceramic factories were two hours by train from London. The article "Stoke-on-Trent, England" reports that Stoke-on-Trent, a unique city in England, is made up of six towns: Tunstall, Burslem, Hanley, Stoke, Fenton and Longton, known as "The Potteries." They had over twenty ceramic factories. I visited only three of the major ones as well as one very important ceramic machinery manufacturer that was located nearby. At Service Engineering, I asked for prices, catalogs, and delivery times. I received this information soon after my return. The information was followed by a visit from a representative of the factory. We had purchased some small and medium sized machinery from this British company.

While in Stoke on Trent, I visited one of the oldest ceramic museums in Europe. To see ceramic products on display that dated back over two-hundred years was very educational and inspiring.

Equally important for me was to visit Frankfurt, Germany. From there I traveled to a small town Kleinheubach am Main, about forty-five minutes by car, to one of the bigger factories, Scheurich Ceramics that employed over 800 workers.

Upon my return I reported to management. David asked me to prepare a comprehensive report. As I also had to be concerned with ongoing sales, reorganizing the sales team, and visiting customers it took me about three weeks to prepare the report.

I was convinced that we had to make many changes including investments in new machinery. The machinery manufacturers from the U.K. visited us, studying each manufacturing step to see what they could supply in a relatively short time. They helped me a great deal, giving details of each machine, productivity, cost, and savings. The Board had previously approved a budget allowing us to purchase some updated machinery, which we did.

Chapter 60
The Smiley Craze

The McCoy factory was making basic kitchen and household products, such as cookie jars, canister sets, and brown drip dinnerware. However, many of the styles were outdated. I hired a Czechoslovakian newcomer to the U.S., Al Kluber, a ceramic engineer, designer, and model maker. Kluber was very talented, and he created new products; some of which became best sellers.

One day visiting a customer in Philadelphia—the Spain brothers, Bernie and Murray—I noticed in their stores a big promoter, the "smiley face." In fact, they claimed to be the creator of the yellow smiley face. Their stores were fully decorated with various printed paper products, such as posters, paper plates, and other party goods. Their store had adopted the logo of the smiley face on the shopping bags they used at the checkout counter. Bernie told me, "This is the most successful product we ever had."

I purchased a number of paper products and took them back to the factory, giving them to Al Klubert, our designer, to develop a group of products incorporating the smiley face. It took Al about thirty days, and we started to pre-sell nationwide with great success.

Chapter 61
Klaus Schumacher

In 1971, during a visit to Cleveland, Ohio, by our major supplier, Ferro Enamel, the general manager, Otto Otavia, told me that he had just returned from Brazil where there were a number of ceramic manufacturers looking for export markets in the U.S. One manufacturer in particular already had his passport and airline ticket. His name was Klaus Schumacher, of Ceramarte, a small but high quality producer of beer steins and ceramic bottles, located in the south of Brazil.

Otto told me, "Mr. Schumacher already has appointments set up with U.S. breweries to offer steins, mugs, and bottles. You have an open door policy for competitors to visit your factories; therefore, I would suggest that you meet Klaus next week."

I wholeheartedly agreed. Otto arranged the visit; Klaus and his German Brazilian interpreter arrived at the airport in Columbus, Ohio (the nearest airport to our factory).

I sent a car to pick them up and bring them to the Zanesville Motel. It was about 6 PM when they arrived. I gave them an hour to wash up, and we met at 7 PM for dinner and drinks. The motel restaurant's bar closing time was midnight. We kept them open for drinks and more drinks until 3 AM. I was known as a generous tipper, so they gladly stayed open.

My first impression of Klaus was very German, blonde, blue eyes, about forty-five years old.

My first question was, "How long have you been in Brazil?"

He said, "I have been in Brazil since 1952."

My first suspicion was that he was a Nazi during the war. I wondered, How many Jews had he killed?

Klaus responded to my questions, "How long are you in the U.S.? Where were you during the war?"

"In Budapest," I replied. "I was in the Jewish resistance, saving Jews from Nazis."

In answer to my next question, Klaus said, "During the war, if you were not with the Nazis, you were against them, so I became a Nazi soldier."

Until three in the morning, the Jewish American Ernest and the German-Brazilian Klaus discussed in depth all aspects of the war. We told each other our stories. We needed no translator between us; we talked to each other directly and openly. We took a liking to each other and respected each other.

Not until the following morning did we discuss business. I drove Klaus to the Mc Coy factory a thirty minute drive. He brought samples to show me. First, I gave him a tour of the factory, showing him products similar to his, beer mugs, bottles, and lamps.

When we entered the office, Peter, Klaus's interpreter, had already unpacked the samples. These were to be shown to the buyers with whom they had appointments. The quality of the samples was very impressive and even more impressive were the prices. I saw a great opportunity.

I asked Klaus about his production capacity. After he told me, I turned to him with an offer to buy his entire production capacity.

I told Klaus, "You do not need to travel any further."

I also showed the samples to Nelson and our management team. Everyone was impressed with the German products made in Brazil with German technology for approximately 50% less than we could produce in Ohio. On top of this the quality was superior.

I mentioned to Klaus, "We must have exclusivity in the U.S.—made for Nelson McCoy Pottery, exclusively in Brazil.

Klaus did not accept my proposal. He was not interested in selling to another manufacturer. His objective was to find a direct market and grow the business with his name. We parted as friends. Klaus had other appointments set up in Pittsburgh, Milwaukee, Seattle, and Washington.

I invited Klaus, on his way back, to meet my family and to stay with us in our home in Philadelphia. Klaus accepted my invitation. When he arrived, he saw that we were Jews from the pictures on the walls as well as the display of a beautiful Israeli bible on a mantle at the entrance to our house.

When Klaus met Sara, she told him about being a concentration camp survivor of Auschwitz-Birkenau and how much she had suffered, losing her parents, grandmother, and all the other family members. Klaus listened with great attention as if it were the first time he had met a survivor and heard the horrendous stories first hand, face to face.

Klaus and Peter were good guests. We warmly received them at our house. Klaus invited us to Brazil for Christmas and New Year's in 1971. We accepted the invitation; Sara and Gil accompanied me.

By the time of our visit, the sale of the McCoy factory was almost finalized and the Mt. Clemens plant was leased out to a Japanese company, so I had more than a social interest in visiting Klaus and his factory.

We spent eight wonderful days with the Schumacher family. They were great hosts. They went out of their way to make us feel at ease, a Jewish American family visiting with a German-Brazilian family. The Schumachers had six children, who also were very friendly. Klaus, Jr., ten years old, and my son Gil, eight, became friends despite the language barrier. Gil did not speak German or Portuguese, and Klaus did not speak English. When Gil was asked, "How do you guys communicate? Don't your tongues get tired?"

Gil replied, "No, my tongue is not tired; my hands and fingers are. We act out everything we are trying to say to each other."

The year 1971 was the first time we had experienced such an extravagant celebration for Christmas through New Year's. For example, we were invited to the famous South American Gaucho Barbeque, in the backyard of the Schumachers' residence. The beer, the music, and the general atmosphere were overwhelming. The Brazilian/German music, the lighting, and the flickering flames of the barbeque large enough to cook three hundred steaks at a time added to the atmosphere.

There was a floating dance floor in the large swimming pool in the backyard of Klaus's spacious home and garden. Because of the weather in Brazil at the time some people even swam in pool.

The Schumachers had close to one hundred guests for Christmas and New Year's. Klaus was the host and also the life of the party that went on to the early hours of the morning.

Our first meeting was a turning point in my life, and I am sure it was the same in his life. Neither of us had imagined in even our wildest dreams that a close friendship of mutual respect and confidence could ever develop between a Jewish man who had fought the Nazis of Germany during World War II, fighting everything the Nazi philosophy stood for and a German who served in Hitler's military.

I drew a difference between an individual and the leaders of those dark pages in the history of mankind, despite the scope of the war that resulted in the murder of approximately six million Jews and five million non-Jews.

In 1939, the Hitler regime declared war on European countries, such as Poland, Czechoslovakia, The Netherlands, Belgium, Great

Britain, and France followed by Yugoslavia in April 1941 and the Soviet Union in June of 1941. They were fighting under the flag and slogan *"Deutschland überall"* ("Germany over all nations"). Before the allies defeated the German war machine and the Axis powers, a total altogether of fifty-five million civilians and military were killed.

Who would believe these mind boggling numbers? Unfortunately the facts and the numbers are recorded not only in Germany and other countries' archives but also in blood and on many monuments and graves. The names of millions are carved in stone. Furthermore, over half a million surviving Jewish witnesses from concentration and death camps, bunkers, and forests can attest to their tragic experiences of those days.

Knowing this did not stop me from believing in an individual, regardless of the fact that he or she was of German, Austrian, or Japanese descent.

History has recorded throughout hundreds and thousands of years that a new page is being written after every tragic event. I chose to believe that there is only one way we can rebuild from the ashes, from the tragic events. Remember: Never forget the past. However, the future must be built on dialogue, trust, and understanding among people. Learning from the tragic past is the foundation of a bridge to the future.

I felt a sense of accomplishment as I saw the good personal relationship between the second generations of the Schumachers and the Pauls, in particular between Klaus, Jr. and Gil, my youngest son.

After studying ceramic engineering in Germany for a year, Klaus, Jr. moved to the U.S. and lived with us in our house in Philadelphia for about six months, while studying English intensely. Klaus, Jr. had to pass an exam before he was accepted to Clemson University (one of the best ceramic universities in the U.S.) from where he graduated in

1988. After graduation he returned to Brazil joining the management team of the family and business, Ceramarte.

In 1954, Klaus had built his home in a small town, Rio Negrinho, Santa Catarina, on the grounds of his ceramic factory, which grew to become the largest beer stein producer in the world, Ceramarte.

Klaus, born in Germany in 1925, was a self-educated intellectual, who followed the daily political and economical events around the world and read many history, science, and engineering books, in German and English. He became concerned about world population growth, sources of energy, and worldwide shortages of the water and decided to acquire a farm about fifty kilometers from his house where neither traffic nor roads exist, in an isolated wooded area.

In 1988, Klaus decided to engineer and build four environmentally friendly homes on the farm (three bedrooms each). The houses were built so that the entrance was on street level, and the rest of the houses was several feet below the ground. During the summer the homes are naturally cooled. During the winter they are warm. From a distance a person would see four man made hills which the homes were sunk into.

The well that he dug was to supply sufficient water for the four homes, in addition to a natural water reserve and a fish pond. The farm grew vegetables such as tomatoes, cucumbers, corn, and mushrooms. It had many livestock: fifty to one hundred pigs, chickens, cows, and horses. The idea was to sustain himself with no dependence on outside suppliers. Furthermore, Klaus had an arsenal of weapons, pistols, rifles, and automatic machines guns. Thus he is prepared for any eventuality.

He built these homes over twenty years ago. The first house was for his wife and him, two others for his grown up children, and one Klaus made available for my family—just in case.

The first years he spent only long weekends and holidays on the farm. In 2006, Klaus, Sr. decided to spend half his days in the factory, devoting his time to research and new product development, and the other half days he would spend at his farm. He built possibly the largest privately owned satellite antenna dish in the world.

Klaus built a concrete foundation for the antenna about two hundred feet high, well anchored deep in the ground to withstand any eventual weather conditions. The dish itself is about thirty-six feet in diameter. One of Klaus's hobbies is to tune in to TV broadcastings from half way around the world from Germany, U.K., France, U.S., Russia, Austria, Hungary, Poland, and all Latin American countries, such as Argentina, Chile, Colombia, Peru, and Paraguay. Klaus speaks German, Portuguese, Spanish and since 1994 English.

Klaus likes the open fresh air on the farm, the quiet surroundings for his reading, and his principle toy: the television with almost worldwide reception.

Chapter 62
Klaus, The Pioneer

Klaus is not only self educated and a pioneer in the ceramic business, constantly involved in research of new technologies, but he also designed and built the factory buildings as well as the production lines and the kilns used to fire the products. At first Klaus built a relatively small factory with three bays. However, he had the vision and hope in mind for expansion.

After we started to sell his products in the U.S., Klaus expanded bay by bay, building by building, as needed to meet the sudden growth of sales. At a certain point, he needed to build across the street from his first factory, so he designed and built a connecting tunnel under the street, to be able to move products from one section of the factory to the other, without traffic interruption, and to protect the product from strong rains which occurred during the winter season.

Because Klaus had built his residence in the back yard of the factory, he was on call 24/7. His house was spacious: a large country home, large swimming pool in the back yard, and a barbeque pit to accommodate three hundred steaks at one time. The outdoor patio shed housed an official size ping-pong table where we played games with Klaus, his children, and many guests.

The barbeque was used on many occasions and celebrations such as May 1, Labor Day, when all the employees were invited for steak, hot rolls, and unlimited cold beer. In the backyard, there were enough seats for over one thousand people; the others found their places on the grass between the trees. In addition to the employees, Klaus always invited the other manufacturers in town, as well as local and national government officials.

Over the years Klaus made special friendships with the Brazilian Air Force. Klaus was made an honorary air force general. Several high ranking officers, including generals, flew in for the May 1 event. The highlight was the Air Force Aerobatic Unit, *Fumansa*, that flew in with several planes and put on a special acrobatic show flying over the factory and town. This was always a special treat for the many kids of the employees and the grownups alike.

Klaus also designed and built a large dance hall with a wooden floor, enclosed with a heavy green canvas. Specially treated straw covered the roof, which from the outside looked like a Japanese pagoda where the large orchestra, dressed in traditional *Bayerische Lederhosen*, played German and Brazilian music loud and clear and with good rhythm

Klaus's house was like a revolving door, open to neighbors, many friends, the pastors and priests of all churches, regardless of their denomination. Klaus himself is an atheist; however, that did not stop him from supporting the churches. Most visits were after work hours, so this became a social gathering. Klaus had an open bar, a good selection of wines, cold beer in the fridge, on standby were the whiskeys and vodkas, liquors, and Myers Rum, one of Klaus's favorites (the rum was my pleasure to supply him). My favorite was the cold Steine-Hage, a typical German drink. To top it off were the national drinks of Brazil—the Cachaça and Caipirinha —made as a lemonade drink and the favorite of most U.S. visitors. There were many empty bottles in his back yard, so the genius architect Klaus incorporated over two thousand bottles in a wall when he built an extension to his recreation room. This was a masterpiece and reflected the number of bottles consumed by Klaus and his guests.

I must note that during my monthly visits with Klaus for years we ourselves had emptied a few bottles of wine and other spirits. It became a habit for us to meet every evening during my stay for a drink, which almost always turned into numerous drinks into the late hours of the evening. We analyzed and discussed the events of the day in the world of politics and economics and our ongoing business issues, for example, new product developments. These brainstorming sessions were most effective, leading to many innovations in Ceramarte's production methods.

Klaus was also an active leader in his town. For many years he was the president of the local hospital that he had helped to build. As the town's biggest employer, at its peak 1200 employees, he was concerned with the well being of his employees. Ceramarte had a full time nurse on the premises as well as doctors and dentists attending his employees. He provided them with free dental care.

Klaus was also founder and president of a local Rotary Club for many years. Klaus had initiated the building of a motel that would be owned by the Rotary for the purpose of having a social club for Rotary members and a meeting place for other social gatherings. This "Park Hotel" was the only lodging place in Rio Negrinho, serving the buyers, salespeople, and visitors that came to town.

During the following thirty years other more modern hotels were built in the bigger neighboring town of Sao Bento; therefore, competition became strong. Because business was slow, the Rotary owned motel was put up for sale. Klaus purchased the hotel and gave it to his oldest daughter Karin to own and manage.

Karin and her husband, Reiner, an industrial design engineer who had emigrated from Germany, did a great job giving the motel a facelift on the inside and the outside. Reiner changed the name to "Hotel Pousada" (the resting place). They fixed up a suite for my wife, Sara, and me because we were frequent visitors. A bottle of Steine Hage, my favorite schnapps, was always in my refrigerator. Reiner turned the Pousada into a landmark, with an unusual eight-foot sized hand-carved wooden statue, a mini golf course, new lighting, and a hot water tank. The motel was clean, spic and span. The food was always delicious; Karin was the chef. The prices were right. The bar had the best selection of liquors, wine, and beer in town.

First time visitors to this hotel had three obstacles to deal with. One was the special keys to open or lock the entry doors to the rooms. When Klaus purchased the motel, he changed the thin fragile doors to typical thick sound proof doors. The thickness of the doors were about twelve inches; however, there were no doors like this in the entire country, so Klaus had to fabricate the special locks and keys. Mechanically they were so tricky that no guest knew how to use the room key.

The second obstacle was the mechanism of the sliding window: half of the heavy window frame was stationery; the other half moved, but to open the window, guests had to use both hands to push the window into an open position. The problem was that the window never locked properly in the open position. In time guests become experts. Some of the guests learned the hard way, like one of our friends the V.P. of Toys R Us, Marty Fogelman. He tried to deal with the window mechanism until the heavy window dropped onto his four fingers, followed by a hysterical screaming, and a painful call for help from his room, "I lost my fingers on my right hand, O my G-d! My golf fingers, O my G-d!" He kept repeating these words, while blood was gushing from his hand all over his shirt and pants.

Marty called to me, "Help! My golf fingers!"

I was in the next room, and, fortunately, Karen who was still at the bar came running to help. We took Marty to a first aid emergency

223

room, which was almost directly across from the motel. Karen, a registered nurse, stopped the bleeding before the doctor could attend to Marty's hand.

Marty wound up with twelve stitches.

"Oh, my G-d," Marty kept repeating. "I am supposed to play in a company golf tournament at home in a couple of days." Marty's injury from the window took six weeks to heal completely.

The third obstacle in the small motel (thirty-two rooms) was the shower. Because there was no hot water tank in the motel, the cold water flowed through electrical wires; therefore, it took a few minutes for the coils to heat up in order to take a shower. This wasn't too bad unless the guest of the motel was six feet or taller. At that height, the six foot tall person's head would reach the open electric wires that were hanging in the shower. If he stood in a puddle of water naked, suddenly he would jump from the electric shot. He would then try to adjust the shower head and would take the chance of being electrocuted. This was quite dangerous, but, fortunately, no one was killed. However, many experienced the shocks of a homebuilt motel, built with no permits or safety guidelines. This was a one of a kind experience.

Chapter 63
Business in Brazil

After our return home I found out that the sale of the McCoy Factory had been completed. I was invited by the new chairman, Bernie Gurlac, to stay on as marketing director.

I respectfully declined the offer. Fresh in my mind was Brazil, Klaus, and the potential with Ceramarte's products as well as the potential to develop new products. I contacted a friend and business acquaintances in Chicago, Harold Roman. Harold owned a ceramic factory in Mayfield, Kentucky, specializing in whisky bottles and ceramic lamp bases.

We knew each other well because I used to supply him products to supplement the needs of his growing business from the Nelson McCoy Factory. At this time, Harold offered me a position in his organization. In addition to the ceramic business, Harold was involved in other successful ventures.

I told him, "No, thanks, Harold. I have other ideas. In Brazil."

Harold asked, "Brazil? What's in Brazil?"

I replied, "I'll tell you when we meet the next time you are in New York."

A few days later we had our meeting in New York at the Plaza Hotel in Central Park. A diversified business man with "deep Pockets, and strong financing," Harold was anxious to hear from me about Brazil, and specifically Ceramarte.

I shared with Harold my findings. I told him that I had liked the people I met in Brazil, particularly at the Ceramarte factory. I explained that I had time and some money to start a new venture, and I wanted him to be my first customer.

I told him, "We will make you better products at a considerable lesser price than I was supplying you from McCoy."

Harold, who was a quick thinker and decision maker, said, "Let's start a new company to handle the Brazilian business 50%/ 50%. We will set up offices in New York; you will be the president of the company."

I had known Harold for a few years, so I said, "Let me think about this. I will get back to you."

Since I was in New York, I decided to make a visit to the Brazilian Consulate Trade Division, where I met the representative in charge of promoting Brazilian trade with the U.S., Marlena Sole. Ms Sole was friendly and anxious to facilitate contacts between U.S and Brazilian business people.

I explained to Marlena about my background in the ceramics business, and the recent visit by Klaus Schumacher of Ceramarte Brazil to the factory, Nelson McCoy Pottery in Roseville, Ohio. Marlena told me about the list she had of other major ceramic factories in Brazil.

Marlena said, "Mr. Paul, I am so pleased to meet you. As a matter of fact I had heard of you and the two factories you are in charge of. Your timing could not be better, Mr. Paul; in two weeks the first Consumer Product Brazilian Trade Show will open in Brussels, Belgium. You must go there. You will be surprised to see ceramics, glass, furniture, textiles, candy, and shoes." Marlena handed me an invitation to the trade fair with a list of over 500 exhibitors.

She continued, "I particularly want you to meet my friend Isa Weiss, who owns one of the largest ceramic factories in Brazil, specializing in hand painted kitchen items, such as cookie jars, turkey platters, flower pots, candy dishes, and other giftware. Besides that Isa is a very attractive lady and speaks English." Marlena told me about an unsuccessful visit Isa had in New York a week before the fair trying to sell her products.

After I had looked through the long list of exhibitors and the variety of products being exhibited, I decided to travel to Brussels to attend the fair. Arriving at the fair, I was very impressed with the opening ceremonies by the Brazilian Minister of Trade and Mr. Benedito Morera, the director of CASEX, the export arm of the Brazilian Government.

The Brazilian Government had made a major effort to bring a significant number of manufacturers to tell the business world that Brazil stands for more than coffee and meat exports. The exhibit was very impressive. Attendance was strong from European countries but not from the U.S. I was a welcome guest everywhere I visited. The display fixtures, the lighting, and the large variety of merchandise were overwhelming. I was very glad I had attended.

More than the merchandise, the friendly people of Brazil impressed me. They were eager to export; however, they had no knowledge of competitive pricing, packaging requirements, the special product requirements in different countries, particularly in the U.S. markets.

The exhibitors were pushing the same product that they were selling on the Brazilian market. It took me three long days trying to explain the American consumers' taste and that even sizes and colors were different from theirs. I needed to explain and emphasize the many changes, such as design and quality improvements, that would have to be made in their factories. The prices they quoted in most cases were almost as high as our retail pricing in the U.S.; therefore, they had to be lowered substantially.

Chapter 64
Primex Is Born

When I was back in the U.S., I contacted Harold Roman for a follow up meeting. This time he invited me to Chicago.

We met at 10 AM when I updated Harold about my successful trip to the Brazilian Fair and a return visit to Klaus of Ceramarte. I presented Harold with details of the preliminary agreements with Klaus. He listened with great interest. Harold reminded me of his offer to set up a new company, which I already had a name for: Primex International Trading Corp. Why Primex? P from Paul, R from Roman, Harold's last name, IM from import, and EX from export.

Harold had given serious thought to this partnership. He had placed a call to his attorney in Chicago to meet with us, if possible, at 2 PM. The attorney was available. During the lunch hour we discussed more details. I agreed in principle to the partnership, knowing that Harold could become a very valuable customer for Brazilian produced products.

The attorney had prepared an agreement of intent to form the Primex International partnership with 50%-50% shares with me as the President. We each agreed to invest $100,000 dollars. The final agreement was signed thirty days later.

My next challenge was to find decent office space in the area where other importers and manufacturers were located. Within a couple of days I noticed an ad in the *New York Times* with a picture of a new showroom building at 41 Madison Avenue, just one block from the well-known gift mart-building at 225 Fifth avenue. I immediately headed over to the location and saw a beautiful thirty-story building. I contacted the rental agent, Harvey Richter, who told me the company was accepting applications from potential tenants; however, the interior of the building would not be ready for 90 days.

Harvey's rental office was on the completed 3rd floor. I turned to Harvey, telling him I needed an office immediately.

I asked, "Can I share part of your space?

Harvey was surprised at my request.

I explained, "Harvey, I started a new company and I need a small space to begin the business."

Harvey looked around. Walking and measuring the space with his shoes, he said, "I can give you approximately 800 square feet."

My next question was, "How much?"

Harvey gave me an excellent deal because I was ready to sign a three year lease once the building's interior was finished.

Harvey had asked me about the size of the space I was looking for.

I replied, "Approximately 5000 square feet."

He responded, "Would you consider the 13th floor?

I said, "Why not? I know the number 13 is considered an unlucky number in the U.S. but I don't think that."

Harvey showed me the stack of leases he already had from companies such as Rosenthal China and Crystal of Germany, Haeger Pottery, Pfaltzgraff pottery, and others.

We made a preliminary agreement; however, Harvey needed approval of our lease from his boss. I was given a special rental cost on the 13th floor. For me the number 13 was a lucky number: Sara and I married on the 13th, and my beautiful daughter, Dahlia, was born on the 13th. It took me a couple of weeks to hire a secretary, to get a couple of phone lines, and to buy some furniture for the small space.

I called Harold told him we were in business in a great location.

Harold said, "Good luck, Ernest. Next week I am coming to New York. I will visit you then. I look forward to seeing you."

1975, NYC: Ernest in his Primex office

Chapter 65
My Baby

Harold had a strong profitable ceramic business of his own: Roman Ceramics. In Mayfield, Kentucky, he manufactured whisky collector's bottles for the major distilleries.

Because I was his major contract supplier at the McCoy Factory, I presented to him this opportunity: the bottle business to Ceramarte and the lamp-based business to Ceramica Weiss, another company I was dealing with. Harold was actually glad to hear of new suppliers in South America, especially with better quality and better prices.

A couple of days later Harold called me from the offices of McCormack Distilleries in St. Louis, Missouri. He told me, "We have the possibility of a sizable order, if we can meet the strict quality requirements. The project is to reproduce the logo of the thirty football (soccer) teams on ceramic bottles. The sensitive issue is to reproduce the exact team colors; this requires considerable hand painting. I cannot commit to these orders to be produced in my factory in Mayfield. Can you do it in Brazil?"

My reply was, "Yes."

Then I asked him for details, size, capacity of the bottles, price objective, packaging, delivery time.

I was as excited as Harold, a potential order for over a half million dollars. Harold committed to the order based on my say so. On the one hand, he was reluctant to make this commitment; on the other hand, he was excited.

Harold flew in from St. Louis to New York that same afternoon. He had a handmade, painted, finished sample with him (prepared by the customer's head designer) and colored art work with detailed line drawings of the other twenty-nine team figures. Harold had had previous experience with this customer; therefore, he felt sure he would be given the order if we showed them a good sample. Looking at this huge project, my first project, I decided to fly to Brazil. I called Klaus in Brazil, advising him of my coming with an exciting potential project.

On Saturday evening I flew to Brazil on VARIG (an acronym for *Viação Aérea RIo Grandense*), the leading Brazilian international airline. After a ten hour flight, I arrived in Sao Paulo at 7AM, and made connecting flight at 8:45 AM to the city of Curitiba, in the state of Paraná, Brazil. Klaus picked me up at the airport.

We were both very anxious. At the airport, we entered the first restaurant we saw. I opened the valuable package with the art work and the one hand-painted sample we had received from the customer.

Klaus said, "Ya! It is totally different from our existing product (a long pause); however; we will make it. I accept the challenge."

We hurried with the precious project to the factory. We arrived at Klaus's house on the factory grounds, where we had a good Brazilian lunch.

It was then Sunday at 2 PM. Sunday or no Sunday, Klaus called up his product development person, his manager of the decorating department, and the model maker—his wife Ettie Schumacher.

Klaus started the meeting, saying, "We all need to look at this project as a life time opportunity to open the U.S market."

My comments were, "We must have a sample ready within ten days (normally it took a minimum of thirty days). If the sample is approved, we will need to start delivering within ninety days and complete the project within six months. The initial order is for 60,000 pieces, with a potential increase (depending on presales) for up to 75,000 pieces."

Harold had told me that the customer was willing to pay a maximum of $6.00 dollar a unit, including packaging, F.O.B. at Port Brazil. The pricing issue was discussed confidentially with Klaus.

Ettie started to work on the first model immediately, on worked through Sunday afternoon into late evening. It usually takes precise detailed work for ten to fourteen days to make a model from which production molds will be produced. She finished the model in a little less than three long days and nights.

In the meantime, I had decided to stay in Brazil, to hand carry the samples back with me. I returned to the other company Ceramica Weiss to see the progress they were making on the two orders and to coordinate the next steps and to prepare new samples for Avon Cosmetics, another new project I had hand carried.

The Weisses were producing the two orders. They themselves could not believe their improvement in efficiency. The production more than doubled per person just by producing thousands of pieces per order per item versus domestic orders at six pieces per order. The consistency of the quality was also marginally improved.

Isa and Leopoldo said, "These look like good orders for us— even at the low prices. Do you think Mr. Paul we could get more orders like this?"

I answered, "Let's see when you get close to completing this order."

Unfortunately, I did not have the same good feeling about this factory that I did with Klaus's. I was pleasantly surprised that the Weisses did meet the shipping date of 90 days.

The Primex success was the success of the factories. The word got around; therefore, the Brazilian government export office, Casex, often directed interested companies to export their products through Primex.

The Ceramarte sample of vodka bottles turned out great. Everyone was as happy as I was, waiting in the factory at the end of the kiln to have the fired final sample in my hands. I congratulated Klaus.

I told him, "The sample is superb."

I had called Harold in Missouri and suggested meeting him in St. Louis at the customer's office. Harold agreed. He made a call, and the meeting was confirmed with the development people at McCormick, including the president of the company. When all had arrived, I gently opened the sample, placing it carefully in front of the president. This project was sizable! The president called the sample "my baby."

The sample was approved; the written order was issued. Harold and I said "Mazel Tov" to each other.

The first order was completed on time. The sales of this ceramic bottle filled with vodka produced by McCormick distillery sold better than projected. Some of the stronger teams sold more than double the forecast. When we were into the second half of production, we received an additional order for 24,000 pieces. The order was very profitable for the factory and Primex.

Chapter 66
The Rumpf Project

Among the first projects I took to Ceramarte was Rumpf. Two brothers from San Francisco, Steve and Norman, came up with an idea and designs for six rustic looking tankards, ones that looked as if they had been carved out of a trunk of wood with carved 3-dimensional handles.

I took the project to Klaus in Brazil. Ceramarte developed new samples, interpreting the designs to everyone's satisfaction. I submitted the samples to our customers; they loved the detailed execution.

As this was a large project both for the Rumpf Company and us, I invited both brothers to visit with me in Brazil where the factory is located. They were very impressed with the warm Brazilian reception. The Churrasco barbeque was on the charcoal, and cold Brazilian beer was on tap. After several beers, we showed our guests the factory. They were overwhelmed; therefore, an order for over half a million dollars was placed. Ceramarte rushed to make more samples to send to the offices of Rumpf in San Francisco, so they could have their order confirmed by their customer.

Ceramarte executed the initial order on time, with exceptional quality. Before the customer received the final shipment of the first order, we had received an additional order for the same quantity as the first one. It was altogether a remarkable experience. Klaus Schumacher and Ceramarte again made history.

There was a third order for about $200,000, which was to be ready to ship upon advice from Rumpf.

Suddenly I received a call from Steven, the managing director of Rumpf: "I have bad news. Disaster news."

Steven told me that during a routine visit to the store by the J.C.P. vice president, he ordered all store managers to stop the sales of the Rumpf products.

He said, "Get rid of the inventory in the stores and warehouse. Cancel all outstanding orders. This merchandise does not meet the standards of the J.C.P. Company. The product borders on pornography."

In addition to the tankards from Ceramarte, on the same display shelf, Rumpf had sold to J.C.P. men's and women's underwear printed with jokes and slogans that provoked the V.P. to order the discontinuation of the entire Rumpf program.

Fortunately there was little merchandise left since this took place six months after the beginning of the project. From Ceramarte's point of view there were no financial consequences. Rumpf Company honored all their commitments; however, along with Ceramarte, Rumpf entered into litigation against the J.C.P. Company, which dragged on for over a year.

Chapter 67
Avon Products

Because Avon Products was an old customer of mine from McCoy and already supplying Ceramica Weiss products, I called Jimmy Flynn the buyer for Avon for an appointment.

Jimmy loved this new concept of collectible beer steins. He called into the meeting the product development manager, Ernie Califano, who was wildly excited with the beer steins' potential catalog sales.

During lunch, we continued to discuss the new opportunities. I gave them an updated report on Brazil in particular on the Ceramarte factory and Klaus Schumacher's integrity.

Suddenly the product development manager surprised us, saying, "We need management approval to sell a vessel for alcohol—beer."

After lunch we called the Executive Vice President, Andy Swanty. Jimmy asked him about Avon policy on selling beer steins.

Andy said, "We never sold beer steins in the past. What kind of steins?"

Jimmy tried to explain.

Andy said, "I would like to see them."

We took the elevator to the executive floor, where Andy's secretary ushered us in. I had met Andy once before at an Avon Christmas party.

Our reception was cordial and professional. Andy looked at the six samples. He said enthusiastically, "I like them. I am a collector of German and English steins. These are made in Brazil?" He was surprised at this, asking, "What is the price?"

I replied, "Depending on quantity, size, style, and packaging requirements, the prices range from \$4.75 to \$6.00, which are workable prices."

Andy agreed to investigate further: "I will check with the president and the legal department about our selling steins."

After a couple of days had passed and we had heard nothing from Avon, I called the vice president directly.

"Andy, I will be in your building tomorrow. Can I drop off a few samples to add to your collection?"

Andy responded, "Yes, come over."

These were different from the ones I had presented to the buyer. Andy was interested in hearing more details about the Brazilian factories and owners. However, he did not accept my gift; ethically he could not accept gifts, but he thanked me anyway. Then I asked about the decision about Avon selling steins.

His reply was, "Give me a couple more days and call me. I like the concept."

Before I walked out of the office, I said, "If the answer is no, maybe you could suggest using the stein as a packaging item. You could drop an after shave lotion in a plastic bottle in each stein."

Andy said, "Good idea, Ernie. I will try my best because I believe it would be a good new category for us. After all, we have over 400,000 sales people out there—mostly Avon 'ladies.'"

One day later Andy told Ernie Califano, the product manager, and the buyer, Jimmy Flynn about management's decision. Ernie called me to share the good news. Avon management had given the green light; however, the stein would be used as a container.

"Great! Good," was my reply.

Ernie Califano was given instructions to design an exclusive Avon stein. Ernie had a design ready in a couple of weeks, when he presented the artwork to his management for approval. Approval was given, and Ernie called me with this good news.

As I had a few additional steins, I invited Ernie and Jim for lunch in our building's five star restaurant. They accepted the invitation and also visited our small showroom. They were quite impressed with the potential of growing new business for Avon in new categories.

Ten days later I was on my way to Brazil. This time my main objective was Ceramarte. Ettie Schumacher as before made a super effort to make the model for the new Avon stein. So within twelve days I was back at Avon, presenting three interpretations and options.

Avon approved one of the samples. Our first order was for 100,000 pieces at $3.75 each. As the stein was photographed and shown in the Avon catalog's Father's Day edition and circulated to the 400,000 Avon sales personnel, the order was increased to 200,000 pieces.

When the stein began selling and first shipment was delivered, the order was increased to 300,000 units. Before finishing the existing order, Avon was in a serious over-sale situation; therefore, the order was increased to 450,000 units. This time because of their commitment to have Father's Day orders delivered before Father's day, we were instructed by Avon to ship by air at their expense.

There was a shortage of air cargo space available, but with the assistance of Avon Transportation International, Avon contracted two jumbo air carriers, allowing Ceramarte to ship the entire order on time, with not one quality claim. We had also shipped a total of 40,000 steins to Avon Germany, Avon U.K., Avon Canada and Avon Australia.

Because of these orders, Klaus had to expand the factory month after month, from less than a hundred people when we started to five hundred people only six months later, and the factory kept growing. Klaus built the addition and also his own kilns, so he had everything under control.

The second stein for Avon was developed for Christmas, 1973, the Steamship stein, bigger than the first stein. The price was up to $4.90. In view of the successful results from the first stein, Avon decided to sell the stein on its own, with no after-shave lotion.

The first order for this stein was 250,000 to be delivered in six months for Christmas. The quality and workmanship was our greatest advertising tool. Avon had very strict quality controls. If we could satisfy Avon's requirements, we could sell to any other company, retailer, or manufacturer, in the world. I made monthly trips to Brazil, to check the quality and production rate to assure timely deliveries.

This second stein blew us away. No one could have imagined the sales of this stein. We made history; never before had Avon or any other company sold a similar product at $24.95 with 1,150,000 sold in the U.S. and another 50,000 to Avon Canada, Germany, U.K., and Australia.

Again Klaus was challenged to increase his production capacity daily, and he did. Ceramarte won Avon's annual award for being the most valuable supplier. The sales of these steins have continued for over twenty-five years. The quantities have dropped over the years, and collectible beer steins are no longer as popular.

Chapter 68
Hand Painted Products by Weiss

I had met Isa Weiss and her husband, Leopoldo, at the Brazilian World Trade Fair in Brussels, Belguim, and had become very interested in their large variety of hand painted ceramics. However, their prices were double, compared to similar products being imported to the U.S. from Italy, Portugal, Japan, Mexico, and other countries.

After a meeting at their exhibit we decided to meet at 7 PM for dinner to discuss further what I saw as their company's potential.

Isa had made the rounds a few days before the fair, meeting with potential customers in the U.S. with the help of Marlena. She came back embarrassed and empty handed. Isa's failure helped me to emphasize that their prices and designs were not suitable for the U.S. market. They quickly realized that my practical experience could help them penetrate the U.S. market. I knew the potential customers and how to accomplish this.

I decided to visit the Ceramica Weiss factory near São Paulo in the city of São José dos Campos in Brazil. The Weisses had already returned home from a disappointing and costly trip, with no orders. The factory, over 200,000 square feet, was in an old building. Mostly everything was handmade; there was no machinery to speak of. Walking through the factory with Isa and Leopoldo, I started to analyze the entire manufacturing process, starting with raw materials through every stage of production, the furnaces, quality control, packaging, and shipping.

The picture became clear to me the first day of my visit. I took many notes at the factories.

Afterwards we sat for a few hours and talked. I asked them about their labor costs, the social benefits for the workers, and the cost of energy, an important component and cost in the ceramic industry.

During dinner at their home, we continued the question and answer session. Leopoldo's father, Leopoldo senior, had joined us because he was in charge of financing. We sat until midnight, when I went exhausted to my room in their house. But I did not go to sleep; I had to plan for the next morning's meeting. My light was on until 3 AM.

By the time of our follow up meeting time the next morning, I had analyzed all my notes and was ready to have a detailed and productive meeting. I realized that with the size of the factory and 300 employees, the total wages would be less than half as much as in the U.S. and lower than other countries such as Japan, Italy, Portugal, and Mexico. It did not take me long to come to some sensible solutions.

I told them, in summary: "You need to make changes in many areas. For export, you must include the cost of special individual packaging as well as the cost of double wall shipping cartons. You must take into consideration the cost of stricter quality control. If you are willing to commit to my suggestions, I am willing to represent your company on an exclusive bases. I will work closely with you to open the U.S. markets. I have good contacts. One more detail: it looks to me at first glance that your selling price per piece will have to be 50% lower than your domestic prices. The Brazilian customers have to pay the higher prices if they want to have this product."

There were no options, no competition, no other large domestic producers, and no imports from other countries. Imports to Brazil were restricted and penalized with duties payable of over 100% of the

F.O.B. cost of products. In the U.S., we had to compete with many countries.

The Weiss family agreed in principle to put their future business in my hands. Leopoldo suggested having a test period of six months. I had confidence in myself. I committed to sending them some samples of American made products, for shapes, sizes, colors, and packaging. I told them once you make the samples, one of you, Leopoldo or Isa, should hand carry them. We will go together to make the first sales call.

A month later Isa arrived with the samples, which were beautiful. I took Isa to Chicago for the first appointment—to the Sears headquarters.

The Sears' buyer was a friend of mine. He looked at the samples and liked them a lot. He called in his merchandise manager. He agreed with the buyer to place an order for 20,000 cookie jars at $3.00 per piece, F.O.B. port of Brazil. Sears would open a letter of credit to Ceramica Weiss for a total of $60,000 dollars, payable upon the loading of the merchandise on the ship.

The second order we received was from Montgomery Ward (also in Chicago) for a canister set and a soup tureen, for a total of $50,000 dollars.

We returned to New York where we visited Avon products at 9 West 59th street. I knew the buyer, Jim Flynn, for I had sold McCoy products to him. We showed him the hand-painted products. Jim liked the samples, so he called in Ernie Calafano, his new product development manager. Ernie's reaction was positive. He saw the potential for new products designed and produced exclusively for Avon.

We also visited the buyers of Macy's, Gimbels, S. Klein, and others. The feedback from all was positive.

I then took Isa to visit stores to show her similar handmade products from Italy, Spain, Portugal, and Mexico. I brought to her attention the quality and prices, explaining how we arrive at the F.O.B. price.

Isa returned to Brazil with the orders totaling $110,000 and the challenge of producing the orders on time, with quality products that were well packaged.

I saw Isa next in January 1974. I had invited her to the Chicago Houseware Show, beginning on January 13. The weather in Chicago was forecasted to be 20° below, with the wind chill factor at 40° below. Our hotel and the exhibition Center were on Lake Michigan.

Prior to Isa's departure from Brazil, I had called to tell her about the extremely cold weather in Chicago, advising her to bring warm clothes, in particular warm thermal underwear. Her first reaction to my phone call was laughter; in fact, she couldn't stop laughing.

At the time of our phone conversation the temperature in Brazil was 88° Fahrenheit. Isa kept on laughing. When she arrived at the Chicago airport, we whisked her away in a warm cab and took her to the hotel. Obviously the hotel was nice and warm.

After breakfast, the following morning at 8:30 AM, everyone headed over to the exhibit, a walk of about 500 feet across a major highway. It didn't take more than two minutes walking for Isa's eyes to tear. A few steps later her eyelashes froze to each other.

She screamed, "O God, I am blind. Please take me back to the hotel or I will die." She was definitely not laughing anymore.

We returned to the hotel, where my wife, Sara, was dressing. Sara took over the handling of Isa. First, Sara sat her down and compressed a lukewarm wash cloth on her eyes, to help her open them. This took five minutes. Sara offered her a warm cup of tea to warm and relax her since Isa's entire body had been shaking for at least ten minutes.

Sara looked at the clothes Isa was wearing and asked "Didn't you know you were coming to Chicago?"

Isa replied, "I could never have imagined this weather. In Brazil, even during the winter, it is about 60 degrees."

Sara gave Isa one of her warm coats and wrapped Isa's face and head with two large bath towels. We made it across the street to the exhibit. Inside the exhibit, Isa must have had ten cups of hot tea. Although indoors was warm, she feared the cold weather outside.

After the fair opened on Sunday, Isa became more relaxed because her products were selling well. She did learn not to take Chicago's weather for granted.

Business with this factory grew for over fifteen years. Our working relationship with management and the owners was especially good. Within two years, the factory grew in sales from two million dollars per year to about ten million dollars, from three hundred workers to over a thousand.

Then the Weisses started to siphon off funds from the factory, buying fancy imported cars, a leisure yacht, their own bar and restaurant, and a beach front second home. They started to neglect the factory, resulting in a serious deterioration of quality and productivity. This was followed by marital problems between the principal owners and managers, Leopoldo and Isa.

Isa confronted Leopoldo in the presence of her three oldest children.

Isa asked him, "Is this true?

With no hesitation, he answered clearly, "Yes!"

For Isa, to say the least, this was an embarrassing and bitter pill to swallow.

Within less than one year, the breakup of the marriage broke the company financially, for both Isa and Leopoldo were pulling in different directions.

The older kids tried unsuccessfully to step in to save both the marriage and the company. For almost fifteen years, I used to be in the factory and their house almost every other month, for a couple of days. I had a good relationship with Isa and Leopoldo. The kids liked me as well and considered me a close friend of the family.

For me it was sad to witness those arguments, which led to the loss of friends as well as a loss of a good income from sales to companies in the U.S. The factory went bankrupt and was liquidated.

Chapter 69
The Breweries

As business was growing nicely, I approached the various breweries in the U.S.

Prior to the meetings, Klaus and I prepared samples for each of the companies with their logo. We presented German quality workmanship at Brazilian prices. Our prices were less than half of Germany's; the products spoke for themselves. We became known as Ceramarte Primex. The names became synonymous, well known in the industry.

However, the one brewery, the biggest in the world, Anheuser Busch (AB), headquartered in St. Louis, Missouri, was missing from our list of clients. When I made the very first contact, I had been told by Jim Bickle, the buyer, that he had no budget to buy in the category of beer steins. Klaus and I came to the conclusion that the only way we would gain this account was to meet with August Busch, III, the president of the company.

Upon my return to the U.S., I fired off a fax to Mr. Busch, sharing with him our success in selling beer steins to Avon cosmetic company. I requested an appointment for Klaus and me, underlining our ability to create a very exciting program with and for Anheuser Busch. Needless to say, I emphasized the Ceramarte quality and price advantages. It took over three months of persistent follow up on my part. Finally I received a phone call from Mr. Busch's secretary arranging a meeting in St. Louis.

Klaus arrived in New York from Brazil a day prior to our appointment with fifty-four quality collectible samples. We flew from New York into St. Louis, Missouri; however, to our misfortune the airport was shut down because of a dense fog. We had to circle for forty-five minutes.

No delay for a business appointment is pleasant or businesslike, in particular when you are meeting with the head of an important company such as Anheuser Busch (AB). Klaus and I became very concerned. The forty-five minute delay could impact our meeting, even subject it to cancellation.

When we finally landed, John Wade, the director of the promotional product division, noticed we were very concerned about the delay. John calmed us down by saying that he had just spoken to Mr. Busch's secretary; Mr. Busch was also delayed because of the weather conditions.

After a thirty-five minute car ride, we arrived at the headquarters of Anheuser Busch. As we approached the entrance of the building, we saw a helicopter landing on the roof.

John pointed to the helicopter, saying, "That is the big boss; he is just arriving."

We took the elevator to the twelfth floor where our meeting was scheduled to take place.

Mr. Bush's secretary ushered us into the meeting room, where we unpacked our samples, and in walked August Busch, III. Everyone in the room became quiet and tense.

Mr. Busch evaluated our samples one by one; he was very impressed with the quality and overall workmanship. Mr. Busch said: "I am a collector of beer steins myself. These are impressive."

My instantaneous reply was, "We hope you will add these fifty-four pieces to your collection."

"Yeah! Okay. Thank you," was his reply.

Klaus and I had a good feeling about Mr. Busch's reaction. Mr. Busch paused for a minute, looked at his watch, and asked, "What are we here for?"

We were all sitting comfortably looking at the steins while sipping on the water or soft drinks that were being served. The server had mentioned that cold beer was available.

I took charge of the meeting telling Mr. Busch that Ceramarte has been selling beer steins to Avon cosmetic company for a number of years. Their sales were in the hundreds of thousands units per promotion. Every Christmas, a Christmas stein theme, and every father's day a different interesting theme was designed by Avon. As a matter of fact, we had just completed a delivery of the 1977 stein that sold 1,150,000 units. I showed Mr. Busch the Avon samples, the promotional material, and the Avon catalog. To say the least he was very surprised to find out that Avon was selling beer steins, let alone the quantities they were selling.

I turned to Mr. Busch acknowledging that Anheuser Busch as the largest brewery in the world could certainly sell more beer steins than Avon.

Mr. Busch looked at his watch again, interrupting my pitching the steins and Brazil's ceramics. He turned to John, his director in charge of promotions, and asked him directly with a strong voice: "What is the problem? Why are we not selling beer steins?"

Before John had a chance to answer the question, Mr. Busch added: "I want to see action! I want results!"

I further commented that AB was selling millions of promotional products, such as t-shirts, hats, belt buckles, and beach towels, but nothing would be more appropriate than beer steins.

Mr. Busch stopped me, saying, "No more!"

He turned to John and instructed him to go to work on this project immediately.

John replied, "Yes, sir."

Before the forty minute meeting was over, Klaus stated that we would be building an extension to his factory, an Anheuser Busch Pavilion.

Klaus invited Mr. Busch to Brazil because Busch was not only a stein collector but also an enthusiastic promoter of soccer, and Brazil is the land of soccer and beer steins. I thanked Mr. Busch for giving up time from his busy schedule to receive us personally.

After four months and seven meetings, the final stein was approved by AB top management. This was about mid-September 1978. AB still had to develop art work for individual gift boxes. In the interim AB marketing people surveyed their distributors. The initial feedback was good, although the distributors did not know how their customers would react and how many each would buy.

Based on the overwhelming sales on this first project, the quality and the price of a comparable product on the market, and Ceramarte's ability to deliver these large quantities, a decision was made by AB to make the holiday concept stein into an annual program, developing a new stein for each year.

Chapter 70
Brazilian Furniture

The largest Brazilian furniture center, with over two hundred small, medium, and large factories, is located in the town of São Bento Do Sul in the State of Santa Catarina. Because we were already active in Rio Negrinho with Ceramarte, the beer stein factory, only ten miles away, and Oxford ceramics in the same town, we decided to expand into the furniture category.

Furniture was a natural move. The region had many good factories with over 4000 experienced workers. The town, São Bento Do Sul, with a population of over 50,000, is heavily populated by families of German descent that immigrated to the region after World War I.

During our initial survey we were very impressed with the friendly factory owners and their desire to export. Since these factories had never exported, their products were designed for the local market. We quickly realized that to become exporters, the factories had to invest new capital.

The first requirement was to build kilns to dry the wood scientifically. They needed to reduce the humidity from 30% to 7%. None of the factories had the knowledge to build these kilns. We contacted Washington State University for assistance. They were helpful in sending us the required details as well as indicating U.S. suppliers of these kilns.

Once the first kiln was installed in the region, the other factories also were determined to export. In addition to drying the wood, we had to provide the factories with designs of ready to assemble furniture items (RTA.) because the shipping cost of the assembled furniture was prohibitively high. We directed them as to the quality of wood to be used for export, proper sanding, and multi layers of finishings, proper hardware, and protective packaging. It was a major undertaking for Primex; however, we had productive partners.

The State and Federal governments of Brazil were instrumental in reforestation programs. They gave incentives and legislated mandatory practices. For each tree cut down, ten had to be planted. This helped to keep prices stable for the wood used for manufacturing furniture, particularly for pine.

The Brazilian climate gave growers an advantage, for the trees in Brazil grew to maturity in ten years, whereas in the U.S. or Canada it takes twenty years. In addition to furniture, we worked with medium size factories on wood related gift items and accessories, such as jewelry boxes, sewing kits, serving trays, and cigar boxes. One of the specialties of the region was butterflies, a plentiful and wide variety of colorful butterflies.

The butterflies were treated to stabilize them, placed under domed glass in beautiful handmade solid wood frames, and made into wall plaques. To enhance the pictures some dried flower arrangements were combined with the butterflies.

One specific factory in Rio Negrinho, Three Roses, decided to devote its entire production to the butterfly, based on the first orders from the J.C. Penney Company. The butterflies flew off the shelves in all 700 J.C. Penny stores and the catalog. The factory could not make them fast enough.

Two months into the program many thousands had sold. Some shipments of forty-foot containers were on the way. We then received the first complaint from J.C. Penney that some frames were warping and breaking the glass. As if this was not enough, a few days later a complaint came in from J.C. Penney that insects, live insects, were under the glass: "Stop shipping!"

Immediately I flew to Brazil to meet with the owners of the factory to analyze the complaints and the returned samples from J.C.P. It was determined that the dry flowers underneath the glass cultivated the insects. The frames' cracking was a result of improper drying of the wood before the frames were made. The factory's claim was that to keep up with the orders and sales the factory had shortened the drying cycle of the wood. It was an expensive disaster. The claim from J.C. Penney was in the hundreds of thousands of dollars. Sales were stopped, and outstanding orders, cancelled. We all had to face a costly set back. The only positive side was that we learned the hard way: we could not cut corners. Wood is alive; we must know how to treat it.

In 1976, I had the pleasure of meeting Luiz Garcia, who worked for one of the largest furniture factories in Sao Bento: Artefama. Luiz, born in São Bento Do Sul, was a twenty-year-old, self-educated, bright, and ambitious young man. He spoke good English, so he was one of the first export managers in the field.

A few months later, we decided to open a Primex office in São Bento. We interviewed a number of candidates, among them Luiz. He was the most obvious candidate, ambitious and self-confident; therefore, we hired him to become the general manager of our office in São Bento.

When Stewart became involved in the furniture business as president of Primex, he realized the wasted potential in the furniture category. He had built a good team in Brazil as well as in the U.S. Our good friend Steven Konigsberg was and is one of our most accomplished account managers in the furniture category—along with Vasso Unks.

Stewart successfully built the furniture business, selling to some of the biggest companies in the U.S. such as Walmart, J.C. Penney, Pier1 Imports, Meijer Inc., Toys R Us, Crate and Barrel, and many others. Stewart set up a separate division within Primex, establishing a sizable permanent showroom at Highpoint N.C., the largest furniture center in the U.S, participating in the largest International Trade Shows.

During the early years of Primex we were known as a housewares company, exhibiting in the major trade shows, cookware, cutlery, ceramics, plastics, and glassware. Under Stewart's management the company also became known as a major source of furniture from South America. At some point furniture became the most significant part of the business.

Luiz managed the furniture business for about ten years until he decided to venture out on his own. Five years later Luiz and Stewart agreed to combine Primex efforts in São Bento with his company, Planor.

An arrangement was worked out with Luiz, and we have been benefiting from a great working relationship with Planor for many years. As important as the successful growth of the business was, equally important was the friendship that grew between our families. Annette, Luiz's wife, plays an important part in our family and business relations, as does their son Raphael, who joined the company about ten years ago.

Primex-Planor was honored by the manufacturers' association and the community for our important contribution to the growth of exports of furniture and the growth of the town. Over the thirty years of our activity in the region, we managed to bring with us to Brazil many, many of the most important furniture retailers in the U.S., as well as furniture manufacturers. Some made two trips a year, some only made annual trips but repeated these were repeated for many years.

Chapter 71
The Dean of Furniture

One of our most prestigious guests was Nat Ansel, the chairman of the Ethan Allan Companies, based in New Haven, Connecticut. In addition to the four hundred franchised and company-owned stores, Ethan Allan had twelve factories of its own. Mr. Ansel was considered one of the leaders in the furniture business, "the dean."

It was quite an effort to arrange an appointment with him. Only with the assistance of a mutual friend, David Chase, did the meeting materialize. I took a couple of small samples and catalogs with me. Mr. Ansel called the V.P. in charge of purchasing into the meeting. This was their first introduction to Brazilian wood. They were considering buying some small furniture items or components to be supplied to one of their factories.

They selected some folding bath trays and a portable bar to be quoted in quantities of five thousand each. I was very encouraged with the potential of selling just about anything to the Ethan Allan Company. The door was opened! I followed up getting prices from Brazil for the items they had selected. Within four weeks I was invited by the vice president to come back for a follow-up meeting; he liked the samples and the prices. An order was written for one container each. I was happy and grateful.

While I was in the building, I took a chance and called Mr. Ansel (I had no appointment that day). He was in a meeting, but his secretary told me: "I will advise him of your request for a meeting."

Thirty minutes later I was in his office. I thanked him for giving us the opportunity to work with his company.

As I was sitting in his office I was looking around the spacious environment, not only at the size of the office but also at his art collection on the walls, the statues and various art objects on each of the many shelves and tables. From wood carvings to ceramic and glass art, the collection was impressive. Mr. Ansel was very much into arts and collectables. He talked about them with knowledge and passion.

This led us into the conversation about Brazil. I told him about the Ipanema Hippie Market in Rio de Janeiro that takes place each Sunday in the *Praca General Osorio*. This market has everything from good leather, clothes, and jewelry to local artwork and souvenirs. Then I told him about the São Paulo Week and Artisan Market, and he became very interested. At 12:30, he asked me to come with him to lunch at his house. At his home I was introduced to Mrs. Ansel, a charming woman, who welcomed me warmly to her home.

As soon as I walked into the house, I noticed another museum, a rich collection of hand painted art with effects that were totally different for those at his office.

The housekeeper then served lunch. During lunch we continued to talk about Brazil. After lunch both Mr. and Mrs. Ansel walked me through their large living room. I noticed a display of precious and semi-precious stones in a glass jewelry-type display case. Each was marked with the name of the stone, the size, the weight, and country of origin.

I noticed quite a number of Brazilian aquamarine, amethyst, topaz, and emeralds. There was a collection of cat eye shaped oblongs, in addition to a large number of over-sized rough and finished stones. Mr. Ansel told me this was his hobby. The rest belonged to Mrs. Ansel.

This played right into my next topic. I told them about the second largest jewelry company in Brazil: Amsterdam Sour. This company had many stores at airports around the world, as well as in the luxury hotels. They also owned a number of mines in the south and north of Brazil.

I told them that I happened to know this company because we had been doing business with them, buying some semi precious stones, hand carved in the shapes of colorful birds, book ends, ash trays, coasters, and clocks. The owners lived in Rio de Janeiro on the Copacabana Beach. I had had a Shabbat dinner at their home. Above their home in the penthouse, they had an impressive collection of Brazilian precious and semi precious rocks and stones, among them a large cats' eyes collection.

Mr. Ansel suddenly became very interested in Brazil.

I told him, "You have several reasons to visit Brazil: the furniture region in Sao Bento and the sources of Brazilian stones." Mr. Ansel asked me to question the Amsterdam family about the possibility of his visiting their home-museum.

The following day I called Mr. Julias Sour and asked him if he would accommodate me again with a visit. I explained that I would like to bring a visitor with me. Obviously I told him a lot about Mr. Ansel, the chairman of Ethan Allan, a collector of stones and art, as well as a Jewish philanthropist. I explained that they had a lot in common.

Mr. Sour gave me the green light to invite Mr. Ansel to a Friday night Shabbat dinner. I was excited to get back to Mr. Ansel informing him about the invitation.

His secretary called me, and we worked out the itinerary. I planned to leave a week earlier with Sara; therefore, I would receive Mr. Ansel at the Rio airport.

Luiz Garcia, the Primex manager in the furniture area, happened to be in New York. I told him about Mr. Ansel's visit. We coordinated his flight back home, so he could be on the same flight as Mr. Ansel's. I described Mr. Ansel to Luiz: seventy-years old and about 6' 3". I told Luiz to meet him at the VARIG Airline's first class lounge. Luiz arrived at JFK airport two hours early to have an opportunity to meet Mr. Ansel.

Mr. Ansel did not appear in the first class lounge, so Luiz assumed that he was delayed and had boarded at the last minute. The door of the plane closed and still no sign of Mr. Ansel.

The flight arrived in Rio at 6 AM. I saw Luiz among the first class passengers but still no sign of Mr. Ansel. While waiting for Luiz's luggage, I noticed Mr. Ansel's big frame at a distance. He approached the passport control area, took the lane designated for the crew, and walked through with the Brazilian crew without presenting his passport.

Luiz asked Mr. Ansel, "Where were you. I waited for you in the first class lounge."

Nat replied, "Who travels first class? I was traveling coach."

Luiz and I looked at each other embarrassed. Then Luiz headed to the domestic airport to get his flight home to Curitiba. I took Mr. Ansel to the Plaza Hotel in Rio, where I was staying with Sara. After checking in and washing up, we decided to meet for breakfast. It was about 8:30 AM. After breakfast, Sara and I took Mr. Ansel on a few hours sightseeing tour.

After lunch Mr. Ansel chose to relax for several hours. He was tired from the nine hour flight in coach. At about 3:00 PM we met to visit the newest shopping mall in Rio. We visited some furniture stores and jewelry stores.

He was not particularly impressed with the furniture nor the decorative accessories, but he enjoyed visiting the Amsterdam Sour Store as well as their number one competitor, H. Stern Jewelers. We went back to the hotel to rest a little before meeting for dinner at 7:30 PM. Mr. Sour's chauffeured car picked us up.

We had a pleasant conversation at the house of the Sour family. Their two children joined us for the Friday night dinner. It was a delicious dinner. Mr. Ansel felt rested; however, he was anxious to get to the penthouse museum. He could not believe the valuable collection of one of a kind Brazilian rocks. Mr. Ansel pointed to a number of pieces that he wanted to buy for his collection. He was told by Mr. Sour that none of the pieces was for sale. This was his private collection. The more Mr. Ansel looked and was told by Mr. Sour about the uniqueness of each piece, size, and color, the more Mr. Ansel bargained for these pieces for his collection.

During the following two hours, the two tycoons discussed and negotiated. One time, Mr. Ansel turned to Mr. Sour and said, "You would not want me to leave here disappointed, empty handed, would you?"

He pressured Mr. Sour for a price for the twelve pieces he had selected. Mr. Sour softened his position, so before midnight a deal was made. They agreed to a price of $45,000.00.

Mr. Ansel was told that he could not take these with him (which he was anxious to do): "They will be shipped officially to Amsterdam Sour New York offices where you will be able to pick them up within the next twenty days."

A big hand shake and a hug sealed the deal. Mr. Ansel was very content with the dinner and the "dessert": the purchases he had made.

On Saturday we took Mr. Ansel to the Ipanema Hippie Market where he purchased several paintings on canvas, as well as some popular arts and crafts. On Sunday we traveled to the south to the furniture area. The following four days we visited several factories and sawmills.

On the third night of the visit a special banquet, a reception dinner with over two hundred people, was given in honor of Mr. Ansel. Most of the manufacturers and the management personnel attended as well as the mayor of the town and journalists from the city and neighboring towns. Everyone was anxious to hear from Mr. Ansel about the factories he had visited, about the quality and pricing. Most importantly, they wanted his opinion regarding the potential of this region to become a major exporter to his company as well as others.

Mr. Ansel spoke very candidly and directly to all the participants. He started off by saying,

You have a long way ahead of you to become a meaningful exporter to the U.S., in particular at the customer level we sell to. To sell a small accessory like a bed tray, shelving unit, or a portable bar is one thing. To make and sell a complete dining room or bedroom set is another. There is no comparison to our detailed precise workmanship, the final look, and the hardware we use. The finishing touches to your product need much improvement. You have some quality woods like the mahogany and the *cerejeira* (similar to our oak), but your trimmings and particularly the finishing must be improved significantly.

The major difference between us is we use, in some products, inferior solid wood or wood veneers. However, once it is finished, it is beautiful with soft corners, a smooth, silky finish. You use good quality wood but pay no attention to the sharp edges nor the final finish. The final product looks like cardboard and to the touch it seems like cardboard.

I did see some well-designed factories, modern buildings with high ceilings, good daylight lighting, automated Italian and American machinery, and good kilns—these drying facilities are essential, particularly when you export from a warm tropical climate to the U.S.

He finished by thanking the assembled guests for their hospitality; he thanked in particular the Primex people, who were persistent in getting him to Brazil.

Mr. Ansel concluded: "If you apply yourselves, learning to meet the U.S. market requirements, you will succeed. I like what I saw here in Brazil: I like your determination and your willingness to improve, and I like your warm friendship. You have a beautiful country to be proud of. I hope to see some of you in the U.S."

For Primex, Sara, and me, Mr. Ansel's visit was an enjoyable six days. Mr. Ansel invited us to stay with his family. We had a reservation to fly home together. I had already learned the Mr. Ansel had a coach ticket. In Rio I had a good friendship with the VARIG Airline manager; therefore, I was able to get an upgrade for Mr. Ansel, so we could sit next to each other.

As passengers passed Immigration Control, they needed to present their passports, which were stamped next to their entry visas. Suddenly a policeman was holding on to Mr. Ansel's passport, asking him, "When did you arrive in Brazil? From where?" These questions were in Portuguese. I became Mr. Ansel's translator.

His reply was, "I arrived on Friday from the U.S."

The policeman got on the phone and five minutes later two other policemen showed up. Mr. Ansel was under arrest. The police ordered him, "Come with us."

I accompanied him to the local police station. I asked to talk to the officer in charge, so we were ushered into the captain's office. The two policemen handed over his passport telling the officer that Mr. Ansel had entered the country illegally because there was no entry stamp on his passport.

I immediately asked the officer to call the VARIG Airline manager, who arrived within a few minutes. The police told him about Mr. Ansel's illegal entry into Brazil. I realized that the situation was getting out of hand. I told the VARIG manager, Nelson Schmidt, whom I knew well that Mr. Ansel was on an important business trip and could not miss his flight home. Mr. Schmidt had to sign a letter that Mr. Ansel was a respectable U.S. citizen, and he guaranteed his good intentions.

This is what had happened: When Mr. Ansel had arrived in Rio because he was "Mr. Ansel," he had not bothered to stay in the long line with the other arriving passengers. He had passed through in the line reserved for the Brazilian crew members.

We boarded and had a good laugh about his being arrested. He enjoyed the trip back, nine and a half hours in first class. We became good friends. Mr. Ansel passed away in 1982 at the age of seventy-four, four years after our trip.

Chapter 72
Brazilian Sweets

During one of my visits to Brazil, I attended the first major South American Candy and Confectionary Show. I was pleasantly surprised to see so many large producers exhibiting their products.

In making contact with some of the major producers, I tried to find out the reason for this strong industry known neither in the international market nor in the U.S. My finding was that most of the raw materials used to produce these products were made from domestic raw material, plentifully available at relative low prices, such as sugar, cacao beans, milk, and wheat.

The domestic consumption of candy was high throughout South America. This attracted companies such as Nestlé's, Hershey's, Cadbury, and General Foods to invest in South America.

I learned that Ancor, an Argentine company, was the leader in South America. I had the good fortune to befriend the president and chairman of this company, Mr. Fulvio Salvador Pagani. I sat down with him to discuss the possibilities of Primex opening the U.S market for his company.

Mr. Pagani and his export manager, Mr. Zeppa, had visited the U.S. before; however, no major sales were made. Thus, Pagani was very interested in our working with him. Upon my return to our New York office, I had a meeting with Stewart, Gil, Steve, and Herb Briggs. I reported to them about my new discovery, the candy and confectionary business potential. After thorough discussions we decided to set up our own candy company. By U.S. law we had to register the company with the State of Pennsylvania's Agriculture Department. We tossed around ideas for a name for the new company. I suggested Mrs. Paul's candies, Gil suggested Sara's candy. We contacted our patent attorney, Norman Lehrer, and instructed him to apply for registration of either of these two names.

A couple of weeks later we were advised by Norman that neither of those names could be registered: in the case of Mrs. Paul's, the frozen food company objected, and in the case of Sara's, the Sara Lee Company objected.

We were back to square one—no name. Suddenly Stewart discussed with Norman as attorney to attorney, "What about Sara Paul's Candies?" Because that was Sara's full name, there was no objection; therefore, the name was approved and registered.

Then began the development of the individual wrappers and bags. We challenged our in-house art department with development of the packaging; they arrived at a good functional design. After making a survey in the U.S. market, we realized that, for the most part, the South American candy had to be changed to match U.S. produced products. The changes were in flavors (we needed stronger flavors), sizes of the individual candy, the wrappers, the overall look, and colors.

After receiving the first production samples, Gil, Herb, and I contacted potential customers. We were successful in selling and reselling the Sara Paul brand candy for many years to customers like F.W. Woolworth, Walmart, McCrory's, T.G.& Y. Variety Store Company, and others.

Primex grew to be the second largest marketing company of imported hard candies in the U.S.

Chapter 73
Oxford Ceramics

The Oxford Factory is located in the neighboring town of São Bento do Sul. Their monthly production capacity was over four million pieces. This factory produced earthenware-dinnerware with the most automated equipment money could buy.

Oxford, considered one of the largest ceramic factories in the world, dominated the South American market. As imports from China and other countries started to compete with Oxford, Ismar Becker looked to other markets. The U.S. was a logical market to penetrate, after having exported to Argentina, Chile, Germany, and other countries.

This is where Primex came into the picture, again in 1974. During numerous visits to Oxford, I had negotiated with Mr. Otair Becker and his son, Ismar, a representation agreement for the U.S. The first trade show where we exhibited the Oxford product was the July 1974 Chicago International Housewares Show.

The pressure was on because when Ismar arrived in Chicago he told us that the factory was in a serious over-stock situation, "We need to sell several million pieces immediately to alleviate cash flow problems."

The reaction at the trade show to the Oxford products was only lukewarm. The inventory in the factory—so many plates, cups, mugs, and salad plates—was packed loose in bins. Because I knew this industry well, I figured they should be sold in sixteen piece sets (service for four).

I knew that it was easier to sell sets than millions of individual pieces.

On the way home from Chicago while standing in line at the T.W.A. counter, I started a conversation with the person next to me. He had visited the Housewares Show. His name was Ike Perelman, the president of a large company with over 500 stores. I quickly told him about the 300,000 sixteen piece sets I had to offer. I asked Ike for an appointment. His offices were in the Empire State Building. The next morning, at 9 AM, I showed up for the meeting with samples. Ike offered to buy the entire quantity of 300,000 sets.

After returning to my office I contacted the factory. I told them about my idea to make up 300,000 sets in gift boxes and asked them to advise me of their best possible price. Expectation and excitement were in the air.

I contacted Ike again, "I am coming over to make a deal."

The price difference between Ike's first offer and factory asking price was 20%. Ike suggested splitting the difference. I accepted Ike's offer, knowing the factory was desperate to liquidate this inventory. Ike had his office issue a purchase order for 300,000 sets at $3.50 per set, over 1 million dollars.

The factory filled the order within the time frame given by the customer. Ike's company opened the letter of credit, guaranteeing payment. To the Oxford Company, we became heroes, almost miracle makers. From then on we developed business with Oxford on an ongoing basis.

Chapter 74
Porcelana Schmidt

The largest porcelain manufacturer in South America was Porcelana Schmidt. When I first came to Brazil, the company was managed by Arthur Schmidt and his brother Harry. The group had three factories, two in the southern part of Brazil and one near São Paulo in Mauá, employing about three thousand people. The main office and central showroom was in São Paulo.

Without a doubt their operation was very impressive, highly automated. The quality of their products was competitive with Japan, at the time the major competition, as well as with European porcelain manufacturers. We built an excellent working relationship with the Schmidt family.

After 1984, as competition became more difficult, Schmidt management was reinforced by Ingrid Schmidt, the daughter of Arthur and her newlywed husband. Nelson Louis Lara became marketing director, and Ingrid was director of new product development.

Ingrid was a very talented, creative designer. In addition, her personal beauty reflected well the new exciting products she had developed for the company. Unfortunately, the Schmidt group had lost market share both on the domestic market and the international market. On top of this Arthur Schmidt, the president of the group, became seriously ill with cancer of the throat and mouth.

One sad day I received a call from Inga Schmidt, Arthur's wife, sharing with me the newly diagnosed illness of Arthur. According to their Brazilian doctor, the only remote chance to save Arthur or, at least, to prolong his life was medical care in New York at Sloan Kettering Cancer Institute.

Somehow after numerous calls to doctors, I was able to arrange an appointment for Arthur. I had also arranged for an ambulance to pick Arthur up at J.F.K. airport. We took Arthur directly to Sloan Cancer Institute, where he was scheduled for surgery the following morning.

After a four hour surgery the professor-doctor informed the family that most of Arthur's tongue had to be removed. Arthur and his family stayed in New York for a total of six weeks. Arthur was adjusting to his new reality in which his only way of communicating was by writing. Ingrid brought him a pad and pencil; he was making as much progress as was expected by the doctor. Before their return to Brazil, I had invited Inga and Ingrid to theirs and my favorite restaurant "The Palm," the original one on 45th and Second Avenue, where my portrait is on the wall.

With an angry look on his face, Arthur wrote: "I am going too."

I said. "Fine, but how are you going to eat your favorite four pound lobster?

His reply was, "Put it in a blender."

We ordered four lobsters.

The chef said he would accommodate us.

We had a very enjoyable dinner with a couple of bottles of chilled Italian wine. As I parted from the Schmidts with tears, hugs, and kisses, they said they would never forget this evening and all my assistance during their unfortunate stay in New York. Our friendship was solidified.

While Arthur was absent from the business the board of directors appointed Arthur's brother, Harry, as president. As soon as Arthur showed up at the office with his note pad and pencil, he instructed his secretary to call a board meeting.

At the meeting Arthur wrote on his pad: "I am back to assume the presidency."

He was unanimously reinstated and continued to run the business for another ten years, despite his handicap, until he passed away in 1983. My friendship with Inga and Ingrid never wavered.

Chapter 75
Tramontina

Visiting the major retailers in Brazil was one way to learn more about locally made products. The Tramontina quality products—stainless steel cookware, serving pieces, flatware (spoons, forks, knives), and a line of cutlery— were in every department store in Brazil. Looking up the address of the factory I realized that they were located in the south of Brazil, close to the Argentina border. I contacted the factory to arrange a visit.

My call was transferred to Raul Scamazone, the director in charge of sales and one of the principal owners. I told him the purpose of my call was to visit the factory.

"No problem," he replied in a friendly voice. "Tomorrow at 7 AM, there will be a Tramontina car to pick you up."

At 7 AM I met the driver. The trip to the main office of Tramontina in Carlos Barbosa, a small town in Rio Grande do Sul (the southernmost state), took two hours. We drove along the winding hilly roads with miles and miles of wineries on the hillsides—a nice ride despite the dangerous ups and downs and the twisting narrow roads with heavy movements of trucks and buses.

Arriving at the main office and showroom, I was welcomed by Mr. Scamazone. I told him about Primex, our good contacts on the American market, and the other business we had already generated in Brazil. I told him that we were looking to expand.

Raul was a friendly host, who made an excellent impression as an intelligent and knowledgeable business man. He took me to visit factory one, the highly automated factory where they were producing steak and kitchen knives, over 50,000 a day; and the second factory, wooden handles for their cutlery factory using hard wood from their own forest in the north of Brazil two thousand miles away. The third factory was the stainless steel factory, one of the largest in South America; the fourth factory produced tools, such as hammers, pliers, wrenches, and screwdrivers.

The common denominator among these four beautiful modern factories was the quality and the gorgeous surroundings: gardens, flowers, and even a small zoo with chickens, turkeys, ducks, and peacocks with a variety of deeply colored feathers.

I learned a lot about the owners: the Tramontina and Scamazone families. They were well traveled and seasoned business people. Management at all levels was of Italian descent, the first, second, and third generations, as were the technical staff and engineers. The outstanding engineer innovator and director of the stainless steel factory was Mario. Mario was friendly, trustworthy, and above all reliable.

The next stop was lunch in a small Italian cantina near the offices. Their *cansha* chicken with rice soup was a delight, the Brazilian barbeque was mouth-watering, and the regional wine was plentiful and tasty. After lunch we went to the well lit showroom. At first I was like a kid in a candy store; I did not know where to look first. Raul pointed out their best selling products. After a couple of hours we selected some samples to be sent to our New York showroom.

After I returned home and the samples had arrived, I sat down with our staff to share with them my impressions of the products and above all the people. I explained that the potential was great, good factories, good products, and competitive prices with Japan,

Italy, Portugal, and Mexico. There were no imports at the time from Korea, India, or China. The first potential customers we had decided to pursue were in New York.

At J.C. Penney Company, the housewares buyer, Art Cummings, committed to buying a six piece steak knife set in a colorful lithograph box. The initial purchase was for 120,000 sets. The program was so successful that we had to ship sets by air at the cost of J.C.P. Company. The orders totaled over 500,000 sets during a period of six months. We also sold to another department of J.C.P. a newly designed stainless steel tea kettle, the Coby Kettle, which became a great seller. In addition we contacted both Macy's and Gimbels in New York. We had a lucky break, selling products to all three companies.

The next stop was Chicago to Sears, Montgomery Ward, and Marshall Fields. The reaction to the Tramontina products was very positive and encouraging for us.

After successful direct sales, we decided to set up an importing company of our own, American Heritage Trading Company, a division of Primex offering South American and Israeli products to independent retailers out of a domestic warehouse. The product mix of American Heritage included ceramics from Ceramarte, Ceramica Weiss, and Oxford, glass from Nadir in Brazil, as well as ceramics, plastics, glassware and gifts from Israel.

Business grew for several years until 1985, when the official exchange rate in Brazil became unfavorable, and about that same time the Chinese and Korean competition came on very strong.

Moreover, Tramontina had decided to set up their company in the U.S. Mr. Scamazone came to the U.S. telling us about their decision to establish Tramontina U.S.A., managed by Antonio J. Galafassi. Mr. Scamazone further told us that Tramontina will buy back from American Heritage the Tramontina inventory which was over a half million dollars. We had no written exclusive contract, so we agreed with one condition that they had to hire Roger Berns, my good friend and our sales manager, for a minimum of two years.

Antonio had rented a warehouse in Houston and established the Tramontina Company. Roger worked for them for four years and then retired. As Tramontina was a strong financial group, Antonio was given all the backing he needed from the parent company. Antonio suggested making the Tramontina name known in the industry. Antonio, who was a protégé of Mr. Scamanzone, practically grew up with Tramontina, visiting often in the U.S. and learning the business from the best: Raul Scamanzone.

To date Antonio is still the president of Tramontina U.S.A., and Tramontina, one of the leading companies in their field in the U.S. The parent company from Brazil is exporting the Tramontina branded products to over eighty countries worldwide.

Our relationship with Tramontina and in particular with Antonio has been excellent over the years so much so that when Primex was forced to lay off our friend and account manager, Kurt Uhlendorf, a talented and hard working American Brazilian, I called Antonio and asked him if at all possible to hire Kurt, explaining that Kurt would be an asset to Tramontina. After their interview, Antonio hired Kurt, replying to my request with kindness. Kurt moved his family, his wife and two children, to Houston and has been working there with mutual satisfaction. I am grateful to Antonio for his friendship.

Chapter 76
Our Helicopter Venture

Throughout my business ventures with other manufacturers, I continued my friendship with Klaus. Klaus's hobby was flying. Therefore, he gathered a few friends in town and decided to build an airport in the small town of Rio Negrinho. A number of friends and Rotary members joined. They built a runway on the outskirts of town on a little hillside.

Klaus and his son-in-law Acirton saw advertising for an American-made helicopter kit made in Phoenix, Arizona. They were so impressed that they decided to buy two helicopters at the price of $18,000.00 each. Klaus sent Rolf, the engineer, to Arizona to learn the assembly process of the helicopters.

When Rolf returned, with the help of a few mechanics from the ceramic factory, he assembled two beautifully painted helicopters, two-seaters, with small engines.

The helicopters were a big sensation in town. First planes, now helicopters, were taking off from the factory grounds, first circling above the factory and then above the neighboring towns. Immediately there were others interested in buying these birds.

During one of my visits, Rolf, the engineer pilot, took me for my first flight. It was interesting to see the surrounding towns from above. I saw the many furniture factories, Ceramarte and Oxford (the other large factory in the neighboring town of São Bento do Sul).

Mr. Shrem, the owner of the helicopter factory, flew to Brazil for a visit. After a lengthy four days and nights we came to a preliminary agreement that we would all meet in Phoenix at the factory with the intention of buying the Rotary Way Company, with all its patents. In the interim, Klaus had ordered six more helicopters, increasing the number of mechanics to do the assembly work. Each helicopter took three hundred hours for one person to assemble, according to the advertisement.

Klaus decided to make a business out of this. He sent an announcement to the press of the official opening date of a helicopter assembly factory in the town of Rio Negrinho. Klaus's intention was to lay the ground work for legalizing the two-seater helicopter for various uses other than for private transportation.

Klaus's idea was great: to sell these choppers to the military for training purposes, to hospitals, police for emergency use as well as a means of transportation. Klaus had a good friend at the Brazilian Air Force: Lieutenant General Roland, the commander in charge of licensing and regulating the Aviation industry; therefore, we flew to Rio de Janeiro to meet with him.. We were asked many questions about safety and given many forms to fill out. We were given positive indications about the possibility of obtaining all approvals necessary within six months or sooner.

The official opening and flight demonstrations by Klaus and others was attended by the governor of the state of Santa Catarina, a number of high ranking Air Force officers including some generals, and the press. Everyone congratulated Klaus for bringing a new industry to town and to Brazil.

Before we made a trip to Arizona, we were negotiating a price with the idea of moving the manufacturing to a special area that Klaus was ready to provide. We had an agreement: Klaus and his family would own sixty percent; my family and I would own forty percent. We arrived in Phoenix—Klaus, his son in law Acirton, his daughter Ursula, my son Stewart (who was also the lawyer for our side), and me.

Klaus asked Shrem to outline exactly what we would see in the factory, what type of machines, dyes, tools to produce the components that go into the kit, the assembly of the helicopter. The dinner session of over four hours turned into a rough business session. Shrem left the hotel at about 10:30 PM, so we decided that our meeting at the factory would start at 9 AM.

Our group, Klaus, Ursula, Acirton, Stewart, and I, continued discussing the issues that Klaus had raised. We sat until past midnight. Klaus had reservations about the entire deal. We decided to re-discuss the deal among ourselves after visiting the factory. We arrived at the factory, where Mr. Shrem was waiting to take us on a tour. That was a terrible disappointment from the beginning to the end.

Although Klaus is not an engineer by degree, it took him very little time to figure out that many of Mr. Shrem's claims regarding patents and blueprints were unfounded. Yes, there were numerous blueprints in various areas of the factory but these were kept in no particular order as related to each component; it was a mess to say the least. We found no filings or proof of approved patents.

The factory was disorganized. There was no specific production flow; many of the components of the helicopter were purchased from outside suppliers. The entire factory looked like a big disorganized garage. The second evening there was another dinner; Klaus had more questions than before. Klaus showed visible anger toward Shrem, the engineer inventor.

Prior to our arrival in Phoenix, Mr. Shrem had set up a meeting at 9 AM in his attorney's office for signing the deal. We had agreed that my son Stewart, our attorney, would meet with their attorney and

Mr. Shrem to review the details of the sales agreement. Klaus and I sat at the bar of the hotel after all the others went to sleep. Klaus and I rehashed the initial deal, the pros and cons among ourselves until 1 AM. Before we walked out of the bar to go to sleep, Klaus turned to me and said, "I do not like this deal."

He was determined not to hand over the certified checks and told me to do the same. At that time Stewart had already arrived to meet with Shrem and the attorney. With no hesitation I agreed with the conclusion Klaus had reached. We decided to go to the airport instead of going to the meeting. I called Stewart at the attorney's office, where he was in the midst of reviewing the agreement. I told him about our decision. I told him to leave everything and meet us at the airport to catch a flight at 9:30 AM to New York.

As it happened, Klaus did not obtain approval from the Air Force authority to sell his assembled helicopters on the Brazilian market. It was a costly and bitter pill to swallow, particularly for Klaus. Looking back at what transpired, we could have faced an even bigger loss and disappointment if we had gone through with the deal. It was an interesting experience for all of us.

Chapter 77
Handicraft Project

I presented some samples at Pier 1's headquarters in Fort Worth, Texas in early 1975. After the presentation, Marvin Girouard, the executive Vice President in charge of merchandising, and two buyers, Jim Prucha and Adrian Long, made the first Pier 1 trip to South America.

They were the first major company in their product categories, other than ceramics, to travel to Brazil. Brazil was not known as an exporter of handicrafts. Our mission was to find interesting products that would complement the mix in their stores.

We decided to travel to Brasilia (the capital of Brazil). We met with the Minister of Labor and the Minister of Social Affairs. Both ministers and staff were very interested in helping the underdeveloped states of Brazil to commercialize the exports of handicrafts, particularly in the North East, where unemployment was over 25% (with no major industries).

We were told by the authorities that a budget was approved by the federal government to fund the handicraft artisans through each state governor. The first ladies of the state, the governors' wives, were in charge of the big effort of exporting handicrafts. The ministers reported to the President of Brazil, Mr. Geisel, as to the potential employment opportunities based on Marvin's report. The President instructed the ministers to take all steps necessary to promote this effort.

The following day we visited a market for handicrafts where many artisans were offering their products for sale to the public. We were quite impressed with the variety of items made of natural, raw materials from that region. These included: straw hats, baskets, hampers, throw rugs, laundry baskets, hand bags, waste baskets, etc. Also, there were a large variety of hand-made ceramics, gifts, figurines, wall plaques, wood carvings, natural soap stone items, etc. There were a large variety of products that the Pier 1 associates became quite interested in, particularly since most of the items were unique and different from those that Pier 1 was already importing from other countries in Asia, Europe or Mexico.

After spending more than a half day at the market, we decided to go back to the handy crafts center. We started to discuss the specific points of each item Pier 1 showed interest in: material cost, labor, availability, quality control, packaging, shipping cost, etc. I realized that there was no infrastructure to get the prices, nor the quantities, Pier 1 would be interested in. The projects needed to be structured to make it interesting for all parties involved, state and federal government, as well as the artisan community.

In spite of the difficulties, I could see the potential opportunity. We had many of the ingredients that it would take to make this into a successful project for the government and the artisans, (employing additional thousands of people), as well as for Primex. The most important elements that impressed me were the federal and state government, the association of the artisans, the availability of natural materials and potentially thousands of talented artisans willing to train their neighbors and friends. In view of the state governor's willingness to invest in this project, I had committed Primex to invest in competent personnel and to manage the project at no charge at all from our part to the government.

In the city of Natal, we hired Edith Schumacher and her husband, Holger, both ceramic engineers with previous experience in managing people, projects, production, and setting up quality control procedures. Both of them were credited to a large extent for the successful project in the handy crafts area.

Pier 1 left us with tentative orders, provided we could meet their price objectives. The unknown factor at that point was the shipping cost for each item. This was a major obstacle for exports from Brazil. Furthermore, the freight from Europe and Mexico were even lower.

We also had found it necessity to take the initiative in contacting the major suppliers of raw materials such as jute, raffia, straw, and box manufacturers to negotiate lower prices based on direct purchases, large quantities, and good payment terms.

We succeeded realizing a savings on of average of 50%. These savings were passed on to the artisans, enabling them to meet the Pier 1 desired prices.

At Natal, we had set up a distribution center to receive goods, and an inspection line to inspect 100% of the product before packing, labeling and shipping.

The big hurdle remained the ocean freight cost. After contacting various shipping lines, I had found out that the government had owned a steam ship line, Lloyd Brazilero. Jointly with the local government, we presented the problem and highlighted the huge difference in freight costs from other countries. We urged them to consider the potential of creating thousands of new jobs in the North East, and mentioned the fact that the federal government, in particular President Geisel, was strongly supporting our efforts. We requested a 50% reduction in the freight cost. We had presented them with the fact of having received already a tentative order from Pier 1 Imports for five 40' containers, with a potential of hundreds more, provided we could get the freight reduction. Pier 1 alone had 350 stores at the time and was growing rapidly.

We made our request, not only as an economic and employment issue for the North East of Brazil, but also as a political objective for the President. With great anxiety we left our request in their hands, as the entire handicraft program depended on their decision.

After fourteen tense days of waiting, our request was granted.

Now we were in business, after all the efforts we had made. The first test orders from Pier 1 resulted in reorders. The first year alone, we had shipped over half a million dollars.

Chapter 78
Our Successful Business Model

Our business model became known in the neighboring South American countries; therefore, we were invited by various manufacturers to open offices in Argentina, Chile, Peru, and Colombia.

The foundation of our business was having the best team money could buy. Prior to opening a Primex office we surveyed each market (country) to pinpoint the specific products they had to offer that were suitable for the U.S. market.

The success of our business was based on a strong, dependable team. My son Stewart worked part-time until he graduated from New York Law School in 1979; my nephew Steve was in charge of financing; my daughter Dahlia, jewelry; my son Gil, candies and other confectionary products. Art Cummings was in charge of housewares. Tony Kreimer was in charge of ceramics and several major accounts. Herb Briggs was Vice President of Primex in charge of textiles and managing some of our biggest accounts. He worked well with Stewart and contributed significantly to the growth of Primex.

At one point we moved my nephew David Paul with his wife, Twila, to São Paulo from the U.S. for a period of six months. Then he was moved to open a Primex office in Los Angeles, California. Gil, my youngest son, with his wife, Dali, and daughter, Elite, were also moved to São Paulo for a period of six months to train the staff on the newest technologies and procedures that Primex New York had implemented.

Michael Grossman had resigned after being with Primex for about five years to venture into his own business. He was replaced as general manager of Primex Brazil by the very professional Heloisa Figuerto. After about ten years with Primex, Heloisa became ill. We decentralized the Primex offices; each office had its own manager. In São Paulo the manager was Elza Godoy, in Blumenau, Adelerio followed by Rubins, and in São Bento, Luiz Garcia.

Chapter 79
Primex in Chile

Our successful activities in Brazil were well publicized in the neighboring countries of Chile, Argentina, Peru, and Colombia by the arm of the Brazilian government, CASEX. One day, in New York City, I was visited by Patricio Fernandez Hernandez, a ceramic manufacturer from Chile. Patricio had in his hand a Brazilian publication outlining some of our many activities in Brazil. We found Patricio to be a very knowledgeable person. Because he had studied in the U.S., he was fluent in English as well as in Spanish.

He argued that we could also build a successful business in Chile. He admitted that Chile was not the same size country as Brazil (population of 150 million versus Chile's twelve million). However, Chile had a strong economy.

Patricio was very persistent, "Come visit Chile, you will like the country and the people."

When we returned to the office, he showed me a few samples produced in his factory Ceramica Espejo. Patricio showed us numerous glazing techniques, decal making, and decorating capabilities as well as some limited hand painting. He answered my question as to how many people he employed and the amount of product he could produce per month. I immediately realized that the decision for Primex and me to become involved with Espejo would be based strictly on potential growth. I took a liking to what I saw, most and foremost Patricio. The product was secondary. I promised him a visit within a year.

In 1984, during my first visit to Chile, I only visited the capital and largest city, Santiago. The first evening of my arrival, Patricio invited me to his home for dinner. He introduced me to his wife, Ana Maria, and his four daughters. Today Patricio and Ana Maria are blessed with married children and ten great-grandchildren.

Ceramica Espejo

The factory was a relatively small facility; everything was handmade with no automated equipment. The kilns were electric, small, and very costly to operate. The factory itself was clean. The production floor was well laid out. Patricio's partner, Pancho, was in charge of production. They also had a third partner, the number cruncher in charge of financing, calculating, and pricing.

We sat around the table at their relatively small showroom evaluating product after product, ones that they were producing for the local market. These included coffee mugs, tea pots, beer mugs, cookie jars, serving pieces, flower vases, and planters. The looks and the finished quality of the products were good. However, most products were not suitable for the U.S. market because of the sizes. An example: our coffee mugs were almost double in size and capacity.

We had to start from the drawing board. We guided them through the process of developing products for the American market. The Espejo management team was eager to learn and implement our recommendations about product development and efficiency improvements; for example, we recommended their buying a continuous kiln that would triple the factory capacity.

The first break we had was supplying an old fashion ceramic shaving mug to Franklin Toiletry, a marketing company in New York. The sales started slowly. Once the customer was satisfied with the quality and timely deliveries, the product was successfully sold into hundreds of gift specialty stores, J.C. Penney Company, and other major retailers. The orders were for over 200,000 units. At the same time the designers, model makers, and mold makers at Espejo were working hard to create the new products we had indicated. Patricio closely followed the development of the new products so the company could start exporting.

Primex became their exclusive representative in the U.S. We sold the Espejo products to chain stores such as F.W. Woolworth, Pier 1 Imports, McCrory stores, Meijer, Inc., and others. The friendship with Patricio continues. However, this business suffered from the Chinese pricing policy.

<u>Fantuzzi</u>

The following day Patricio introduced me to a large manufacturer of porcelain and steel cookware, pots and pans, and washing machines. The factory was Fantuzzi, a sizeable factory with over three hundred workers, established for over one hundred years.

Unfortunately they had made only minor changes over the years in terms of automation. Roberto Fantuzzi, the president of the company, was one of the four Italian descendants who owned the company. They were friendly brothers, intelligent, and well educated. One of the brothers, Angel, was a popular politician and a senator. Roberto was the president of the Chilean Manufacturers' Association. As the computer age was ushered in, the Fantuzzis were up to date in their offices but not in production. They were very interested to hear my opinions as to their potential for exporting their products.

I had visited similar factories in the U.S., Mexico, Italy, and Portugal as well as at international trade shows in Frankfurt, Germany, and in Canton, China, Milan, Italy, and Chicago. In a few days I came back to the Fantuzzis with my findings, evaluations, and recommendations based on my observations. The Fantuzzi management accepted my basic recommendations.

I had purchased numerous samples in the U.S. of the most popular items in their category of products, as examples of what direction Fantuzzi must take, for example, an oval roaster, with a reversible usable lid, in three sizes. The two smaller sizes were sold all year around, whereas the larger size was a hot seller for Thanksgiving and Christmas. Second, a seven piece cookware set, a very popular seller in the U.S.

The Fantuzzi were willing to make the investments in the new tooling requirements. Business was generated successfully for several years. Based on this first potential supplier, Stewart, Herb Briggs and I made a follow-up trip to Chile,

We decided to open a Primex office in Chile in 1985. We interviewed to hire a general manager. We were lucky, meeting a bilingual (English & Spanish) person by the name of Juan Eduardo Undorraga. Juan Eduardo and his wife Vivian's family owned Fourcade, one of the major furniture factories in the south of Chile. He turned out to be a great manager and a trustworthy lifetime friend.

Juan was instrumental in identifying for Primex management the opportunities in the furniture category, since Chile had vast resources of raw materials.

We hired an additional two very capable partners and friends: Isabel Lanas and Marriete Argelery. They were with us for twenty years. After Juan Eduardo decided to venture into his own business, Isabel became general manager.

At a later stage we hired Maria Eugenia Lanas to specialize in the furniture end of the business. At Primex New York, my son Stewart was in charge of the furniture business. He had worked at *Kibbutz Yasur* in their furniture factory, which gave him a good foundation to become a *maven* (expert). Chile benefited a great deal because Primex had developed a strong furniture business first in Brazil.

Stewart made sure that Chile learned from our experiences in Brazil, for example, not to repeat our fundamental mistakes, such as the improper drying of wood, improper finishing, assembly instructions, and packaging.

Stewart managed the growth of the Primex in sales of furniture. We became a successful major player in the disassembled or "knock down" (K.D.) furniture business by selling to a broad spectrum of customers such as Pier 1, J.C. Penney, Target, Walmart, Williams-Sonoma, Crate and Barrel, Toys R Us, and others.

Chapter 80
The Presidential Palace

The news traveled fast from Brazil to Chile regarding our successful involvement in the handicraft category. Our manager, Isabel Lanas, made us aware of a handicraft center in Santiago. I made a visit with her to the center housed in a large government owned building. The very attractive architecture accentuated the various handicrafts on exhibit. Chile had different handicrafts than either Brazil or the Orient.

We were impressed with their wide range of wood carvings, large variety of ceramics, candle holders, wind chimes, candy dishes, hammocks, copper wall plates, and other items. We started to discuss with the person in charge of the handicraft center the possibility of copying some of the items into large production, suitable to sell in the U.S., particularly to Pier 1 Imports. Obviously this would employ hundreds of additional people. We discussed their cost strategy, the method of buying the products from the individual artisans, and financing.

The manager of the center told us, "I must discuss this entire concept with my boss."

The boss was no less than Mrs. Pinochet, the first lady of Chile. I suggested a possible meeting with the first lady and the President of Chile. A couple of days later, Isabel, our manager in Chile, received a call that the president and the first lady were interested in having a meeting, especially because unemployment in Chile was high.

On my return to the U.S., I contacted the executive V.P. of Pier1, Marvin Gerard. I shared with him the handicraft activity in Chile and the potential for Pier 1. I suggested he visit Chile to discuss the potential directly with President Pinochet and the first lady, who was in charge of the growing employment in the handicraft category.

Marvin's reply was, "Good. I am interested."

We set a date suitable for all parties. About three days later Marvin advised me that the trip was approved, "I'll be bringing with me Adrian Longe, my V.P." I contacted Isabel to coordinate the visit. She was able to set up the meeting within a couple of weeks.

When Marvin and Adrian arrived in Chile, they were picked up by the Primex car. I arrived in Chile ahead of time and, together with Isabel Lanas, greeted our guests at the airport. We all stayed at the 5 star Sheraton Santiago Hotel. At the hotel we were visited by the Chilean secret service. They had asked us to surrender our American passports two days prior to our meeting at the Presidential palace in order to get security clearances. This was their procedure.

The meeting was specified for 8 AM. We were all excited to visit the palace and to meet the president and Mrs. Pinochet. At 7:30 AM, sharp, a presidential limousine came to pick us up. Marvin, Adrian, Isabel, and I dressed up properly for the anticipated historic meeting.

When we arrived at the palace, we were ushered in by two security officers dressed in Chilean Navy dress uniforms. We were taken through the gate of the palace and down a long wide corridor. Numerous flags flew on both sides of the corridor. The flag bearers stood at attention, saluting us as American dignitaries. We walked to the door of the President's office on the fourth floor.

The door was opened at exactly 8 AM. The room was decorated in good taste: gold decorated furniture and a crystal chandelier. The flags added to the atmosphere. We were standing as we waited for the president. Mrs. Pinochet walked in alone, apologizing that the President was not here to greet us. Overnight there had been a serious damaging earthquake in the north of Chile. The president had to fly there.

"He sends his *Bienvenido*, greetings and apologies for not being with us," Mrs. Pinochet explained.

Mrs. Pinochet asked us to sit around a large handcrafted table covered with Chilean leather, on comfortable heavy chairs. Coffee and breakfast rolls were served. Mrs. Pinochet had with her the person in charge of the handicraft center. After introductions, Mrs. Pinochet told us she was anxiously awaiting to see what we could do for her country and artisans whose livelihoods depend on handicrafts.

Marvin elaborated on Pier 1, the largest purchaser in the world of handicrafts. Pier 1 traveled the world to find unique products for over 500 Pier1 stores. A number of questions and related issues were discussed including the financing that the Chilean government needed to provide to the artisans so that they could buy low cost raw materials, packaging, and a reasonable freight cost so they could be somewhat competitive. Mrs. Pinochet was thankful to Marvin and Primex for showing an interest in Chile. She promised the head of the handicraft center more financial assistance.

We thanked the first lady for graciously receiving us in the early morning.

Later in the day we visited the center. Marvin and Adrian selected some items indicating the quantities per item and approximate price objectives. The rest of the follow up was left with Isabel of Primex Chile.

Business with the artisans never developed to be as big as in Brazil. The first difference between Chile and Brazil was the size and diversification in the different states. Also the Chilean artisans were accustomed to selling their limited output on the local market at higher prices, without the strict quality control that was required by Pier1. However, we did generate some business successfully.

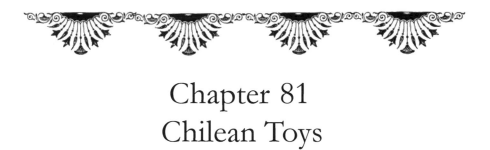

Chapter 81
Chilean Toys

We had found a number of wooden toy manufacturers in Chile. These companies were family owned and focused on making products for their local markets. We helped each one in developing products for the U.S. market. We identified meaningful potential business. However, as individual small factories, they were not capable of exporting. We urged them to organize into an association that we would be interested in representing. We exhibited their products at the annual and the most important U.S. Toy Fair in New York City at the Jacob Javits Center and sold those products to our major customers. Once they formed the association they received financial assistance from the Chilean government to expand and modernize their factories.

One of the first customers in the toy field with the largest purchasing power was Toys R Us. We presented some of the Chilean products to their buyers, and their reaction was positive. They reported their findings to their V.P. of merchandising.

Thirty days later Marty and I were on a plane to Santiago, Chile. Mariette Argelery, our Primex person in charge of textiles, had set up a meeting with a small textile manufacturer, Smart. This company made woven fabrics, pre-cut to order and gave them out to hundreds of workshops to be sewn and returned to the factory for final inspection, packing, and shipping

The company specialized in making infant ware, specifically infant bodysuits, often called "onesies"®. This was a strong product category for Toys "R" Us. Marty, who was impressed with the quality and prices, decided to place an order for a container of these products.

The business grew beyond our expectations. Once we had sold to Toys R Us, we confidently contacted J.C. Penney Company, Walmart, and others and succeeded in selling their production capacity. For Primex, Chile became the second most important country.

We frequently visited Chile with buyers. We increased our Primex staff a number of times and also expanded Primex offices and showrooms. In addition to furniture, we successfully developed a wide range of product categories, such as candy, chocolates, wafers, plastic housewares, ceramics, tools, apparel, and toys. In 1995, Primex was honored by the Chilean Manufacturers' Association, at a special gala dinner, in the presence of over two hundred guests as well as ministers of trade and industry, for our major contributions in spearheading the export of Chilean consumer products for over fifteen years.

Chapter 82
The Trade Shows

We attended many trade shows over the years, including The Hardware Show, The Home Improvement Show, The Highpoint Furniture Show, The Toy Fair, The Premium Show, The China and Glass Show, The Gourmet Show, and The Frankfurt Fair.

In fact, every year we visited the international Frankfurt Fair in February and August, where we met with some of our suppliers from Brazil and Germany, as well as some of our important clients from the U.S., such as Pier 1 Imports, Crate and Barrel, Macy's, and Williams-Sonoma. The first international show of the year was always in Chicago. Primex exhibited with American Heritage, a subsidiary of Primex, in an impressive setting at the Chicago Housewares Show. This show always took place around January 14, my birthday, and the second show around July 13, our wedding anniversary. In addition to me, my wife, Sara, my sons Stewart and Gil, my nephew Steve, my brother Emil, Tony Kreimer, Herb Briggs, Art Cummings, Rich Koval, Harold Rose, Steve Konigsberg, Harry Botoff, Roger Burns, Ken Sopher, Ulysses Gadoy, Harvey Klein, and in later years, Frank Adgida and Kurt Uhlendorf, office managers, all participated in this event. The trade shows in Chicago were the most important in our business; each show attended had over 2,000 exhibitors and over 50,000 buyers from all over the U.S. Canada and other countries. The Primex and American Heritage Company had a strong clientele following.

The show always started on a Sunday and ended Wednesday at the McCormick Exhibition Center on the Michigan Lake. We had to arrive the latest Friday to help set up. In January it was 10 to 20° below zero, in July it was in the mid 80s. In order to meet our customers in a private room after the show closing in the evening, we always occupied a large suite and many rooms at the McCormick Hotel across the way from the exhibition center. To interface and show our appreciation to our customers, we set up a buffet at the hotel. The buffet had plenty of food and drinks, wines, liquors, and champagne. Supervising this was Sara's job.

At 7:30 in the evening we had a secluded dinner with specific customers and suppliers. Chicago was known for a great variety of restaurants, such as the Bakery Hungarian Cuisine, Gene and Georgetti's Steak House; however, our favorite was the Italian Village on Monroe Avenue. I had visited the Italian Village for over fifty years, so I knew the owners well, altogether three generations of Frankie's. This three-story beautiful building had three different restaurants with different managers on each floor; our choice was always the second floor—the main floor.

When one of our people called for reservations for Mr. Paul, we were always given a room, most of the time a private room that seated thirty people, who filled every chair. The food and the special service we got from the owners and the maitre d' was second to none. When the Paul family with guests walked in, their attention was given to us. The maitre d' lined up numerous bottles of our favorite chilled white wine and rich aromatic red Italian wines.

The inside of the restaurant had Italian wood paneling, gold leaf covered wood carvings, almost like a church. The wall décor was warm and pleasing. The overall atmosphere, the lighting, and the music were an experience. However, the best experience was eating the food.

The freshly prepared antipastos with extra large shrimp and Italian cold-cuts were a great start, followed with a mouth watering manicotti. The main course was offered with almost a singing heavy Italian accent by Lorenzo, the head maitre d'. Lorenzo told us what to eat, and we always had the best. When Lorenzo retired after over thirty years of service, Frankie the maitre d' continued giving us superb service.

The accordion player was Bartello. When we arrived, he dropped everything, playing and serenading us all evening. He knew my birthday was in January, and July, our anniversary. In 1978, Bartello retired; however, knowing the dates of the housewares show, he knew Mr. Paul would be coming to the restaurant. He left a strict message with the owner, Frankie, to call him when we arrived. Bartello showed up with his accordion and entertained us for hours. He always looked forward to the crisp new $100 bills; this became a tradition, twice a year, for many years.

This restaurant was also Sara's favorite. We had many, many memorable evenings in this place. Dancing and singing spontaneously followed our emptying a few bottles of wine. Friends made our evenings at the Italian Village more memorable, friends such as Agi Johnson, Rita Bole and the Rusten Lloyd group, Jerry Glasberg, Fred Gould, and our Primex and American Heritage group.

These were just some of the fringe benefits of meeting and knowing a large number of people; many of whom have remained our good friends until this day.

Chapter 83
Scheurich Keramik

One of the largest ceramic factories in Europe was located outside Frankfurt in a small town called Kleinheubach am Main in Bavaria, Germany. They specialized in manufacturing over-sized decorative vases, umbrella stands, cache pots, and decorative and functional flower pots, as well as oven bake ware.

I had the pleasure of meeting the managing director and owner of Scheurich Keramik, Dr. Herbert Bauman, during his visit to the Nelson McCoy stand at the Atlantic City China and Glass Show in 1968. We struck up a friendly conversation, and I invited Dr. Bauman to visit the McCoy Factory located in Roseville Ohio.

During the visit to the McCoy Factory in Ohio, Dr. Bauman was my guest. He was an intelligent individual, very polite and friendly. The main purpose of his visit was to see the first Ram press, produced in Columbus, Ohio, that had been installed in our factory. This press was a major innovative breakthrough in the ceramic industry for semi-automatic production of kitchen items, such as mixing bowls and bakeware. The Scheurich Factory was just starting to produce a new clay pot for baking, so Dr. Bauman was looking to buy automated equipment to give him an edge in competing with another German company that had already marketed the same product—the *roemer topf* (a clay casserole dish)—successfully in Germany and the U.S. We at McCoy also produced a version of that clay pot with the new Ram press.

Dr. Bauman was impressed with the performance of the press and purchased two presses from the U.S. company at $40,000 dollars each, with an option to buy five more presses within a year for the same price.

Dr. Bauman had spent a couple of days with me, so during this time, we had discussed many other subjects than ceramics, mostly and above I was anxious to hear from him about his upbringing, and his parents' and family's involvement in the Nazi regime during the war.

He was a very modest, progressive, and realistic person. He had told me with no hesitation that he was only thirteen years old when the war ended. His father had died before the fascist regime took on international dimensions. By then, his mother was managing their ceramic factory with his in-laws.

Dr. Bauman, a believer in social justice, admitted that the Nazi philosophy left a black mark on Germans. He was a good businessman, and we developed a good mutually respectable and friendly relationship, maintaining contact particularly through my visits to Frankfurt and the factory twice a year. Bauman was a great host, who loved good restaurants and good entertainment.

The Scheurich Factory was located in the center of the town of Kleinhaubach (forty-five minutes from Frankfurt) in a four-story building. I was told when they had first started in business the factory was out of town; however, as the town grew, housing was built around the factory. The factory had expanded numerous times, building one level above the other; at its peak, the company had employed over 1,000 people. Scheurich Ceramic became known worldwide for their products; they were the leaders in the field. In particular they became well known for their innovative designs, their colorful glazes, large vases, and the cache pots.

Little did I know when I first met Dr. Bauman that I would one day be the exclusive representation of his company in the U.S. In 1971, when we had already sold the Nelson McCoy Factory, Dr. Bauman had invited me to represent them and help them to develop the U.S. market. At that time Scheurich had a capable and friendly export manager, Rudolf Shader, who came to the U.S. numerous times, helping us to learn as quickly as possible the specific strengths of the Scheurich products.

I had assigned a fellow German, Tony Kreimer, to work with Rudolf on a day to day basis. We suggested selling the Scheurich products in the U.S. to many large and medium size retailers. We had also imported their products and warehoused them in our own U.S. distribution company, American Heritage Trading Company. This enabled us to sell to the smaller independent retailers, with the exception of the *shlimer topf*, "the clay baker."

One of Dr. Bauman's hobbies was flying planes and helicopters. On May 7, 1980, he had purchased a newly rebuilt helicopter, and the engineer who had rebuilt the copter took Dr. Bauman up for a flight. We received a message from his office about the tragic crash and his death. This was obviously a terrible shock to his family. We lost a good friend.

Mrs. Bauman managed the factory for ten years until their young son, Peter, grew up and completed his university education; he graduated with a degree in business administration. Before assuming management of the company, he traveled worldwide, visiting and learning the industry.

I had previously met Peter when he came into the trade shows with his father or mother. We had always enjoyed our meetings with him twice a year during the Frankfurt Trade Fair (German: *Messe* Frankfurt).

Peter took charge of the factory in 1990 and was successful in creating innovative new products. Despite the world becoming smaller, and competition, more difficult, Peter succeeded in keeping his company a leader in the world. He is a bright and aggressive businessman.

During the first year of representing Scheurich, I was lucky to meet at the Atlantic City China and Glass Show, an impressive businesswoman by the name of Rita Bolle. Rita was born in Germany; yet after years in the U. S., she still had a heavy German accent, which only enhanced her charming personality. Rita was friendly and beautiful, but, most important ,business-savvy. Her ex-husband was the exclusive representative of the other big German manufacturer that produced the original clay pot marketed in the U.S.

Rita was available to sell the Scheurich clay pot. We had worked out the arrangements with the factory whereby Rita had exclusive representation from us on the oval *Shlimer topf* (red clay baker).

Rita started a new company by the name of Reston Lloyd based in Sterling, Virginia. She built up a successful business with a great organization and exhibited at all the important trade shows, such as the Atlantic city China and Glass Show, the Chicago Housewares Show, the west coast Gourmet shows, and others.

In the last ten years she brought her two sons, Calvin and Kurt, into the business. For over thirty-five years we enjoyed our friendly business and social contacts. Rita and her team were welcome guests, participating during the trade shows with our Primex guests. They contributed to our party's good humor, laughter, and joy.

Chapter 84
Israel

In 1984, we opened an office in Israel managed by my good friend Zvi Prizant. We had more than one reason to open in Israel: first we wanted to conduct some business in Israel. Second, a free trade treaty was signed between the U.S and Israel granting Israel duty free status on all products manufactured in Israel; no other country had the same advantages of trade with the U.S. The agreement did include Jordanian manufacturers; thereby finished products for export to the U.S. could also become duty free provided the Jordanians used a minimum of 10% added value of Israeli components or raw materials. Dov Lautman, special emissary of Prime Minister Rabin, spearheaded and negotiated the agreement with the U.S. government on behalf of Israel and Jordan. In Israel, we developed textile products such as bed sheets, bath towels, kitchen towels, bathing suits, men's and women's underwear, ceramics, glassware, and gold and silver jewelry with small diamonds. Our first customers for Israel were the J.C. Penney Company, Williams-Sonoma, Pottery Barn, and Pier 1 Imports.

Labor costs in Israel were never competitive with South America and Asia nor with most of the exporting European countries, such as Turkey, Italy, Portugal, Eastern Germany, and Czechoslovakia. In spite of this hurdle we tried very hard to establish a business in Israel. Because ceramics were my specialty, I had contacted the two largest, well established factories.

Lapid Ceramics was located in Tel Aviv-Yafo (Jaffa), a city on the Mediterranean, called the White City, also a UNESCO World Heritage site. Most of the workers were Jewish; however, a number were Arab. The factory was managed by Eli Gur, a young, smart, hard working executive. The factory was owned by the *Histadrut*—the Israeli Federation of Labor or trade union congress, the Koor Division (Conglomerate of Israeli Federation of Labor). The director of this product category at Koor was Joska Givol, a confident, ambitious businessman. Givol was the first Israeli Trade Consul in Budapest, Hungary. Givol was also in charge of the porcelain factory near Acre (Akko): Naaman Porcelain Company, established in 1945.

Both factories had excellent quality products. Lapid produced stoneware; Naaman, fine porcelain equal to the famous Rosenthal china of Germany. I noticed a strong commitment between Eli and his boss Givol, that is, the desire to export, keeping the nearly five hundred people in the two factories working.

Their production capacity was larger than their domestic market could consume; therefore, exports were very important for their survival. We spent a couple of days in both factories working to identify the items suitable for export to the U.S.

Realizing the difficulties but with a strong desire to increase their exports, Givol and Gur re-calculated the costs of some of the products I had selected. As we had our wholesale distribution company in southern New Jersey with a national sales organization and participated in the major U.S. trade shows, I placed an order for the first container of assorted items to be included in our American Heritage Company catalog, a company managed by my brother Emil and our friend Harry Klein.

For Stewart, Gil, Emil, and me, our love for Israel was a special reason and a strong motivator to push the Israeli products. Givol was a sincere, hard working, and effective manager; his sense of humor was always enjoyable and appreciated. When the time came for lunch or dinner, Givol was the guide; he knew and he was well known in the restaurants that he frequently patronized. In Tel Aviv-Yafo, at the harbor, we enjoyed the best hummus and *dag Moshe Rabbeinu* (the fish of Moses, our rabbi), which is a fillet of flounder grilled to perfection. When in the Naaman Factory near the historic port city of Acre, he patronized the Arab restaurants, where he was always greeted with a big hug and "*As Salaam Alaikum*," in Arabic, "Peace be with you."

It was not easy to reciprocate when Givol or Gur came to the U.S.; however, we always tried to take them to my favorite restaurants: the Palm, Joe's Pier 54, Smith and Wollensky, or the Brazilian *churraco-rodizio* restaurant: Churrascaria Plataforma on W. 49 and 8th Avenue. We enjoy our friendly personal relationship until this day.

Phoenicia

The glass company, Phoenicia, was the largest glass supplier in Israel and also was part of the core group. One morning the newly retired Brigadier General (Res), the former Israeli Defense Forces (IDF) chief artillery officer, Oded Tira, showed up in our New York office, and introduced himself as the newly appointed manager of this large Israeli glass factory.

Tira said that our name had been given to him by the Israeli Trade Consul in New York. I immediately called in our management for a meeting: Stewart, Gil, Herb Briggs, Art Cummings, and Tony Kreimer. The general's approach to business was very direct and professional; his military background was obvious in his approach.

The major work of the glass factory was producing flat plate glass for construction. The consumer product division was a facility with little automation, high energy and labor costs, and working at only 50% capacity.

We agreed to send him some physical samples in advance of my visiting the factory. I had visited this factory once before with no results; however, this time I liked the ambitious approach of the new manager. I believed our joint efforts could meet the challenge, taking the company to the next step by developing specific products for the U.S. market.

Business was good for two years; unfortunately, Koor management decided to close the factory because of domestic market difficulties (at the same time they had closed a number of their other factories).

The Israeli Textile Business

In textiles, at first we worked with the Kitan Textile Factory located in the south of Israel. This was a highly automated facility specializing in printed flannel sheets, bath sheets and other bedding products. Because of the quality we were able to develop special items for the J.C.P. Company that continued successfully for a few years; the duty free status of Israel helped to meet the J.C. Penney price points. Unfortunately, Portugal became an effective competitor primarily because of a 50% lower labor cost.

We also worked with David and Steven Greenstein, owners of Fabrite Fabrics, a small factory outside of Tel Aviv. Their specialty was also bedding. Most of their production was sub-contracted to workshops in Arab villages. The two young brothers impressed me as aggressive, hard working individuals determined to develop a business mainly for export to the U.S. They were in the early stage of business; therefore, I suggested that David come to the U.S. and visit us and meet with my son Stewart and Herb Briggs, our V.P. in charge of textiles. David accepted my invitation.

We met in our office and discussed David's business and his ability to increase production for the U.S. market. We came to an agreement, whereby Primex would establish a Fabrite office within our showrooms at 230 Fifth Avenue and whereby Primex would become the exclusive representative in the U.S. Steven was running the business in Israel, mainly in charge of production, and David was in charge of marketing.

It was not long before Herb Briggs set up meetings to show the Homestead product line. Both Herb and David, who were knowledgeable in the field, did their homework before the meeting. The meetings were with Macy's stores, J.C. Penney, Pottery Barn, Target, and others. The results were positive. Orders were immediately placed by a number of customers—a good beginning. However, Steve had a problem increasing production as the sales grew beyond his supplier's capacity.

David moved his family to the U.S. and worked at their offices within Primex. Business grew with major accounts such as Macy's and Target.

David worked under this stress for almost two years. Business was good but the pressure on David became unbearable. A couple of years later David and Steve started a new company called Homestead.

Primex became the representative of the new company, Homestead. The business continued for three years until our agreement expired. Both Dave and Steve are now with Li and Fung Company, managing the textile division in their New York office.

Dov Lautman

To meet and do business with Dov Lautman was a special privilege; as a specially appointed ambassador by Yitzhak Rabin (at the time the Prime Minister of Israel), Dov spearheaded Israeli efforts to help the Jordanian government reduce their unemployment problems by building a free zone industrial park in Jordan near the border with Israel.

Mr. Lautman was a strong advocate of strengthening peace and friendship with Israel's Arab neighbors. Dov Lautman's company, Delta Galil Industries, located in Carmel, Israel, was one of the largest textile producers in the world specializing in underwear and hosiery and the first Israeli company to invest in Jordan. Delta invested in the most modern machinery and in a plant over 200,000 square feet employing almost one thousand Jordanians. Other Israeli companies followed.

The combination of Israeli technology, the supply of raw materials from Delta Textiles, his factory in Kiryat Gat in the southern district of Israel, with the low Jordanian labor costs made sense economically and politically. The products produced in Jordan from Israeli precut fabrics were shipped back to the Israeli factory for final inspection and exported duty free to the U.S. At one point, Delta employed over 1,000 workers in Israel.

Delta Textiles also has a factory in Egypt where they employ over 500 people. Dov has become the expert at building bridges between Israel and its Arab neighbors, succeeding in convincing other Israeli manufacturers to extend their businesses to Jordan.

Dov Lautman was recently recognized and awarded the Israeli Prize by the government and the Federation of Manufacturers in Israel for his leadership and lifetime achievements.

<u>Plastic Products</u>

Israel was a leading producer in the plastic industry. Keter Plastics, ZAG, Schwartz, and Katz were the leaders in the industry. As a result of their successes, thousands of workers were employed by large numbers of medium and small companies, including a number of *kibbutzim* that had become a part of the growing plastic industry in Israel. Primex was successful in selling their plastic products to a number of major U.S. chain stores such as Walmart, K Mart, F.W. Woolworth, McCrory's, and others.

<u>Candles</u>

Hechal Haner, owned by Shalom Fisher, in the city of Beersheba, was one of the largest automated tea light candle producers in the world. During one of my several visits to Israel, I had the pleasure of meeting Mr. Fisher, a *Shomer Shabbat* (a Jew who adheres strictly to *Shabbat* laws) and a seasoned businessman.

We were able to sell some of his product to a number of major companies in the U.S. among them K-mart. The business continued for several years until Mr. Fisher purchased candle companies in the U.S. These companies had established a strong presence on the U.S. market. So Mr. Fisher decided to combine all his business efforts in the U.S. through his newly purchased U.S. companies.

POLGAT Israel

During the early 1950s with the increase of aliyah (immigration to Israel), the major challenges of the Ben Gurion government were housing and jobs. The government made special efforts to establish new towns and cities to the south and the north.

One of these new towns was Kiryat Gat, located half way between Tel Aviv and Beersheba. My brother in law Avraham Argov was the first secretary appointed to the city Kiryat Gat. The government had ambitious plans to build Kiryat Gat into one of the major industrial centers in the south of Israel.

After hundreds of homes had been built, employment was the major concern. The very aggressive and capable Minister of Finance, at that time, Eliezer Kaplan, decided to travel, meeting with world Jewish industrialists and bringing them to Israel. One of his trips was to Chile, where he met with the Polack brothers, the largest producers of fabrics for men's and women's clothing in South America.

Mr. Kaplan invited the Polack brothers to Israel to set up a factory, creating employment in the new city of Kiryat Gat, thirty-five miles south of Tel Aviv. The Polack brothers, as good Jews, favorably responded to Mr. Kaplan's pleas.

The factory was built: an over 200,000-square-foot building with modern machinery, a state of the art facility. POLGAT Textiles opening was a great source of pride and accomplishment; this was one of the most modern factories specializing in men's and women's suits and sportswear. POLGAT employed over 500 people; one of them was my nephew Shalom Argov. The company grew to employ over 1,000. We brought the J.C. Penney Company's Vice President Rolf Larivera to POLGAT where a good business relationship developed.

Chapter 85
Partnership with Shaul Eisenberg

In 1989, I received a call from the Israeli Trade Council in New York, from Mr. Dudi Litvak. Dudi had visited us at Primex offices and showrooms numerous times. Stewart and I had befriended him as he was a strong promoter of business with Israel and had introduced a number of Israeli manufacturers seeking to market their products in the U.S.

This call was a special call from Dudi; he told us that he had a very important person from Israel visiting the U.S., one of the wealthiest people in the world. This person wanted to increase his business in the U.S. the fastest way possible. This person wanted to buy a running business in the U.S. that had a structure to market products from various parts of the world. The person was Shaul Eisenberg, Austrian-born, who had fled Austria in 1938, jumping ship in Japan. Eisenberg's company name was Asian Enterprises. Dudi elaborated: because he knew Primex and our subsidiary, American Heritage Trading Company, he believed we had a good marketing organization and a strong customer base. He thought we would be a good fit for what Mr. Eisenberg was looking for. I thanked Dudi and agreed to meet with Mr. Eisenberg.

The meeting lasted for almost two hours. He took a liking to us and suggested a follow up meeting within a couple of days. At the meeting his secretary took many notes. In the meeting also was Mr. Diamond, Mr. Eisenberg's son in law and the managing director of the Eisenberg

Company in the U.S.: U.D.I. (United Development Industries). Mr. Eisenberg instructed his New York Company's financial manager, Ron Knettle, and Mr. Diamond to visit our showroom, offices, and distribution center in Glassboro, New Jersey. Mr. Eisenberg asked us for financial information reflecting the last three years of our business activities, including financial statements.

We made some inquiries about the Eisenberg companies. In Israel the Eisenberg group companies had controlling interest in a number of major companies, such as Zim Lines, the Haifa Oil Refineries, and the national company, *Ha Chevra Ha Leumut*, that controlled insurance companies and financial institutions. The Eisenberg companies traded in commodities, airplanes, weapons, etc., throughout Japan, Korea, China, Germany, Austria, Bulgaria, the Soviet Union, the U.S., and Israel.

I visited with Mr. Eisenberg in his Israeli headquarters, the Asia house, and in an impressive relatively new twelve-story office building in the district of foreign embassies on Rothschild Avenue. Six of the floors were occupied by the Swiss embassy; the other six floors by the Eisenberg Company. Mr. Eisenberg became aware that my wife, Sara, was with me in Israel staying at the Sheraton hotel. He instructed his secretary to send a beautiful bouquet of flowers to her hotel suite with an invitation to his home for Friday night *Shabbat* dinner. This took place while I was sitting in his son Erwin's office. When I was ready to leave on Friday after our early meetings, Mr. Eisenberg told me, "My driver will pick you up at 6:30 PM to bring you and your wife to my house for *Shabbat* candle lighting and dinner."

It was a wonderful, surprising gesture. Sara and I were picked up and driven to the northern part of Tel Aviv to Zahala, a suburb where many of the high ranking military officers and the wealthiest families of Israel lived.

As we approached Zahala, we saw reinforced security positions in addition to armed private guards. Many of the homes had private guards, including the Eisenberg's estate where Mr. Eisenberg's married daughter and son lived. The entrance to the Eisenberg's three level house was through a heavy steel gate and a beautiful garden of flowers, shrubs and trees.

As we entered through the large hand carved doors, I saw that numerous pairs of slippers for men and women were lined up at the door. The housekeeper assisted us with removing our shoes. When we arrived, we were greeted by Mr. and Mrs. Eisenberg with the Hebrew greeting of "*Shabbat Shalom.*" To our surprise we learned that Mrs. Eisenberg was Japanese. She had converted to Judaism thirty years earlier. Mrs. Eisenberg spoke perfect Hebrew.

Everyone was invited by Mrs. Eisenberg to be seated. Mr. and Mrs. Eisenberg were seated at the head of the table and near them were Sara and me, and the children and grandchildren. In front of each of us was a *Siddur* (a prayer book), with the pages turned to the blessing for the candles.

Mrs. Eisenberg stood up, placed a scarf on her head, and chanted the blessing for the candle lighting; Mr. Eisenberg made the blessing over the two challah loaves. The blessing over the wine was made by their son Erwin.

Dinner was served by two housekeepers. The desserts and coffee were served in a different area—a tatami area (raised tatami-floored seating area or traditional raised platform Japanese seating area with sunken leg room). In this area, we ate at a Japanese-style table surrounded by natural tile and potted plants. We were sitting comfortably, with our slippers on our feet, on the ledge that surrounded the sunken in area, the *Horigotatsu*.

The dinner, the atmosphere, and the Eisenbergs' hospitality were unforgettable. About 10 PM we were driven back to the Sheraton by Mr. Eisenberg's chauffeured black limousine.

On Sunday morning we had one more round of meetings with Mr. Eisenberg and some members of his team. Mr. Eisenberg started the meeting by asking me how Sara and I enjoyed the *Shabbat* dinner. I thanked him for his gracious hospitality.

Without any doubt the friendship he had extended to us influenced my approach to the potential partnership. I felt quite comfortable and reassured that I was partnering with a scholar, a gentleman, and a good business man.

After a few weeks of back and forth, Mr. Eisenberg made us an offer to buy our company, Primex. My son Stewart, a lawyer and the president of the company, had influenced the other board members of Primex, my son Gil, and my nephew Steve, to oppose selling Primex.

The Eisenberg group came back with a new offer: buying fifty percent of Primex. A deal was worked out whereby the Eisenberg group was to buy fifty percent of Primex, and the existing management and staff would continue to run the company. Eisenberg was given the option to appoint a chief financial officer (CFO). He delegated Ron Knettle from his U.S. company as CFO.

Stewart, Gil, and Steve were not happy with the deal. However, I was controlling share holder of Primex and chairman of the board, so they had yielded to my decision to make the deal.

One important paragraph that saved my family from making a disastrous deal was one that Stewart insisted on including in the agreement: the option of our buying back Primex within two years. After our partnership agreement was signed, I traveled to Israel for a meeting to discuss details and the objectives of the new Primex.

Primex had overseas offices in Israel, Brazil, Argentina, Chile, Peru, Colombia, Guatemala, and Mexico. The Primex office in Israel was moved to the Eisenberg building. Per the agreement, a Primex office was to be established in each of the Eisenberg offices in China, Hong Kong, and Germany.

Before the agreement, Primex sourced products from the countries where we had our offices. The new partnership was to expand our international activities to the European countries and Asia, wherever the Eisenberg group had a presence.

During the first year of our partnership, in 1990, I traveled to China and Hong Kong six times to identify and develop product sources. My expectation on these trips was also to establish the presence of Primex in the Eisenberg offices. The managers at Eisenberg gave me a cold reception. They looked at the Primex Company as a "step-child." Only later did I discover that the employees in the Eisenberg offices were working on retainers and paid fat bonuses based on performances. The Eisenberg offices were involved in big business at the government level; their business included sales and purchases of arms, airplane leasing, government-controlled commodities, such as copper, silver, pewter, and modern turnkey factories built and financed by Eisenberg.

Many of these transactions were in the millions of dollars, so the Eisenberg personnel were not interested in "wasting" their time on the consumer products that Primex was involved in. I made a number of trips with Mr. Eisenberg in his private jet. He planned to give instructions to his office managers or at least try to convince them of the need to set up in each office a Primex desk and have adequate personnel to focus on consumer products. Not even Mr. Eisenberg's personal instruction convinced his managers to engage with Primex. In addition to China, I traveled with Mr. Eisenberg to Yugoslavia, Bulgaria, and the Soviet Union. Mr. Eisenberg was well connected with the top government officials in these countries. He was known as an international "flying tycoon." The Eisenberg personnel did not hide from him the fact they had no time to waste on Primex. Within a year I realized that the Primex partnership would not benefit me or my family.

Stewart was proven right. After discussions, we decided that we must exercise our buyback option. Stewart pushed me hard to open discussions with Mr. Eisenberg about the breakup of the partnership.

I made an appointment in Israel to meet with Mr. Eisenberg; our meeting lasted for several hours. Mr. Eisenberg was angry; therefore, he called in his corporate attorney and some of his financial people, including his son Erwin and his son-in-law, Mr. Diamond. I stated that the Eisenberg group failed to contribute to the partnership, and we wanted to exercise our buyback rights for one hundred percent control of Primex.

Mr. Eisenberg showed another side of himself, trying to dominate and dictating the continuation of our partnership. For hours, we discussed and argued, even raising our voices; at one point I turned to Mr. Eisenberg and asked him politely and professionally, not to force us to take expensive legal action.

I placed a call to Stewart in New York because he, Gil, and Steve were waiting anxiously to learn the outcome of the meeting. I shared with Stewart the difficult position Mr. Eisenberg was taking, requesting Primex to give it more time.

Stewart was very determined to end the partnership.

As angry as Mr. Eisenberg had been, he surprised me by instructing his team to work out the details of the break up, pay back terms, dates, etc. Thanks to Stewart's legal background we managed after months of negotiations to buy back the fifty percent of Primex we had sold.

Primex continued to grow by relying on our own resources and business model while focusing our business activities in North and South America.

Chapter 86
Crystalline, Israel

In 1992, we became aware of the Crystalline Company, owned by the Mali family, which had offices in Tel-Aviv. They manufactured personal care products. Most of the raw materials for these products are derived from the Dead Sea in Israel. In the beginning, production was sub-contracted. They had set up a production facility on the Golan Heights in 1997.

Similar products are manufactured by Ahava Company. The Crystalline Company started to market their products very successfully to tourists visiting Israel. They then began selling their products in the U.S. and other parts of the world.

I had the pleasure of meeting with Ilan, the manager of Crystalline, who told me that they were in the early stages of production. They had just hired the best known chemist in the industry, focusing on developing original products such as facial creams, hand creams, and bath salts—with the aim of marketing private label products at competitive prices. Ilan, at that time, already had an office in the Empire State Building.

Ilan's father was one of the pioneers of Israel, arriving from Poland in the early 1920s. He manufactured bricks for buildings. Later he organized the largest public transportation company, EGED, or Egged, for which he was the managing director for over twenty-five years. His next venture was to establish the first public telex service in Israel, starting with one machine and growing to fifty machines in a short time. Ilan followed in the footsteps of his father and mother, in the telex service business. However, he had inherited the pioneering spirit from his parents and went on to establish a manufacturing facility, Crystalline, in the Golan Heights. By moving to the Golan Heights, on the border with Syria, he was responding to the call of the government for a patriotic effort to re-enforce the already existing businesses and settlements on this disputed territory. This territory had been captured by Israel during the Six-Day War in 1967.

On one of my trips to Israel in 1998, our office in Israel renewed contact with Ilan and coordinated a meeting. For me, it was a memorable ride: a three hour drive from Tel-Aviv on a new road, through the beautiful valleys of Emek Israel, passing kibbutzim, moshavim, farming coops blooming with fruit trees, and the green fields of farm land. During the ride I had the pleasure of Ilan's sharing with me his feelings about his pioneering accomplishment.

As we drove up almost 10,000 feet on a winding one lane road, he pointed out the Syrian border and the Israeli part of the occupied mountain. The Golan plateau encompasses about 700 square miles. Over the last ten years, the Israeli population was about 40,000 co-existing with 80,000 Syrians.

During my visit to Crystalline, I saw an impressive, clean research and development department, as well as their relatively small but efficient product line. In discussing business opportunities, we came up with the idea of Primex's becoming Crystalline's exclusive representative in Chile, one of the countries where Crystalline was not represented and where Primex had already established businesses in other product categories. Primex had set up a separate division within our company in partnership with our Chilean management team, headed by Isabel Lanas.

Our business with Crystalline lasted only a couple of years. Chile was the test market for the other bigger countries in South America, such as Argentina, Brazil, etc. The product line did not sell to our expectations; however, our friendship with Ilan and recently with his son, Asaf, who joined the company after completing his military service and education, continues.

Asaf took charge of the U.S. market, working closely with my son, Gil, with some special accounts. They succeeded in selling the Crystalline products to Pier 1's over 1000 stores.

Continued friendship exists between our families, and new business efforts are continuing.

Chapter 87
Primex Argentina

In Argentina we are represented by Sebastian Salas. We opened our office in Argentina in 1982; initially we had high hopes because Argentina was a country rich in resources. In addition, as a traditional exporting country, the standard of living was the highest among all South American countries.

During our first years in Argentina, we generated some business in the furniture category, housewares, ceramics, glass, and confectionary; however, overall, business was not up to our expectations.

Inflation in Argentina during this period reached over 30%. The powerful labor unions tried to protect their achievements of high wages and costly social benefits. Major labor strikes across the country contributed to the deterioration of the economy. Main sectors of industry were shut down by the labor unions for months, and some never re-opened.

At the same time the economies of the two principal neighboring countries, Brazil and Chile were booming. The exports of Argentina in the most important category, commodities—wheat, soy, meat, and sugar—were unable to compete.

Chapter 88
Primex Colombia

Our business in Colombia was limited to one blown glass company that supplied to Pier 1. This business had continued for several years until the Chinese copied our items and offered them direct to Pier 1 at prices 40% below Colombia.

The political environment did not help our efforts in Colombia. A number of major U.S. companies had listed Colombia as a security risk because of drug and guerrilla activity; therefore, for security reasons, buyers were not permitted to travel to Colombia.

During one of my trips, I had an interesting encounter at the airport with the Colombian police. I was traveling with Bob Hewes, the Pier1 buyer; we had checked out from the Intercontinental Hotel after breakfast, leaving our luggage at the hotel to be picked up in the afternoon on our way to the airport.

At the airport we checked our bags in as usual. Then we stood in the waiting room for thirty minutes past our scheduled boarding time, waiting for the announcement of our flight. Instead of the flight announcement, the Colombian Police announced my name on the loud speaker: "Mr. Ernest Paul, come to the entrance of the waiting room." Bob went with me. When we arrived at the entrance, two policemen were waiting for me.

They ordered me to come with them. They spoke no English, but my Spanish was good enough to understand their orders to follow them. Bob kindly stuck by me. Following the policemen, we walked and walked for more than fifteen minutes.

Bob and I were hot, sweating, walking in about a 90 ° temperature. We finally arrived at the baggage ramp, at the point where they load the baggage onto the plane.

One of the policemen pointed to my bag and asked, " Is that bag yours?"

My American Express name tag was clearly visible.

I answered, "Yes, it is."

The policeman ordered me to open it. As I was about to open the bag, I heard a ticking sound coming from my bag. The ticking sounded like a time bomb—Tic, tic, Tic, tic. On and on. I stopped near the bag, listening to it.

Bob asking me, "What is going on?"

My reply was, "It sounds like a time bomb."

I turned to the policemen and told him, "No, you open it."

Before I opened the bag, I told the policemen that I had stored my bag at the Intercontinental Hotel and was concerned that a bomb had been tucked in by some terrorist or drug smuggler.

He became angry, unbuckling his pistol holster and ordering me again, "You open it, and fast."

As he pointed the pistol at my head, my heart was pounding like the "bomb." I finally opened the main zipper to my bag. The ticking became louder; however, I saw nothing. I opened the second zipper where I had my overnight toiletry bag. I unzipped it and suddenly saw my electric shaver vibrating and ticking. Both Bob and I were relieved.

When the bomb scare was all over, we were ushered back to our waiting room to catch our flight. We had been delayed for an hour and a half.

Other than this incident, our first visit to Colombia was pleasant; however, since then I have stopped carrying an electric shaver with me.

Chapter 89
Primex Peru

The Primex office in Peru has been managed by Emilia Bellido for over twenty years. Our visits to Peru were productive; most of the time, we found new products. The social aspects of our visits were always enjoyable: nice accommodations, friendly hospitality, great restaurants and food; Peruvians that we met were simply nice people.

Peru was not known as a great business destination for U.S. buyers. However, once we visited, we did not hesitate to recommend Peru.

There are in Peru a number of medium-sized textile manufacturers that export their products, such as the Peruvian alpaca products, blankets, cotton beach towels, kitchen towels, polo shirts, and underwear. However, most of the exports were in the handicraft category, such as handmade typical Peruvian silver and gold jewelry, and unique ceramics as well as pottery particularly from the Chulucanas region. Chulucanas pottery comes from Chulucanas, a small village on the side of Mt. Vicus in northern Peru. Other handicrafts that were exported were hand carved wooden mirrors, picture frames, wood carvings, hand painted small furniture, accent pieces, hand- knitted Christmas ornaments, glass items, and wind chimes.

The individual artisans exported through trading companies. Thousands of artisans in small towns were producing special products according to the export needs of the trading companies. Some of the most active trading companies were Allpa SAC, R. Berrocal SAC, Raymisa SA, and Inter-American Trading Company.

Because the individual artisans were organized in cooperatives (co-ops), they had no knowledge of the international market and no means of buying raw materials or the specially required packaging. The trading companies with the assistance of the government purchased and supplied the artisans with raw materials and packaging. Then they purchased from the co-ops the finished products and exported these to various parts of the world.

During one of my visits with the ceramic buyer of Pier 1 imports, Bob Hewes, we decided to travel to the Chulucanas region where the ceramic vases for Pier 1 were produced. The purchases, through Allpa and other trading companies, amounted to about $300,000 per year, F.O.B. Peru. At an almost $2 million selling price, these ceramics had been a successful product category for over twenty years.

We flew from Lima, a two and a half hour flight on an old D.C.9— quite a choppy flight. During the flight, Bob, a heavy smoker, must have smoked a pack of cigarettes. We landed on time at 10 AM. We traveled with Nelly from Allpa and Emilia from our Peru office. According to the article "Allpa," *Allpa*, from a Quechua Indian word that means "earth," is a fair trade company, a "Peruvian craft trading company providing marketing assistance to artisan groups and family workshops throughout Peru."

A co-op van picked us up to take us to the Indian tribal settlements. After more than two hours, mostly on unpaved dirt roads, we arrived at the co-op regional offices where a typical lunch was waiting for us: wild boar, pig's feet, rice and beans, and who knew what else was in the homemade casserole.

After lunch we were driven about a half an hour to the "factory," several sheds covered with large green leaves. The ceramic vases were hand turned on manually operated wheels and then dried in the sun. After that, they were moved to the hand carvers, who were working on long wooden tables under the open skies. Next the vases were carried to primitive homemade kilns, fired with wood and green leaves to give the fired product a unique two-tone hand carved finish. Some parts of the vases were hand polished to give the pieces a three dimensional look. More surprising and interesting than the products were the artisans.

Young and old females were all topless, sitting on their behinds with small scarves wrapped around them. Young and old males used only natural green leaves on a string to cover themselves.

For the first half hour we focused on the "show"—the artists. In this location over three hundred workers were scattered. At first, for us, it was certainly a most embarrassing scene. For them, it was natural. We were told that this is how they live and work because of the over 90° heat and high humidity.

Bob the buyer's comments were, "I have been traveling to China, India, Thailand, Mexico, and many other countries, but this was my most unique and memorable visit; however, so is the finished product."

Chapter 90
L'Chaim!

In 2008 after reviewing the pros and cons, I decided to retire. I now live at our condominium in Atlantic City, still convenient to New York. I enjoy swimming in the condominium pool and walks on the boardwalk. I still get up early and have a regular routine. I need to do that to accomplish all that I want to do—reading, writing, lecturing in schools and colleges, and talking with friends and family.

My children telephone me every day, and I visit them often. I still love to go into New York City and enjoy the wonderful restaurants the city has to offer. I talk with my friends around the world once a week.

I read extensively: books about politics, about Israel, about Hungary, about WW II, and especially books about the *Shoah*. Recently my reading has focused on research for the book I wrote about my wife, Sara, titled *Sara Triumphant!* published in 2009 and for my book, *Ernest Triumphant!* in 2010.

Students are reading *Sara Triumphant!* and I am often invited to speak to classes. For example, I have spoken frequently to my granddaughter's middle school classes and also to classes at The Richard Stockton College of New Jersey.

In 2009, I participated in an evening presentation with the Chief Justice of the New Jersey Supreme Court, Stuart Rabner. I was one of three Holocaust survivors who were interviewed by him at Stockton College before a standing room only audience. These interviews became a film *From Despair, Hope*.

I have a full and rich life. Since I retired, I have more time for the things that I enjoy. I am enjoying time with my children and their partners as well as with my grandchildren and great-grandchildren. I find writing to be a great pleasure. I also love traveling to visit my friends in Israel, Europe, and South America. In May 2010, I will participate in a Stockton study tour to Germany.

Life, despite the torture and horror of the Holocaust years, has given me a bountiful harvest: not only plums and *cholent*, but also, and most important, the love of my wife, my beloved Sara, and the love of my family and friends. All this and the State of Israel! Bountiful, indeed!

Chapter 91
An Interview with my
Saba-Grandfather—Eitan Paul

On December 26, 2009, I sat down with my *saba*-grandfather and asked him about the people, experiences, and values that guided him throughout his life.

1. How did family life before the war compare to modern family life? What lessons can we learn from your upbringing, from your mother, and your father?

At the time, during my childhood, the world was a different world in terms of technology and in terms of standard of living. But we didn't feel that we were missing anything. We adjusted to the life that the time had to offer and adapted to the land and the way of living. We made the maximum within our ability to cultivate the lands. We felt that the land gave us so much. We had a wonderful life.

My parents were busy with the lives of others in the community. Although my father was blind, he was like a front door for anyone who needed some advice. There were many people without education, without financial means, or in need of medical attention who came to my father. My father was able to open doors with regional and federal government authorities.

As a child, I didn't appreciate what my parents were doing. But later, when I was on my own, I looked back and saw how much love and care they had. But they were sharing that. Nothing was too difficult for them. There was nothing they wouldn't do to make us happy. We were a happy family. I learned to respect the fact that they were not just looking out for their own family; they were looking out for all the needy people in town. That is the most fundamental characteristic that I got from them.

2. What aspects of your Jewish upbringing were important to you and stuck with you?

We were a traditional conservative Jewish family. We supported the small Jewish community. Jewishness was felt in our home—in the way we lived. *Shabbat* was a precious time to spend with family and with the Jewish community. The Jews stuck together very closely. Our parents were leaders in the community and they supported, with everything they could, the Jewish community.

The entire community looked up to my father, especially because although he was Jewish, he was devoting his time and his life to the non-Jews, even though some of them were anti-Semites. He didn't pay them back in their own way; he paid them with kindness and assistance. Morally, he was committed to helping the non-Jews as well as the Jewish community.

What gave you the courage to act with such bravery as a teenager in the Underground?

Upbringing at home definitely had an impact. The role model for me was my father because he was so active and devoted to the wellbeing of the whole town. When I moved away from home, I was alone and I realized that I had to carve out for myself a way of life. I realized that the way to do that was to stand on my own. I didn't want to depend on my relatives or my friends. I had to plow a way and find my own way and stand on my own. There was no choice, no option in a way. That was a driving force for me—that either I'm going to make something out of myself and become somebody that could help in the Jewish community or I'm going to waste my life and my time. I chose to stand up and do whatever was in my power, within my limited abilities, to help and to be counted.

There were two ways of trying to live an independent life. One was just to let things happen. And, in my case, I made things happen instead of just going with the flow. I took the initiative of getting involved and learning about the issues and trying to analyze and realize what was ahead of me and what I had to do to survive—and what I had to do to help others to survive. We had seen the handwriting of the Nazi sympathizers on the wall.

How did your experiences in the Resistance shape the rest of your life? What gave you strength to keep hope throughout difficult times?

Experiences as a youngster, living alone and trying to make something of myself and of my life that was meaningful, even at my early age, helped me to be strong and to be motivated. I was only thinking in one direction—the positive direction of being strong, being helpful and effective, getting involved with the youth movements, which I embraced and I shared with others, realizing that we had to be organized and we had to be able to defend ourselves.

That experience taught me and affected my decisions after I was liberated. I was very active in *kibbutzim* in Romania and Italy. I was active for two years from Romania to Israel, organizing immigration. In Israel, as a result of my activities in the youth movement, they realized the strength of my character, so I was appointed to a position in the Federation of Labor at a very young age.

My first preference was to continue to fulfill my dreams and my Zionist beliefs by joining a *kibbutz* where I had friends from the underground. However, my wife, Sara—your *savti*—had other aspirations.

When I came to the United States, I couldn't think of anything other than adjusting to the new reality and trying to carve out a living for myself and my family. There is no doubt that my experiences and my life as an independent youth had impacted my decision-making in business as well.

In addition to your father, who else served as role models and influenced your life decisions?

Hannah Senesh

Even though I had not known her personally, Hannah's spirit was living in me as an individual. The movement taught us collectively about her lifestyle, her common sense, her dedication to follow and willingness to sacrifice, her leading by example, leaving her family, her home, making *aliyah*. In Israel, she chose a pioneering lifestyle. Knowing that she was from Hungary and one of the founders of the movement, we followed her spiritually and mentally. Educators used her life as an example of what we needed to do and what we should be doing even in the most difficult circumstances. Volunteering to go back to Budapest to become a paratrooper with the objective of helping to save the 750,000 Hungarian Jewish people was another shining example of Hannah's spirit.

David Ben-Gurion

The person that impacted my life when I came to Israel was David Ben-Gurion. Throughout the years in Israel, I met Ben-Gurion numerous times in the Central Committee, where I was a member of the Mapai Party. I listening to him speak. Ben-Gurion's vision that he reflected impacted me so much that I was ready to follow him blindfolded. Years later, I remember visiting him in Kibbutz Sde Boker, with a delegation from Haifa, to try to bring him back for the third time because twice he had resigned. The way he expressed himself; he told on a number of occasions, "Don't cry for me. Come with me. Join me." Ben-Gurion was the one who led the nation and the armed forces to independence. He decided to fight the Egyptians and the other Arab forces against all odds, against all military advice. His actions were heroic, including sacrificing the last years of his life in becoming a personal example, believing that the only way Israel would stay a solid country is if we transformed the south of Israel, 50% of the land, to a productive, intricate part of the country. He believed that that was the last mission in his life. Because of his pioneering example, many thousands moved to the south. His life and name are commemorated with the airport in Tel-Aviv, as well as the Ben-Gurion University in Beersheba, one of Israel's most important research centers for higher learning.

Klaus Schumacher: In the business world

I was very impressed over the years by Klaus Schumacher. He built and designed facilities without any engineering background. He was a pioneer and innovator. He took pride in everything he did. Above all, he was an honest hardworking person.

How did you reconcile fighting against the Nazis in World War II with having as one of your best friends in life, Klaus, who is German and who was involved in Nazi Germany?

The evening Klaus and I met, I found out that Klaus was a German Brazilian. During World War II, he was sixteen to eighteen years old and served in Hitler's military. I introduced myself as a Jewish survivor of the Nazi regime who during the war was an active member of the Zionist Underground Resistance Movement in Budapest. From 7PM to 3AM, we discussed the past. I questioned him about his role during the war. I quickly learned that as a youth, he had no decisive role during the Nazi regime.

I could not hold against Klaus the atrocities of the Hitler regime. I believed then, as I believe now, of the need to differentiate between the past, the present, and the future. We worked together for over thirty-five years, learned to trust each other, and respect each other. We became the best of friends for life.

I remembered the cooperation between Ben-Gurion and the first Chancellor of the Federal Republic of Germany, Konrad Adenauer. Ben-Gurion told the Knesset, the Israeli parliament, that, in Adenauer, he had a partner he could trust. Adenauer agreed in his sincere efforts to make good for some of the atrocities the Nazi government committed against the Jewish people by paying reparations to Israel and helping build a strong foundation for the State.

History will tell us that we cannot hold a nation at fault for leaders who are no longer here. I understood that there has to be a line drawn between the past, the present, and the future. There is no other way. An individual has to be judged on his own and not by the crimes his nation committed.

Do you feel as if you achieved the American dream and did you feel as if you were chasing it at the time?

Within my limitations, I think I lived the American dream. I learned early in the days of being in the U.S. of the unlimited potential within American society. Everything is possible. It depends on the individual—how hard he or she wants to work and how big are the mountains the person wants to climb. I was always looking to maximize the conditions of the market related to my own ability to take advantage of it. In my daily life, I had to adjust. There were ups and downs in my business life—but I always believed in myself: I knew that I could navigate through even the stormiest weather to achieve the best possible results.

What lessons did you learn from maintaining a relationship with my grandmother, Sara, for over sixty years?

It was a give and take situation. Nothing through the 62 years was a one-way street only. It was a life of compromise, love, respecting each other, as well as the determination to forge the best partnership between us, to be an example to our children.

Has the world learned the lessons of the Holocaust?

I certainly hope so. I believe that we have learned despite the fact that we could have done much more and should have learned more. There are still atrocities in the world, which have no justification or room to exist. Darfur, other tragedies and illnesses, AIDS—I still believe that the free world, the rich nations, are not doing as much as they should be doing. Looking back at history, at what life gave us—we should be doing more to elevate the standard of living of these people. There is still so much misery and poverty and suffering. Maybe it is lack of education—people do not comprehend the depth of the problems. For the sake of the future, each and every one of us must believe that one person can make a difference in this world.

Postscript

I had the most wonderful fortune of first meeting my father-in-law when, at the young age of fifteen, I fell in love with his son Stewart. I have been quietly in awe of my father-in-law ever since.

I knew of his heroism during World War II from his family and friends. He rarely spoke of his actions in the Hungarian Underground and only through his work on this book did more details emerge as to just how courageous he was as a very young man.

When I asked him how he was able to do what he did to save others and at such a tender age and when I wondered aloud about where that kind of superhuman bravery came from, he simply and quietly said, "I had no choice."

But of course there were choices to be made—whether to run and try to save oneself or stay and fight to save others. My father-in-law chose what seemed to him to be an unquestionable and clear path. So clear, that he saw no other option.

I had a glimpse of that hellish time through his eyes when he became very ill with seizures toward the end of my mother-in-law's tragic illness. He lay in the hospital in a room next door to her, but he was very far away—in time and place. He was back in Nazi Hungary, and Nazi soldiers were everywhere coming to harm him. Every nurse and doctor was the enemy. When he looked out the window, he saw buildings exploding, including his home. And while he was anxious being back in the streets and forests of his frightening youth, he was also incredibly strong. His hand would grip mine with the strength of an Underground fighter and there was a determination in his body language that fairly shouted that he would neither give in nor be taken.

This was an extraordinary thing to witness. This very sick and sad man, whose beloved wife lie dying in the room next door, was again fighting Nazis with every fiber of his being. We worried about him. Would we lose him too in the days ahead? Would the *Shoah* be the last thing he would remember?

Once, after being especially agitated about another patient in the room, whom he believed to be a Nazi commander, he suddenly burst into singing the Israeli national anthem. I gazed at his face in amazement and now it was shining. He was safe in the Jewish homeland. For a few moments, his body relaxed and I heard the voice of a young man, full of hope. My dear father-in-law survived this awful period of seizures, and then he went on to bury our wonderful Sara, mere days after. We didn't know how he would survive without her. She was his love, his friend, his everything.

There were more losses to come on the heels of this greatest loss of all. He needed to give up his home in New York City and his work. Each one of these losses by itself could have been the hardest of challenges. Taken together, my father-in-law could easily have fallen into great despair and torment. He could have given up.

But not Ernest Paul!

He showed his children and grandchildren how not only to survive the darkness of excruciating loss, but also how to go forward, continuing to make a meaningful difference.

My father-in-law threw himself into completing my mother-in-law's memoir, adding to her work, which had never been finished. He fleshed out her story with his commentary on the events of her life. He researched places and people who were part of her journey. He chose photographs to share with the world.

He speaks of her life to students of all ages and does book-signings.

It was very important to my mother-in-law to have her story known and he did this for her—an extraordinary labor of love. Now many more would know of her own ability to triumph over horrifying circumstances; to believe in love, when she could have been bitter.

My father-in-law then set out to write his own memoir as a companion volume. He sat for hours a day, day after day, month after month writing and editing his own journey. He showed the same discipline in tackling this as he did everything in his life. If there was a job to do, he did it, never tallying the hours.

So at the age of eighty, my father-in-law reinvented himself as a writer and lecturer. Without any prior education or experience in writing, researching, or speaking in academic circles, there he was— doing this and doing it well—with charisma, charm, and wisdom. Students from middle school through college have been made the wiser by his talks on the importance of tolerance and education, the need for compassion and understanding.

These days my father-in-law is learning computer skills and sending emails. We can't wait to see what is next!

His and my mother-in-law's stories show us that the human spirit can triumph when tested, again and again. It is an important and inspiring message for all of us. There are so many who sadly turn to darker choices when suffering one dreadful thing after another. The gift of these companion volumes is to remind each of us that it is possible not only to survive, but also to deal with terrible circumstances and losses with grace. One need not succumb to despair. It is possible to engage in new, important endeavors. Each has this capacity to go forward and to make a difference.

Nancy Z. Paul, 2010

(Still in awe of my father-in-law after all these years)

Appendix

I had the privilege of accompanying the Stockton Study Tour to Germany and the Netherlands, from May 11 to May 23, 2010. This study tour opened dormant wounds in my heart. The memory of the Nazi era is still living in me—I heard the cries and felt the suffering of the innocent victims, as we were guided through the Bergen-Belsen Concentration Camp and Buchenwald Concentration Camp Memorial, as well as at the Euthanasia Killing Center of Bernburg and the many other memorials and museums.

In the Netherlands, I will never forget the Oldebroek Farm and the Vierhouten Woods, where Jewish families were hidden, and the former Synagogue Museum in Elburg. In Berlin, among other sights, we went to Rosenstrasse where German women resisted the deportation of their Jewish husbands and the Wannsee Conference House where the Final Solution was planned. The touring and seminars hosted by German historians and professors were educational for me and, in particular, for the Stockton College undergraduate and graduate students. Everyone was fascinated and horrified about the numbers and the methods of mass murder but especially about the resistance.

Notable in Berlin are the number of Jewish memorials and museums, centrally located at the most important government sites in the city. These are well publicized and visited by millions of Germans, including students, in addition to the millions of visitors from around the world. This signifies that the German government is embracing the importance of educating about the Holocaust. Not only have they financed most of the memorials, building and financing the upkeep, but also have included financing for newly built and renovated synagogues. Most important are their efforts in mandatory education, legislation and enforcement of the laws, and keeping the lights of the memorials burning. These symbolize a new Germany. As we walked through Berlin, East and West, we noticed street signs, such as David Ben-Gurion Boulevard, Yitzhak Rabin Street, Sara's Street, and Chana's Street; these warmed my heart and opened my eyes concerning the new reality of Germany. I could see and feel that a large majority of the people and political leaders in Germany are committed to avoiding the reoccurrence of the dark and terrible days of the Nazi regime.

The study tour of twenty-seven students, one Stockton administrator, and three Holocaust survivors was organized and led by two most capable Stockton professors: Gail Rosenthal and Michael Hayse. For them, this was their fifth study tour to Germany, Poland, The Netherlands, as well as to Israel. For the students and me, it was a most painful educational trip.

Over 90% of the graduate and undergraduate students were not Jewish; therefore, it was remarkable to see their active interest and focus on learning about the Holocaust. Because the majority these students will become teachers, they will be teaching the present and future generations of students. In addition to the text books and memoirs, they will teach from their own witnessing and visiting of those many Holocaust sites that are still soaked with the blood and the ashes of millions.

Both of the leaders of the group made my trip more meaningful by allowing me to interact with the students by speaking to them, sharing with them my mother-in-law's experiences in Auschwitz-Birkenau and my wife Sara's experience in Auschwitz and Bergen-Belsen, and her suffering of typhus, lice, and tuberculosis. I shared with them highlights from Sara's book, *Sara Triumphant*, that was published last year, as well as highlights from my book that will be published in July 2010. The students made an important impact on me, which I will remember and cherish for the rest of my life. The help they extended to me physically by watching over me every step of the way, carrying my luggage, sharing and caring for me, made me feel as if I was traveling with my own children. The pinnacle was when they handed me a beautiful gift, a *Kiddush Cup* and a *Tallis Clip,* which symbolize life and security, with a Book of "Remembrance." Each student and the two leaders wrote a page of comments about getting to know me and the impact of my life story.

My praise to all of them. My mutual love, respect, and appreciation to all.

Maps

Czechoslovakia, 1928. Nové Selo indicated.

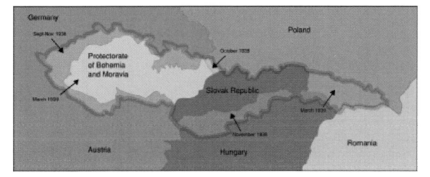

Partition of Czechoslovakia, 1938-1939, by Germany, before WWII began.
—sfpa.sk/dokumenty/publikacie/22

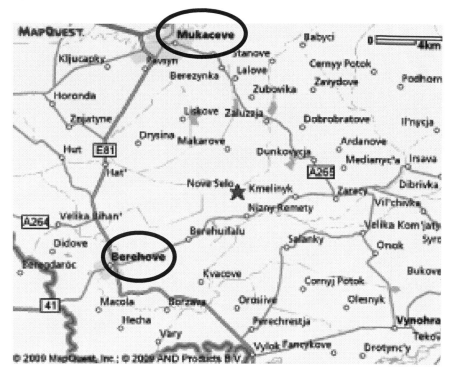

Ernest's home town: Beregújfalu (Berehuifalu) circled, near Nove Selo, indicated with a star. Berehovo (circled), 9 miles WSW. Mukaceve (Munkács) circled, 12 miles NNW.

From Beregújfalu, Czechoslovakia, Ernest went to Budapest, Hungary (circled), when he was thirteen years old. —cia.gov

Ernest and Sara lived in DP Camps in and around Bari and Tricase, Italy (circled), before immigrating to Israel. —images.google.com

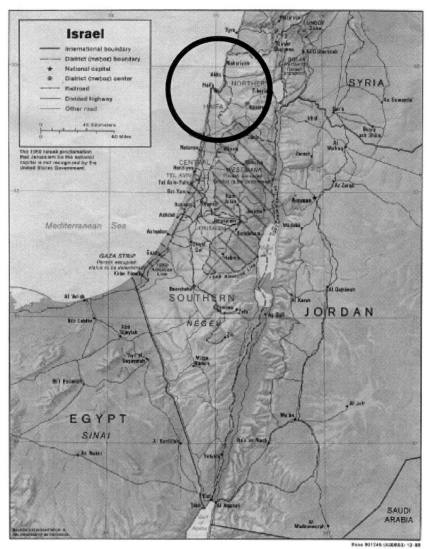

Israel—modern map; Haifa where Sara and Ernest lived is circled.—itradio.org

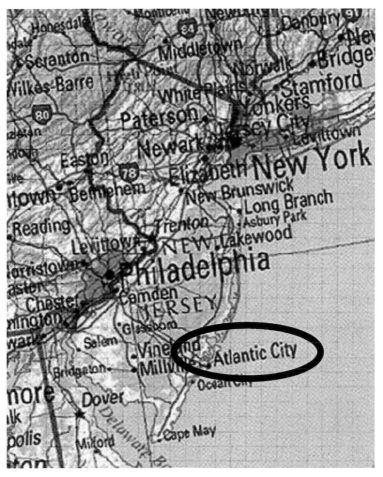

Ernest and Sara lived in Philadelphia, New York, and Atlantic City (circled), where Ernest retired. lib.utex

Works Cited

"Allpa." Ten Thousand Villages. 2009. Web. 2 Jan. 2010.

Gur, David. "Resistance and Rescue Operations by
    Hungarian Zionist Youth." Fax . January 2010.

"Jezreel Valley." Enwikipedia. 28 Feb. 2010. Web. 5 Mar. 2010.

Lapidot, Yehuda. "The Acre Prison Break." Jewish Virtual
    Library. 2010. Web. 22 Feb. 2010.

Palgi, Yoel. *Into the Inferno: The Memoir of a Jewish Paratrooper
    behind Nazi Lines.* New Brunswick: Rutgers UP,
    2003. Print.

"Stoke-on-Trent, England." The Potteries. Web. 20 Feb. 2010.

"Turnkey Definition." Investor Words. Web. 2 Jan. 2010.

Endnotes

¹ Nové Selo/ Beregújfalu

Before WWI (c. 1900):	Beregújfalu Bereg	Hungary
Between wars (c. 1930):	Nové Selo	Czechoslovakia
After WWII (c. 1950):	Novoye Selo	Soviet Union
Today (c. 2000):	Berehujfalu	Ukraine

"Nove Selo." Jewish Genealogy. Web. 28 Apr. 2010.

² Beregovo, or Berehove "a city in the Sub-Carpathian Ruthenia region, now part of the Ukraine. Prior to 1918, the town was part of Hungary and known as Beregszasz. Between 1918 and 1938, the town was part of Czechoslovakia. Between 1938 and the end of World War II, the town was once again part of Hungary. The Jewish population in 1930 was about 5,700. After the Hungarians regained control in 1938, most of the Jewish males were sent to Hungarian labor battalions." "Berehove." *Encyclopedia Judaica.* 2007. Web. 28 Apr. 2010.

Further reading: Arad, Yitzhak. *The Holocaust in the Soviet Union.* Lincoln: U of Nebraska P, 2009.

³*Gabbai* (Heb/Aram. Attendant/tax collector) Title of the person in charge of organizing synagogue services. A *gabbai*'s other roles include calling individuals up to the Torah for an aliyah and standing beside the reader to monitor for mistakes." "*Gabbai*." Jewish Virtual Library. Web. 28 Apr. 2010.

⁴Challah "traditional Jewish braided bread eaten on Shabbat and Jewish holidays (except Passover, when leavened bread is not allowed). This association with Judaism is most prevalent in the United States, as challah is also traditional bread in numerous European countries, such as Hungary, among local non-Jewish peasant populations. On Shabbat every Jew is commanded to eat three meals (one on Friday night and two on Saturday). In Judaism, a "meal" includes bread. Hence, Jews will traditionally eat challah at the beginning of their Shabbat meal. As with any other type of bread, the blessing '*Baruch atah Adonai, eloheinu melech ha'olam, hamotzi lechem min ha'aretz*'is recited before the challah is eaten. Translated, it means "Blessed are you, Lord, our God, king of the universe, who brings forth bread from the earth." "Challah." Jewish Recipes. Web. 28 Apr. 2010.

⁵Kiddush "(means sanctification) the ritual of sanctification, with blessings recited over a cup of wine, that is performed at the beginning of Jewish Sabbath and Jewish festival meals. The purpose of the kiddush is to remind Jews of the sanctity of the day. Traditionally the head of the house recites the kiddush over a cup of wine immediately before the Sabbath or holiday meal. Following recitation of the kiddush, each person sips wine from the kiddush cup." "Kiddush." Jewish Virtual Library. Web. 28 Apr. 2010.

[6]**Cholent** "The traditional stew for the Sabbath midday meal and [traditionally] the only hot dish of the day, prepared on Friday and left to cook overnight." "Cholent." My Jewish Learning." Web. 28 Apr. 2010.

[7] *Shomer Shabbat* a Jew who adheres strictly to *Shabbat* laws.

[8] *Pesach* "(Passover) "The major Jewish spring holiday (with agricultural aspects) also known as *hag hamatzot* (festival of unleavened bread) commemorates the Exodus or deliverance of the Hebrew people from Egypt (see Exodus 12-13). The festival lasts eight days, during which Jews refrain from eating all leavened foods and products. A special ritual meal called the Seder is prepared, and a traditional narrative called the *Haggadah*, supplemented by hymns and songs, marks the event." "Passover." Jewish Virtual Library. Web. 28 Apr. 2010.

Further reading: Ziefert, Harriet. *Passover: Celebrating Now, Remembering Then*. Illustrator: Karla Gudeon. San Francisco: Blue Apple Books, 2010.

[9] **Ark** "(Heb. *Aron hakodesh*, lit. holy chest) The cabinet where the Torah scrolls are kept." "Ark." Jewish Virtual Library. Web. 28 Apr. 2010.

[10] *Succoth or Sukkot* "(Tabernacles) (Heb. booths, tabernacles) Seven-day Jewish fall festival beginning on Tishri 15 commemorating the *Sukkot* where the Israelites lived in the wilderness after the Exodus; also known as *hag haasiph*, the Festival of Ingathering (of the harvest)." "Succoth." Jewish Virtual Library. Web. 28 Apr. 2010.

[11] **Bar (Bat) Mitzvah** "(Heb. son (daughter)-of-the-commandment(s)). The phrase originally referred to a person responsible for performing the divine commandments of Judaism; it now refers to the occasion when a boy or girl reaches the age of religious maturity and responsibility (thirteen years for a boy; twelve years and a day for a girl)." "Bar (Bat) Mitzvah." Jewish Virtual Library. Web. 28 Apr. 2010.

[12] *Eretz Yisrael* (Heb. The land of Israel) "(Heb. The land of Israel) A maximalist term used by some right-wingers to refer to the borders of the ancient kingdom of Israel which includes all of the West Bank and parts of Jordan." "*Eretz Yisrael*." Jewish Virtual Library. Web. 28 Apr. 2010.

"This term should not be confused with historical Israelite kingdoms or with the modern nation state of Israel (*Medinat Yisrael*).

"Prior to the foundation of the Jewish State, now Israel, the term *Eretz Yisrael* was used by religious Jews to refer to the area then generally termed

348

among others and non-Jews as Palestine or as the Holy Land. Since 1967, the English term *Eretz Israel* particularly has been associated with the political right in Israel. Historically, another commonly used name, referring to both the land of Israel and Jerusalem, was Zion." "*Eretz Yisrael.*" Enwikipedia. Web. 28 Apr. 2010.

Further reading: Penkower, Monty. *Holocaust & Israel Reborn: From Catastrophe to Sovereignty.* Champaign, IL: U of Illinois P, 1994.

Govrin, Yosef. *In the Shadow of Destruction: Recollections of Transnistria and Illegal Immigration to Eretz Israel, 1941-1947.* Portland, OR: Vallentine Mitchell, 2007.

[13] **Yom Kippur** "(Heb. Day of Atonement) Annual day of fasting and atonement, occurring in the fall on Tishri 10 (just after Rosh Hashanah); the most solemn and important occasion of the Jewish religious year." "Yom Kippur." Jewish Virtual Library. Web. 28 Apr. 2010.

[14] **Synagogue in walking distance** According to Jewish law, the operation of a motor vehicle constitutes multiple violations of the prohibited activities on Shabbat. Though Jewish law is based on texts that existed long before the existence of the automobile, various writings prohibit during Shabbat the actions that take place as a result of driving. The Torah thus prohibits driving on the basis that a labor is being performed by the act of operating a motor vehicle. However, Jews of varying backgrounds have taken differing views on the matter, either finding various interpretations to permit and justify at least some driving on Shabbat, either solely for synagogue attendance or for other personal reasons as well, or else by disregarding the Jewish laws altogether. In Israel, approximately 80% of Jews drive on Shabbat. "Synagogue and walking." Judaism. Web. 28 Apr. 2010.

[15] **Zionist Movement** "(Mount) Zion is an ancient Hebrew designation for Jerusalem, but already in biblical times it began to symbolize the national homeland (see e.g., Psalm 137.1-6). In this latter sense it served as a focus for Jewish national-religious hopes of renewal over the centuries. Ancient hopes and attachments to Zion gave rise to Zionist longings and movements since antiquity, culminating in the modern national liberation movement of that name. The Zionist cause helped the Jews return to Palestine in this century and found the state of Israel in 1948. The goal of Zionism is the political and spiritual renewal of the Jewish people in its ancestral homeland." "Zionism." Jewish Virtual Library. Web. 28 Apr. 2010.

Further reading: Laqueur, Walter. *A History of Zionism: From the French Revolution to the Establishment of the State of Israel.* New York: Schocken, 2003.

Hertzberg, Arthur. *The Zionist Idea: A Historical Analysis and Reader.* Philadelphia: Jewish Publication Society of America, 1997.

[16] **Fall of Hungarian government in 1944** "In April 1944, Hungarian authorities ordered Hungarian Jews living outside Budapest (roughly 500,000) to concentrate in certain cities, usually regional government seats. Hungarian gendarmes were sent into the rural regions to round up the Jews and dispatch them to the cities. The urban areas in which the Jews were forced to concentrate were enclosed and referred to as ghettos. Sometimes the ghettos encompassed the area of a former Jewish neighborhood. In other cases the ghetto was merely a single building, such as a factory.

Conditions in these ghettos were terrible. Most of the ghettos were outdoors without shelter or sanitation. "Food and water supplies were dangerously inadequate; medical care was virtually non-existent." Police guarded these temporary ghettos; most were liquidated after a few days. Jews were subjected to rape, torture, and extortion. None of these ghettos existed for more than a few weeks and many were liquidated within days.

"In mid-May 1944, the Hungarian authorities, in coordination with the German Security Police, began to systematically deport the Hungarian Jews. . . . . In less than two months, nearly 440,000 Jews were deported from Hungary to Auschwitz, but thousands were also sent to the border with Austria to be deployed at digging fortification trenches. By the end of July 1944, the only Jewish community left in Hungary was that of Budapest, the capital.

"In light of the worsening military situation and facing threats (from Allied leaders) of war crimes trials, Horthy ordered a halt to the deportations on July 7, 1944. . . . . In August, the Germans sponsored a coup d'etat. They arrested Horthy and installed a new Hungarian government under Ferenc Szalasi, the leader of the fascist and radically antisemitic Arrow Cross party.

"In November 1944, the Arrow Cross regime ordered the remaining Jews of Budapest into a ghetto which, covering an area of 0.1 square miles, became temporary residence to nearly 70,000 people. Several thousand Budapest Jews were also marched on foot under Hungarian guard to the Austrian border during November and December 1944. Many who were too weak to continue marching in the bitter cold were shot along the way. "Hungary after the German occupation." *Holocaust Encyclopedia*, USHMM. Web. 28 Apr. 2010.

Further reading: Braham, Randolph L., and Scott Miller, eds. *The Nazis' Last Victims: The Holocaust in Hungary*. Detroit: Wayne State UP in assoc with USHMM, 2002.

Braham, Randolph L. *The Politics of Genocide : The Holocaust in Hungary*. Detroit: Wayne State UP in assoc with USHMM , 2000.

[17] **Tricase** "a mid-sized DP camp at the southern tip of Italy, founded in 1944 by the Allied Commission. This small camp quickly outgrew its quarters in requisitioned holiday villas. 'During the most recent visit made in January 1946 it was definitely established that Tricase could not accommodate more than 800 persons during the winter season since the unused villas were considered uninhabitable,' stated the UNRRA, which assumed management of the camp in late 1945. Tricase housed many members of the Betar kibbutz and the camp's Zionist orientation was evident in the many lectures and activities conducted by Israeli envoys. Like other southern Italian DP centers, Tricase also served as a staging ground for illegal immigration to Palestine. Two of the camp's kibbutzim bought radios that aided communication with Palestine and clandestine charter ships. Cultural life in the kibbutz focused on sports, including organized table tennis and boxing tournaments, and a three-week-long chess competition in the summer of 1946." "Tricase." *Exhibit,* USHMM. Web. 28 Apr. 2010.

Further reading: Wyman, Mark. *DPs: Europe's Displaced Persons, 1945-1951.* Ithaca, NY: Cornell UP, 1998.

Kochavi, Arieh J. *Post-Holocaust Politics: Britain, the United States, and Jewish Refugees, 1945-1948.* Chapel Hill: U of North Carolina P, 2000.

[18] **UNRRA** "The Allies chartered the United Nations Relief and Rehabilitation Administration (UNRRA) at a 44-nation conference at the White House on November 9, 1943. The express purpose of the agency was the repatriation and support of refugees who would come under Allied control at the war's end; UNRRA was charged with coordinating relief efforts and managing the camps. UNRRA was also responsible for certifying welfare agencies for operations in the camps. UNRRA was designated as the principal provider of care for the survivors following the Harrison Report. . . . . . The protracted relief effort cost the United Nations billions and eventually led to the insolvency of the UNRRA. In late 1947, its tasks were delegated to its successor agency, the International Refugee Organization (IRO), which undertook similar responsibilities but concentrated more on financial security. The agencies and their officers . . . set important precedents for the care of refugees." "UNRRA." *Holocaust Encyclopedia,* USHMM. Web. 28 Apr. 2010.

[19] **Ladispoli** "a town and commune in the province of Rome, 55 kilometers from Roma, in the Lazio region of central Italy. Ladispoli occupies the area where the ancient port of Alsium, an Etruscan port, existed. Alsium was later a Roman colony cited by Cicero.

Modern Ladispoli was founded in 1888 by Ladislao Odescalchi, from whom its name stems." "Ladispoli." Enwikipedia. Web. 28 Apr. 2010.

[20] **Cyprus** "an island in the Mediterranean Sea, south of Turkey. A former British colony, Cyprus became independent in 1960 following years of resistance to British rule."

"Cyprus." CIA Report. Web. 28 Apr. 2010.

"In most cases, the British detained the refugees—over 50,000—in detention camps on the island of Cyprus in the eastern Mediterranean Sea. The British use of detention camps as a deterrent failed, and the flood of immigrants attempting entry into Palestine continued.

"The internment of Jewish refugees—many of them Holocaust survivors--turned world opinion against British policy in Palestine. The report of the Anglo-American Commission of Inquiry in January 1946 led U.S. president Harry Truman to pressure Britain into admitting 100,000 Jewish refugees into Palestine.

"The British authorities held Jewish "illegal" immigrants in detention camps on Cyprus from 1946 to 1949. This policy was part of an effort to deter Jewish immigration to Palestine, under British control, as was Cyprus. During that time over 53,000 Jews passed through the barbed wire camps, held against their will, with a quota of only 1,500 per month permitted to leave Cyprus for Palestine.

"The Jews considered illegal immigrants by the British were intercepted by British naval forces and turned back from the shores of Palestine and escorted to Cyprus or temporarily imprisoned in Palestine (Atlit) before being deposited in the camps of Cyprus. "The two major camps were Caraolos, north of Famagusta, and in Dekhelia, outside of Larnaca. The compounds stretched for several miles. The story of these camps has been well documented as an episode in the history of the modern state of Israel. "Cyprus." Holocaust Encyclopedia, USHMM. 28 Apr. 2010.

Further reading: Laub, Morris. *Last Barrier to Freedom: Internment of Jewish Holocaust Survivors on Cyprus, 1946-1949.* Berkeley, CA: Judah L. Magnes Museum, 1985.

[21] **Arab-Israeli War 1947-1948** "Violence in the Holy Land broke out almost immediately after the UN announced partition on November 29, 1947. The United States, the Soviet Union and most other states immediately recognized Israel and indicted the Arabs. The United States urged a resolution charging the Arabs with breach of the peace.

Bard, Mitchell. "The 1948 War." Jewish Virtual Library. Web. 28 Apr. 2010.

Further reading: Morris, Benny. *1948: A History of the First Arab-Israeli War.* New Haven, CT: Yale UP, 2010.

Morris, Benny. *Making Israel.* Ann Arbor, MI: U of Michigan P, 2007.

22 Fedayeen "a term used to describe several distinct, militant groups and individuals in Armenia, Iran, and the Arab world at different times in history. It is sometimes used colloquially to refer to suicide squads."

"(Arabic. Self-sacrificers) Palestinian militants who carried out attacks on Israel during the 1950's and 1960's from across the Jordanian and Egyptian borders." "Fedayeen." Jewish Virtual Library. Web. 28 Apr. 2010.

23 Garin, or Gareen "(Heb. Core or seed) Small group of young Jews dedicated to establishing something new (usually a settlement or community) in Israel. "Garin." Jewish Virtual Library. Web. 28 Apr. 2010.

24 brit milah (literally, Covenant of Circumcision) commonly referred to as a *bris*. Even the most secular of Jews, who observe no other part of Judaism, almost always observe these laws. Like so many Jewish commandments, the *brit milah* is commonly perceived to be a hygienic measure; however the biblical text states the reason for this commandment quite clearly: circumcision is an outward physical sign of the eternal covenant between G-d and the Jewish people. It is also a sign that the Jewish people will be perpetuated through the circumcised man. "Brit Milah." Jewish Facts. Web. 28 Apr. 2010.

25 Masada (Hebrew for fortress) "situated atop an isolated rock cliff at the western end of the Judean Desert, overlooking the Dead Sea. On the east the rock falls in a sheer drop of about 450 meters to the Dead Sea (the lowest point on earth, some 400 m. below sea level) and in the west it stands about 100 meters above the surrounding terrain. The natural approaches to the cliff top are very difficult.

"The only written source about Masada is Josephus Flavius' *The Jewish War*. Some 75 years after Herod's death, at the beginning of the Revolt of the Jews against the Romans in 66 CE, a group of Jewish rebels overcame the Roman garrison of Masada. After the fall of Jerusalem and the destruction of the Temple (70 CE) they were joined by zealots and their families who had fled from Jerusalem. With Masada as their base, they raided and harassed the Romans for two years. Then, in 73 CE, the Roman governor Flavius Silva marched against Masada with the Tenth Legion, auxiliary units and thousands of Jewish prisoners-of-war. The Romans established camps at the base of Masada, laid siege to it and built a circumvallation wall. . . . In the spring of the year 74 CE, the legion moved a battering ram up the ramp and breached the wall of the fortress.

"Josephus Flavius dramatically recounts the story told him by two surviving women. The defenders . . . decided to burn the fortress and end their own lives, rather than be taken alive. "The Zealots cast lots to choose 10 men to kill the remainder. They then chose among themselves the one man who would kill the survivors. That last Jew then killed himself.

"The heroic story of Masada and its dramatic end attracted many explorers to the Judean desert in attempts to locate the remains of the fortress. The site was identified in 1842, but intensive excavations took place only in 1963-65, with the help of hundreds of volunteers from Israel and from many foreign countries. To them and to Israelis, Masada symbolizes the determination of the Jewish people to be free in its own land." Telushkin, Joseph. "Masada." Jewish Virtual Library. 2010. Web. 28 Apr. 2010.

Further reading: Seward, Desmond. *Jerusalem's Traitor: Josephus, Masada, and the Fall of Judea.* Cambridge: Da Capo P, 2009.

Ben-Tor, Amnon. *Back to Masada.* Washington, DC: Biblical Archaeology Society, 2009.

[26] **Hillel** (born in Babylon traditionally c.110BCE–10CE in Jerusalem) "a famous Jewish religious leader, one of the most important figures in Jewish history. He is associated with the development of the *Mishnah* and the *Talmud.* Renowned within Judaism as a sage and scholar, he was the founder of the House of Hillel School for *Tannaïm* (Sages of the *Mishnah*) and the founder of a dynasty of Sages who stood at the head of the Jews living in the land of Israel until roughly the fifth century of the Common Era.

"He is popularly known as the author of two sayings: 1) 'If I am not for myself, who will be for me? And when I am for myself, what am I? And if not now, when?' and the expression of the ethic of reciprocity, or 'Golden Rule': 2) 'That which is hateful to you, do not do to your fellow. That is the whole Torah; the rest is the explanation; go and learn.'" "Hillel." Enwikipedia. Web. 28 Apr. 2010.

Further reading: Telushkin, Joseph. *Hillel: If Not Now, When?* New York: Schocken, 2010.

Buxbaum, Yitzhak. The Life and Teachings of Hillel. Lanham, MD: Rowman & Littlefield, 2008.

[27] *Yom Ha'atzmaut* Israeli Independence Day. "the national independence day of Israel, commemorating its declaration of independence in 1948.

"Celebrated annually on 5th of the Jewish month of Iyar, it centers around the declaration of the state of Israel by David Ben Gurion in Tel Aviv on May 14, 1948 (5 Iyar, 5708), and the end of the British Mandate of Palestine.

"It is always preceded by *Yom Hazikaron*, the Israel fallen soldiers Remembrance Day on the 4th of Iyar. "Yom Ha'atzmaut." Jewish Virtual Library. Web. 28 Apr. 2010.

Further reading: Troen, S. Ilan. *Imagining Zion: Dreams, Designs, and Realities in a Century of Jewish Settlement*. New Haven, CT: Yale UP, 2010.

[28] *Mohel* "Traditionally, parents hire a *mohel* to perform a *bris*, circumcision. A *mohel* is usually a rabbi who has received medical and religious training specific to performing a *bris*.

"Circumcision is an outward physical sign of the eternal covenant between G-d and the Jewish people. It is also a sign that the Jewish people will be perpetuated through the circumcised man." "Mohel." Jewish Facts. Web. 28 Apr. 2010.

[29] **Shiva** (Heb. seven) "Seven days of mourning after the burial of a close relative (as in, 'to sit shiva')." "Shiva." Jewish Virtual Library. Web. 28 Apr. 2010.

[30] **Bimah** "platform in the synagogue on which stands the desk from which the Torah is read. Occasionally, the rabbi delivers his sermon from the bimah, and on Rosh HaShanah the shofar is blown there." "Bimah." Jewish Virtual Library. Web. 28 Apr. 2010.

[31] *Chazzan* **or** *hazzan* (Hebrew: ח_ר.וֹ ḥazzān, Modern Hebrew hazan, Yiddish khazn) "(Lat. one who sings) In Judaism, a chanter/singer of liturgical materials in the synagogue; also used similarly in Christian contexts (choir leader, etc.)." "Chazzan." Jewish Virtual Library. Web. 28 Apr. 2010.

[32] *Havdalah* (Hebrew: separation) "To mark the beginning of sacred time, we light two candles and recite a *berakhah* (blessing) which praises God who commanded us to kindle the lights in celebration of the occasion. We mark the end of that sacred time period with a ceremony called *Havdalah*, which means 'separation.' It, too, begins with light, as we kindle a braided candle. The most common time to perform the ceremony of *Havdalah* is weekly at the end of Shabbat when three stars appear in the sky. *Havdalah* is also performed at the end of other festivals, such as a Bar Mitzvah, and on holy days." "Havdalah." Jewish Virtual Library. Web. 28 Apr. 2010.

[33] **Sabbath** (Hebrew: *Shabbat*) "The seventh day of the week (*Shabbat, or rest*), recalling the completion of the creation and the Exodus from Egypt. It is a day symbolic of new beginnings and one dedicated to God, a most holy day of rest. The commandment of rest is found in the Bible and has been elaborated by the rabbis. It is a special duty to study Torah on the Sabbath and to be joyful." "Sabbath." Jewish Virtual Library. Web. 28 Apr. 2010.

Further reading: Shulevitz, Judith. *The Sabbath World: Glimpses of a Different Order of Time.* New York: Random House, 2010.

[34] *Mentschen* (Yiddish: pl. of mensch) "A special person with worth and dignity. One who can be respected." *"Mentschen."* Jewish Virtual Library. Web. 28 Apr. 2010.

Photographs

1943, Budapest: Ernest on motorcycle

1948, Israel: Ernest in IDF uniform

1949, Israel: Sara

1951-1955: 3 best friends, co-workers at the Histadrut – Federation of Labor in Israel; L to R: Moshe Wertman, Arje Glazer, Ernest

1952, Jerusalem, Israel: Visiting Moshe Wertman at the Knesset in the Majority Leader's home; L to R, Wertman's son Elisha, his wife Malka, Ernest, Sara

1959, Philadelphia: L to R, Steve (Villi's son), Imre Resler, Villi

1970, Philadelphia: L to R, Bernie (Nancy's father), Sara, Buba Chava, Ernest, Nancy, Edith (Nancy's mother)

1975, Philadelphia: Moshe Wertman and his wife Malka visiting us. Friends are greeting them; Top L to R, Villi, Malka, Manci, Wertman, Barry; Bottom L to R, Frida, Ernest, Trudy, Sara, Rachel, Lily, Simon

1982: Sara Rasmovich (Sara's cousin)

1982, Israel, Adi's Bar Mitzvah: L to R, Zipi, Gil, Shalom, Anat, Adi
(Ronnie & Zipi's son, our nephew), Chaja, Ronnie, Stewart, Sara, Ernest

1984, Lebanon:Stewart in IDF

1985, Israel: L to R, Ernest, Yochevet (Eva) Prizant, Sara, Zvi Prizant

1988, Philadelphia: Moshe and Malka Wertman visiting us from Israel: L to R, David, Twyla, Ernest, Malka, Lili, Moshe, Emil, Rifka, and Sara

1995, July 15, Atlantic City, 50th Wedding Anniversary: Sara and Ernest

1995, July 15, Atlantic City, 50th Wedding Anniversary:
Ernest and Sara, holding their photograph from 1945

1995, July 15, Atlantic City, 50th Wedding Anniversary:
The Paul children   L to R Gil, Dahlia, Stewart

1995, July 15, Atlantic City, 50th Wedding Anniversary:
L to R, Stewart, Eitan, Nancy, Ari

1995, July 15, Atlantic City, 50th Wedding Anniversary:
Ilana, Dahlia, and Tara

1995, July 15, Atlantic City, 50th Wedding Anniversary:
L to R, Neal (Emil's son), Rita (Emil's daughter), Emil, Lili, David (Emil's son)

1995, July 15, Atlantic City, 50th Wedding Anniversary:
L to R, Standing, Steve Paul, Joyce Paul, Harry Fineberg, Miriam Fineberg, Esther,
Rifka, Seated: Rita, Ed, Lili, Emil

1995, July 15, Atlantic City, 50th Wedding Anniversary:
L to R, Rachel, Tikva, Paula, Sara, Elaine, Frances

1995, July 15, Atlantic City, 50th Wedding Anniversary:
L to R, Joyce, Steve P, Chaya, Ernest, Sara, Christian, Juan Eduardo

1995, July 15, Atlantic City, 50th Wedding Anniversary:
L to R, Rear: Frida, Belle, Miriam, Miriam's friend;
Front: L to R, Lili Goldfarb, Sara Katz, Moise Goldfarb

1995, July 15, Atlantic City, 50th Wedding Anniversary:
L to R, Rear, Christen Chaigneau, Patricio Fernandez, Herb
Briggs, Viviana, Hirsh, Adrian Long;
Front, Carrie Ranz, Isabel Lana, Juan Undorraga, Carol Long

1995, July 15, Atlantic City, 50th Wedding Anniversary: L to R, Dan Ranz, Mary Murphy-Houlihan, Carrie Ranz, Belle, Sara, Ernest, Iris, and Klaus

1996: L to R, Ilana, Dahlia, Sara, and Tara

1997, June 26, Masada, Israel: Ari's Bar Mitzvah: a reading by Nanci, Ari's mother

1997, Masada, Israel, Ari's Bar Mitzvah: Sara and Ernest presenting Ari with a miniature Torah

2003, Hyatt, Princeton, NJ, Eitan's Bar Mitzvah:
L to R, Ari, Ernest, Eitan, Sara, Nancy, Stewart

2003, Edison, NJ, Elite's Bat Mitzvah:
Elite and Gil

372

2003, Edison, NJ, Elite's Bat Mitzvah:
L to R, Dali, Gil, Elite, Daniel

2003, Edison, NJ, Elite's Bat Mitzvah:
Elite with her Savta Sara

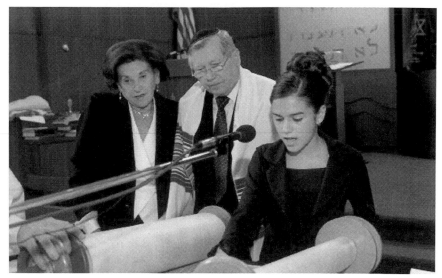

2003, Edison, NJ, Elite's Bat Mitzvah: L to R, Sara, Ernest, and Elite

2003, Edison, NJ, Elite's Bat Mitzvah: L to R, Ilana, Tara, Elite, Eitan, Ari

2004, Jerusalem, Israel: Zvi Prizant receiving the Medal for Courage from the Hungarian government representative, Peter Kiss.

2005, Atlantic City: L to R, Barry Ickovics, Rachel Ickovics, Jeanette Ickovics Thorpe, Tyler Charles Thorpe, Ethan Ickovics Thorpe, Samuel Ickovics Thorpe

2005, New York: Steve, Louis, Ernest, Stewart, Gil, Sara, Annette

2005, Crystal Line Cruise: Sara and Ernest

2006, Haifa: Meeting Moshe Wertman and his wife Malka at my sister's during one of our visits in Israel; L to R, My sister Chaya, Malka, Sara, Ernest, Wertman

2006, December 23-30, *Queen Mary 2* cruise: Sara and Ernest

2006, December 23-30, *Queen Mary 2* cruise: Sara and Ernest

2006, New York: Gil with motorcycle club, The Hillel Angels

2007: Award for Gil and Hillel Angels for the donations they collected

2007, Princeton, NJ: Eitan, saxophonist

2007, Atlantic City: L to R, Rear, Sara and Ernest; Front, Lili, Rachel and Barry

2007, Thanksgiving: Sara & Nancy

2008, Atlantic City: L to R, Rachel, Sara, Lili, sitting; Frida, standing

November 2008, Haifa, Israel, with the Argov Family: L to R, Top, Natty, Shalom, Gail, Noga, Neama, Avraham, and Ronnie; Bottom, Rachel, Chaya (my sister), Ernest

2008, Princeton, NJ: L to R, Eitan, Ari, Nancy, and Stewart

2008, Denver, CO: Nancy Pelosi and David Paul,
Ernest's Nephew

2008, December 20, Neve Shalom, Metuchen, NJ, Daniel's Bar Mitzvah:
L to R, Cantor Levine, Elite, Daniel, Rotem, Rabbi Zelezer

2008, December 20, Neve Shalom, Metuchen, NJ, Daniel's Bar Mitzvah:
L to R, Elite, Daniel, Ernest

2008, December 20, Neve Shalom, Metuchen, NJ, Daniel's Bar Mitzvah:
L to R, Dali, Gil, Daniel, Elite

2009, Atlantic City: Dahlia's Sixtieth Birthday: Dahlia and Steve

2009, Atlantic City: Dahlia's Sixtieth Birthday: L to R, Steve, Dahlia, Ernest

2009, Atlantic City: Dahlia's Sixtieth Birthday: L to R, Gil, Dahlia, and Stewart

2009, Atlantic City: Dahlia's Sixtieth Birthday: Ernest and Dahlia

2009, Atlantic City: Great-grandchildren,
Bottom, left to right—Cole, Roman, Ryan Sara, Sean;
Top, left to right—Tara, Jake, Ilana

2009, Pomona, NJ: The Richard Stockton College of NJ, Holocaust event:
L to R, Stewart, Gil, Chief Justice Stuart Rabner, Ernest, Dahlia, Steve

2009, Pomona, NJ: The Richard Stockton College of NJ, Holocaust event.
L to R, Ernest, Gail Rosenthal, Director of the Holocaust Resource
Center, and Dr. Jan Colijn, Dean of the College of General Studies

2009, Pomona, NJ: The Richard Stockton College of NJ, Holocaust event,
L to R, Steve, Stewart, Gil, Ernest, Dr. Jan Colijn, Dean of the College of
General Studies, Dr. Herman Saatkamp, President of Stockton College, Sharon
Schulman, Director of the William J. Hughes Center for Public Policy,
and Leo Schoffer, Esq.

Business Associates

1972, Germany: Ernest with Dr. Bauman

1975, New York: Ernest shaking hands with Brazilian Consul General

1993, São Bento Do Sul, Ernest accepting an award from the
Furniture Manufacturers: L to R, Sara, Pedro Skiba, and Ernest

1994, Brazil: L to R, Klaus, Jr., Ernest, Klaus, Gil

1998, Chile, Toys 'R Us visit: L to R, Marty Fogelman, V.P., Roger Goddu, President, Ernest, Isabel Lanas, Juan Undorraga, Maria Eugenia

1999, Chile, Reception honoring Ernest: L to R, Ernest, Isabel Lanas, Alvaro Garcia (Minster of Trade), and Patricio Fernandez

1999, Brazil: Ernest in Natal, visiting handicraft fair

1999, Chile: L to R, Robert Fantuzzi, president Chilean
Manufacturers Assocation, and Ernest

2001, North Carolina Primex, Highpoint Furiture Showroom, Top Floor

2001, Chile: L to R, Marcelo Furcade, Jr., Stewart, Marcelo Furcade, Sr., Ernest, Juan Undorraga, in the Furcade Furniture Factory in the south of Chile

2002, Chile: L to R, Juan Undorraga, Kurt, VP Pier I Adrian Long, Ernest, Viviana, Marvin Girouard, president of Pier 1, Carlos

2002: L to R, Patricio Fernandez, president of Cermica Espejo, and Ernest

2006, New York: L to R, Louis Garcia, Ernest, and Stewart

2008, Brazil: L to R, Klaus, Klaus, Jr., and Ursula at Ceremarte Factory

Primex Logo

Ceremarte Collection—Mickey

Ceremarte Collection—Bud Man

Ceremarte Collection—Liquor bottle

1968, Ohio: Smiley Face with Tara, Dahlia's daugther, at Nelson McCloy Factory

1975, Brazil: Avon/Tall Ship Stein, produced
by Ceremarte

Rumpf Project, produced by Ceremarte

Sara Paul's candy marketed by Primex
International

PRESENTED TO

PRIMEX
INTERNATIONAL CORP.

IN RECOGNITION OF
A DECADE OF
OUTSTANDING SERVICE
1984 - 1994

Our Sincere Appreciation,
CUI, Inc.
Wilmington, N.C.

Primex Award

Brazil: Planor Wall of Awards

1975, New York: Avon Award, L to R, Ernest,
two Avon representatives, Acriton, Klaus, Art
Cummings, Stewart

1988, Chile: Ambrozole Chocolate Factory,
Primex International

1992: Toys 'R Us Award to Primex

2005, St. Louis: Anheuser Busch Award, given to Primex for Ceremarte

L to R: Gail Rosenthal, leader, Thomasa Gonzalez, vice-president for Student Affairs, Fred Spiegel, Holocaust survivor, Ernest Paul, Professor Mike Hayse, leader, Andrea Mehrlönder, Checkpoint Charlie Museum, Rolf Hanselmann, Magdeburg, Maud Dahme, Holocaust survivor, in Berlin.

—Photograph by Randee Rosenfeld.

Ernest Paul and Fred Spiegel, Holocaust survivors, reciting Kaddish at Track 17 in Berlin, the main train station from which Jews were deported.

—Photograph by Randee Rosenfeld.

Ernest embracing the president of the state of Saxony an Halt, Dieter Steinecker, for his leadership role in promoting education for present and future German generations about the Nazi atrocities, advocating clearly and loudly throughout Germany that "Never Again!" will this happen in Germany.
—Photograph by Randee Rosenfeld.

Ernest speaking to the study tour participants. —Photograph by Randee Rosenfeld.

Ernest, return to the hula-hoops of his earlier days, 2010 Germany
—Photograph by Randee Rosenfeld.

Nitzkor Le Natzach-Netzachim—Remember forever and ever!